FORD Big-Block
COVERS ALL FE, MEL & 385 SERIES ENGINES
PARTS INTERCHANGE

George Reid

CarTech®

CarTech®

CarTech®, Inc.
838 Lake Street South
Forest Lake, MN 55025
Phone: 651-277-1200 or 800-551-4754
Fax: 651-277-1203
www.cartechbooks.com

© 2016 by Tony Thacker and Michael Herman

All rights reserved. No part of this publication may be reproduced or utilized in any form or by any means, electronic or mechanical, including photocopying, recording, or by any information storage and retrieval system, without prior permission from the Publisher. All text, photographs, and artwork are the property of the Author unless otherwise noted or credited.

The information in this work is true and complete to the best of our knowledge. However, all information is presented without any guarantee on the part of the Author or Publisher, who also disclaim any liability incurred in connection with the use of the information and any implied warranties of merchantability or fitness for a particular purpose. Readers are responsible for taking suitable and appropriate safety measures when performing any of the operations or activities described in this work.

All trademarks, trade names, model names and numbers, and other product designations referred to herein are the property of their respective owners and are used solely for identification purposes. This work is a publication of CarTech, Inc., and has not been licensed, approved, sponsored, or endorsed by any other person or entity. The Publisher is not associated with any product, service, or vendor mentioned in this book, and does not endorse the products or services of any vendor mentioned in this book.

Edit by Bob Wilson
Layout by Monica Seiberlich

ISBN 978-1-61325-737-1
Item No. SA379P

Library of Congress Cataloging-in-Publication Data

Thacker, Tony, author.
Ford flathead engines : how to rebuild and modify / authors, Tony Thacker & Michael Herman.
pages cm
ISBN 978-1-61325-287-1
1. Ford automobile--Motors--Design and construction. 2. Ford automobile--Motors--Modification. 3. Hot rods--Design and construction. I. Herman, Michael, 1977- author. II. Title.

TL215.F35T53 2016
629.25'040288--dc23

2015006502

Written, edited, and designed in the U.S.A.
Printed in the U.S.A.

Title Page:
This cool little track-nosed, turtle-deck T, known as the Woody Lee T, raced in the late 1940s and early 1950s hitting a top speed of 133.136 mph at Bonneville in 1951. NASCAR and TV personality Ray Evernham now owns it. He hired H&H Flatheads to build the engine so that it can be raced again. (Photo by Tim Sutton)

Back Cover Photos

Top Left:
Vic Edelbrock was one of the first to see the potential of the speed equipment business. He experimented with his own parts before even World War II. Here's a Bay Area hot rodder with Edelbrock heads and intake with three deuces. (Courtesy GhostracksUSA.com)

Top Right:
Before he does anything with an old crank, Mike checks the mains and rod journal sizes to see if it's even useable. This one was good at 2.497 for the mains and 2.1385 at the journals.

Bottom Left:
A follow-up Magnafluxing operation clearly reveals the crack-fixing screw in position. Obviously, you've sealed a big crack by making a smaller one, creating the need to pressure seal the block after the stitching process.

Bottom Right:
A pickle fork compresses the valvespring. Note how the tangs of the fork go between the coils of the spring and locate in the machined groove in the bottom of the guide. The elbow of the fork pushes against the block.

Author note: Some of the vintage photos in this book are of lower quality. They have been included because of their importance to telling the story.

CONTENTS

Acknowledgments 4
Introduction 4

Chapter 1: General Data and Specifications 8
   360/361/390/410 8
   406/427 9
   The 428 10
   FT Series 12
   The MEL 13
   The Super Duty 15
   427 SOHC Cammer 16
   385 Series 19
   Boss 429 20
   Gross Horsepower/Torque versus SAE Net 21

Chapter 2: Cylinder Block 26
   FE Series 26
   429/460 35
   Boss 429 37
   The MEL 39

Chapter 3: Rotating Assembly 43
   FE/FT Rotating Assembly 43
   429/460 Rotating Assembly 50
   MEL Rotating Assembly 54

Chapter 4: Lubrication 57
   FE Oiling System 57
   429/460 Oiling System 61
   MEL Oiling System 62

Chapter 5: Cylinder Heads 63
   FE Series 63
   The MEL 76
   385 Series 78
   Boss 429 81

Chapter 6: Camshaft and Valvetrain 83
   FE Series 83
   The MEL 89
   385 Series 429/460 90
   Boss 429 91

Chapter 7: Induction 92
   FE Intake Manifold 92
   MEL Induction 103
   429/460 Induction 106
   Air Cleaners 110
   Thermactor/IMCO 110

Chapter 8: Ignition, Charging and Starting 111
   Starting 111
   Generator and Alternator 113
   Distributor 120

Chapter 9: Exhaust 129
   Mufflers and Pipes 132

Chapter 10: Cooling 134
   Radiator 135
   Water Pump 137
   Cooling Fan 143

Source Guide 144

ACKNOWLEDGMENTS

It goes without saying that a book like this is an enormous undertaking, taking nearly a year to write and a lifetime to research. I've been an automotive technical writer for most of my life and have found that I've never stopped learning. When I examine the first *High-Performance Ford Engine Parts Interchange* book written nearly 20 years ago it is proof we never stop learning. I've learned so much about these powerful Ford V-8 engines through the years making updates and corrections as I've learned back from you, our valued readers. And thanks to you, this book series has endured in the marketplace. In fact, the Ford Engine Interchange Series has performed so well that CarTech decided to break it up into separate small-block and big-block books.

A book like this doesn't happen without help from knowledgeable people in the industry: Jim Grubbs, Ryan Peart, Jeff Latimer, and Vinnie Vicedo of JGM Performance Engineering in Valencia, California; Jay Brown of FE Power in Minnesota; Robert Pond of Robert Pond Motorsports in Arizona; Ray McClelland of Full Throttle Kustomz in Fillmore, California; Craig Conley of Paradise Wheels; brothers Bill and Jeff Sneathan of SEMO Classic Mustang in Southeast Missouri; Dave Stribling in the great state of Indiana; and John Vermeersch of Total Performance just outside of Detroit.

Special thanks to Garrett Marks at Mustangs Etc. in Van Nuys, California, who has developed a sharp eye for the Ford Master Parts Catalog to help sort it all out. Mark Jeffrey of Trans Am Racing has assisted me with FE builds more times than I can count. I consider Marvin McAfee of MCE Engines one of the most knowledgeable engine builders I've ever known. There's also the gang at Ford Performance in the motherland of Detroit; Jesse Kershaw and Mike Delahanty, who have helped me countless times through the years.

Despite the great challenges of a book of this caliber and depth, it has proven to be a very successful publication that has helped thousands with their engine-building projects. I have read your letters, emails, and posts in the forums. I have taken your comments to heart and enlisted help from some of the best minds in the business.

There's an old saying and it is surely true. Put 50 engine builders in a room and approach a given subject and you will get 50 opinions. Our job is to take what we learn from engine builders and knowledgeable people in the industry and bring it to you.

Many thanks to all of you who have helped me with these extensive book undertakings through the years. Additional thanks go to those of you with enough faith in me, and in CarTech, to have purchased these books through the decades. I will never take any of you for granted.

INTRODUCTION

Ford's big-block story consists of four basic engine families: the FE, MEL, Super Duty, and the 385 Series. The FE/FT, MEL, and Super Duty Truck big-blocks were all introduced in 1958. The 385 Series big-block was introduced later in 1968 as a replacement for the MEL.

When the FE/FT Series, MEL, and Super Duty big-block Fords were introduced there was no such thing as a small-block or a big-block. At the time, there were the Ford and Lincoln Y-block V-8s and the enduring legacy of the classic flathead V-8 first introduced in 1932. The Lincoln Y-block was also produced as a truck powerplant.

The FE

The FE Series big-block with its skirted block entered production with plenty of room for growth. During the FE's 18-year production life spanning 1958–1976, it was produced in displacements of 332, 352, 360, 361, 390, 406, 410, 427, and 428

INTRODUCTION

Ford's 429 Super Cobra Jet was produced for just two model years (1970 and 1971) and made huge amounts of horsepower and torque for a big-block production engine. It was fitted with Holley carburetion and a hot flat-tappet hydraulic cam that enabled it to put a lot of power to the pavement.

ci for a wide variety of missions, ranging from basic utilitarian function in cars, trucks, and stationary applications to world-beating Le Mans–winning performance.

The FE was a continuing tradition of skirted Ford Y-block designs that were as rugged as they came. It remains loved for its durability and reputation for making whopping amounts of power. As the FE engine grew in terms of displacement in the 1960s it also became more durable. Ford gave the FE thicker main webs, cross-bolted main caps, a steel crank, heavy-duty rods, and an improved oiling system. The result was race-winning performance starting with the lightweight Galaxies and Thunderbolts in the early 1960s, through the 427 Cobras and 428 Cobra Jet Mustangs, and culminating in four consecutive wins at Le Mans, where the 427-powered GT-40s ended Ferrari's domination in the mid- to late 1960s.

What makes the FE Series engine so popular is its historical pedigree and the wide variety of displacements and cylinder head variations that were available from Ford over the engine's lifetime. When it was introduced, the FE was available in displacements of 332 and 352 ci, which was rather modest, considering that it gained nearly 100 ci of displacement in the years to follow to wind up at 428 ci. Ford achieved these displacements by playing with bore and stroke combinations.

The FE was produced in four bore sizes: 4.000, 4.050, 4.130, and 4.230 inches, with strokes of 3.300, 3.500, 3.780, and 3.980 inches. Ford managed eight displacements with these bore and stroke combinations. And, if you're creative enough you can come up with more than 450 ci using the 427 block and a 428 crank. Opt for an aftermarket stroker kit and you can take the FE to the moon in terms of displacement and raw torque.

You can ask a lot of the FE without consequence as long as you amass the correct parts and infuse proper building technique. Although there are four bore sizes, basic engine block architecture is the same with the exception of the 406, 427, and 428 Cobra Jet, which are higher-displacement high-performance versions of the FE Series big-block. Cross-bolted main caps and heavier main webbing arrived late in the 1962 model year with the 406, then, ultimately the 427 in 1963.

NASCAR-driven performance improvements included High Riser heads available over the counter from Ford starting in 1963 (replacing the earlier Low Riser versions), and then Medium Riser heads in 1965, with a NASCAR rule change. In 1964, in the wake of the Chrysler Hemi's NASCAR performance, Ford developed the 427 Single Overhead-Cam (SOHC) engine during a crash program, in just 90 days, to take back NASCAR dominance. Rules issues in NASCAR at the time prevented it from being used in stock car racing, but it became a legendary drag racing engine, piloted by Don Prudhomme, Mickey Thompson, "Sneaky" Pete Robinson, Connie Kalitta, and others.

The 427 Side Oiler, which featured an improved oiling system over the FE wedge engines, arrived in production cars in 1965. The 427 Tunnel Port came online next in 1967 as a NASCAR alternative to the SOHC. The 428 Cobra Jet, which arrived in 1968 in the Mustang and distinguished itself on the dragstrip, used a unique heavy-duty block with heavier main webbing for rugged durability.

The FE's closest sibling, the FT Series (Ford Truck), produced in 330, 359, 361, 389, and 391 ci for medium- and heavy-duty trucks, was a stouter version of the FE with a heavier block and a steel crank. The beauty of the FT is its interchangeability with the FE. The FT's steel crank will fit the FE with the talents of a good machinist who can machine the snout down to the FE's diameter and length.

INTRODUCTION

The FE big-block was eliminated from high-performance factory applications after 1970. In fact, 1970 was the last year for any kind of high-performance FE; it wrapped up with the 428 Cobra Jet, which was replaced with the 385 Series 429 Cobra Jet and Super Cobra Jet in 1971. In 1971, the 390 FE was replaced in passenger cars with the tall-deck 400-ci middle-block derived from the 351 Cleveland program. The 390 and lower-displacement 360-ci FE big-blocks, which were factory installed only in trucks, were all that remained of the FE program through 1976. The FT engine program wound down to a halt around the same time.

It can be safely said the venerable FE big-block is the most legendary high-performance engine in Ford's history. It started out as a mild-mannered passenger-car grocery-getter engine in 1958 with the 332, 352, and 361 (Edsel). It wasn't long before Ford engineers and product planners realized the great performance potential of this engine given displacement and a hotter cam. Racing history was made as Ford began adding displacement and brute high-performance components.

The MEL

The MEL (Mercury-Edsel-Lincoln) big-block, produced from 1958 to 1967 to replace the Lincoln Y-block V-8, is the most unusual Ford big-block ever produced. With displacements of 383, 410, 430, and 462 ci, the MEL was available in the Mercury, Edsel, Lincoln, and even Ford Thunderbird. When this engine entered production at the beginning of the 1958 model year at Ford's new Lima, Ohio, engine plant, it wasn't officially known as the MEL. In fact, based on Ford documentation from the period, the Mercury-Edsel-Lincoln Division of Ford didn't exist until January 1958, when it was officially announced. The MEL was once a very popular racing engine, especially in powerboats where its torque and durability were unbeatable. It could make torque all day without breaking a sweat. These days, the MEL is often built more for automotive and boat restorations than anything else. Die-hard MEL performance buffs still look to these engines for torque. Parts for the MEL are becoming increasingly scarce.

What makes the MEL different from any other Ford V-8 of the period is the absence of combustion chambers in the cylinder heads, which employ a flat deck like a diesel cylinder head. The block deck is cut at a 10-degree angle off the piston crowns to where the top of each cylinder bore is a wedge combustion chamber. Chevrolet did the same thing with its "W" series 348- and 409-ci big-block where the top of the bore was also the chamber.

The MEL went through a series of revisions with its cylinder heads and pistons to reduce detonation and hard-starting issues early in production. The flat-deck cylinder heads got a small pocket chamber briefly during the course of production to help reduce compression and help quench. It wasn't long before Ford went back to the flat-deck cylinder head and made changes in piston design.

Early on, the MEL was an option for the Mercury in 383 ci. Mercury received the 430-ci Super Marauder with 6V carburetion, along with the distinction of being Detroit's first real muscle car engine. In the 1958–1959 Edsel, the MEL was 410 ci; in the Lincoln and the 1959–1960 Thunderbird, 430 ci. After 1960, the MEL was a Lincoln-only 430-ci powerplant until 1966 when Ford grew it to 462 ci. Production ended in mid-1968 when the 462 MEL was replaced by the 385 Series 429/460.

Super Duty Sleeper

When you think of Super Duty, thoughts turn to the current F-250/F-350 Series pickup trucks. However, 50 years ago Super Duty meant big heavy-duty cast-iron 401-, 477-, and 534-ci big-block Ford V-8s for medium- to heavy-duty trucks. You've heard and seen them in delivery trucks, school buses, garbage trucks, and a host of other duties including marine use if you've been around a while. The behemoth Super Duty gas types were very popular marine engines.

The Super Duty engines, produced from 1958 to 1982, made big torque for gasoline engines and were about as inefficient as it gets. These low-revving high-torque engines burned a ton of fuel and did a tremendous amount of work tirelessly. Although they have been out of production for more than three decades, there are undoubtedly thousands of them still operating around the world.

Ford promoted the Super Duty 401-, 477-, and 534-ci engines as "similar to modern diesels in performance, economy, and durability." Although the Super Duty remains a very common engine still in use worldwide, it doesn't enjoy the kind of following seen with the 385 Series and FE big-blocks. These low-revving high-torque V-8s did their work at low speeds yet made tremendous amounts of power. They are in no way a high-performance engine. The Super Duty V-8s were workhorses long on brute twist.

INTRODUCTION

When the 401-ci Super Duty was introduced for 1958, it was rated at 226 hp at 3,600 rpm along with a whopping 350 ft-lbs of torque at 2,300 rpm. These were grunt engines developed to make torque for tough jobs where low-RPM twist was needed. The larger 477-ci Super Duty delivered 260 hp and 430 ft-lbs of torque. The largest of them all, the 534, made 277 hp along with 490 ft-lbs of torque. In marine use, these were available with twin turbochargers for unending amounts of power.

The Super Duty engine family for big trucks was a mix of MEL and FE nuances that had no interchangeability with the FE/FT or MEL. Although Ford produced untold millions of Super Duty gasoline V-8s back in the day, they aren't very common today. As a result, they aren't covered extensively in this book.

The 385 Series

In the years leading up to 1968, Ford produced old-school big-block V-8s. The FE, MEL, and Super Duty engines were heavy, outdated designs at a time when Ford was looking for improved efficiency from high-displacement V-8s. When you study the 385 Series big-blocks displacing 429 and 460 ci closely, they are little more than an enlarged version of the skirtless, lightweight small-block Ford V-8. The belief in those days was to eliminate the block skirt and excessive weight in this new gray wall iron casting.

The 385 Series big-block debuted in displacements of 429 and 460 ci offered in Ford, Mercury, and Lincoln automobiles. Both engines had the same bore size of 4.360 inches with the displacement difference being in stroke. The 429 had a 3.590-inch stroke with the 460 coming in at 3.850 inches. The nice thing about the 429/460 big-block is interchangeability thanks to the use of the same block casting and the same cylinder heads and induction. These engines were hardy workhorses from the Dearborn iron foundry and Lima, Ohio, engine plant. They witnessed hard use across a broad array of car and truck applications throughout their production life.

Boss 429

Although not many of you are going to be building a Boss 429 engine it is important for you to know a little something about this rare limited-production high-performance hemispherical-head engine. The Boss 429 began life as the Blue Crescent with iron cylinder heads during development. The Boss 429 was developed strictly for NASCAR competition as an answer to the Chrysler 426-ci Hemi, which had been beating the pants off the competition since 1964.

Ford's ill-fated 427-ci FE SOHC was a significant setback for Ford when it attempted to compete with this unusual single overhead-cam big-block mill when NASCAR chief Bill France said no. France viewed the Ford SOHC as too powerful for NASCAR and gave it the thumbs down. The Boss 429 was a renewed attempt at the winner's circle in stock car racing.

It is important to remember that Ford won five NASCAR championships in the 1960s, all with FE big-blocks. The 427 SOHC had more than a 100-hp advantage over the Chrysler hemi. NASCAR became afraid that the speeds attained by the cars powered by that engine would exceed the vehicle's tire and suspension technology and would cause many deadly crashes. After the death of Fireball Roberts, NASCAR was very sensitive to this, and it is generally believed that this is the reason why the 427-ci SOHC was never permitted to run in NASCAR.

The Boss 429 was a purpose-built hemi-head racing engine developed specifically for NASCAR competition. In pure racing form the Boss 429 is a strong performer. To compete in NASCAR, Ford had to produce at least 500 streetable examples of the Boss 429 along with a corresponding number of Ford Torino Talladega and Mercury Cyclone Spoiler II fastbacks. Short-term Ford President Semon E. "Bunkie" Knudsen felt that Ford could get more promotional mileage by building at least 500 Boss 429 Mustangs and at least 500 Torino Talladegas fitted with the 428 Cobra Jet, which were required for homologation of the aero packages. Cyclone Spoiler IIs were fitted with the 351W V-8 small-block.

A Legacy of Great Ford Big-Blocks

Ford can be credited with the development and mass production of some of the greatest big-block V-8s ever produced. No other North American automaker can claim that it went up against some of the most legendary automotive marques in the world at Le Mans and won with an American pushrod V-8 four times straight, handing Ferrari a defeat each time. Ford's big-block story is about adversity, learning from it, practicing what was learned, and coming back with an even better engine than before. Ford's reputation for durability and longevity comes from more than a century of research, development, and a commitment to refinement and engineering.

CHAPTER 1

GENERAL DATA AND SPECIFICATIONS

Ford's FE Series big-block arrived in 1958 in three displacements: 332, 352, and 361 ci. The 332 ci had the shortest stroke of any FE Series big-block at 3.300 inches with a 4.000-inch bore. The 352 with the same 4.000-inch bore had a 3.500-inch stroke. In the beginning, the 332 and 352 were fitted with mechanical lifters with blocks void of oil galleys for hydraulic lifters. Throughout the 1958 model year 332/352 blocks were drilled for hydraulic lifters in order to meet higher passenger car standards of the period. Car buyers did not want the hassle of periodic valve adjustment in a marketplace full of V-8 engines with hydraulic lifters.

When you're shopping for a 332/352 block, pay close attention to important elements such as hydraulic lifter oil galleys along the cam bore. Blocks designed for mechanical lifters cannot be upgraded to hydraulic lifters.

360/361/390/410

The 360, 361, 390, and 410 engines are grouped together because they have the same 4.050-inch bore. The 361 was an Edsel engine option with a larger 4.050-inch bore and the 352's 3.500-inch stroke. The 361 was also available as the Ford Police Interceptor for 1958 only. The 360, virtually the same displacement, was introduced strictly for pickup trucks from 1968 to 1976. FE production ended in 1976.

The 390, introduced in 1961, differs from the 332, 352, 360, and 361 in terms of stroke, which was greater at 3.780 inches. The increase in stroke made the 390 FE something of a powerhouse for its time. The 2- and 4-barrel versions of the 390 were most common followed by the 401-horse 6-barrel 390 High Performance V-8 made possible by a trio of Holley 2-barrel carburetors and a progressive throttle linkage. The 390 High Performance engine for

When the FE was introduced in 1958, the 292/312-ci Y-block V-8 (shown) was the Ford industry standard with its skirted block, mechanical tappets, stacked port heads, and simple design. The FE Series big-block dwarfed the Y-block even though it employed similar engineering.

The Ford FE Series big-block was introduced in 1958 looking a lot like this custom-built 428-6V with Mallory ignition. This 428 demonstrates what you can do with the FE Series big-block given budget and imagination. In its most basic form the FE Series big-block was available with 2-barrel carburetion as a 332, 352, 360, and 390 ci.

FORD BIG-BLOCK PARTS INTERCHANGE

1961–1962 had mechanical lifters in a mechanical lifter block. The 390-6V was a flash in the pan because this engine was never as powerful again.

There were many variations of the 390 produced in this engine's 15-year production life, including the Police Interceptor, Thunderbird Special, and the 390 Special. There were also industrial, stationary, and marine versions, each being distinctive in its application. Some ran on natural gas while others were fired by propane instead of gasoline.

The 410 was a Mercury-only displacement available in 1966–1967, which was little more than the 428's long-arm 3.980-inch-stroke crank in the 4.050-inch-bore 390 block. A soul mate to the 390 is the shorter stroke 360 truck engine, which is little more than a 390 4.050-inch-bore block destroked with the 352's 3.500-inch crank.

406/427

The 406 and 427 are grouped together because they were purpose-built high-performance V-8s with many of the same nuances. The 406 sported the 390's 3.780-inch stroke with a larger 4.130-inch bore, thicker main bearing webs, and larger oil galleys for improved oil volume to the main journals. Toward the end of the 1962 model year, Ford revisited the 406 block's architecture and gave it cross-bolted main caps for bottom-end strength. You may never have heard of a cross-bolted 406 block but they were produced in low numbers toward the end of production in 1962–1963.

In its quest for power, Ford developed a new big-bore block casting with a 4.230-inch bore and the 406's cross-bolted main caps to get 427 ci. The 427 was a big-bore FE like never

Ford introduced the big-bore 427-ci FE in the Galaxie and Marauder as a midyear sales booster in the spring of 1963. The 427 arrived with Ford's new Total Performance program ushering in a new era of excitement. Ford was back in racing and the 427 proved this out. This 1966 427 Side Oiler is fitted with pent-roof steel valvecovers.

before with a new approach to stress relief during the casting process, which came via a slower cool-down process at the Dearborn foundry.

When the casting process was complete, 427 blocks were machined and assembled on a 427-specific line at the Dearborn Engine Plant. Each 427 engine was hand-assembled with close attention to detail. The 427 block has a thicker deck to handle extreme compression ratios. Down under, much thicker main webs were employed to handle the power.

Despite the 427's cross-bolted main caps and stress-relieving efforts, these engines still came apart at high RPM, scattering parts all over racetracks across the country. This was when Ford engineers discovered these engines had a serious oil starvation problem at high RPM. The 427 Side Oiler was a major engineering and manufacturing commitment to durability with a redesigned block equipped with a single oil galley down the driver's side of the block. The Side Oiler supplied the crank,

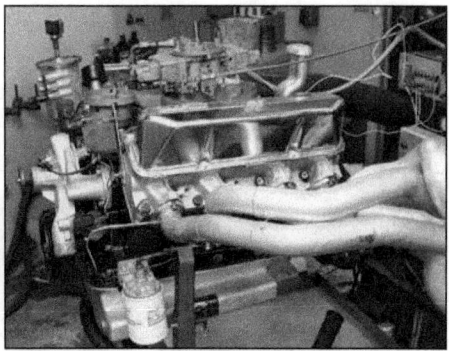

Here's the 427 FE on the dyno at JGM Performance Engineering. What makes this 427 unique is its Side Oiler block and rare factory aluminum heads from the mid-1960s. This is a Le Mans–bowl Holley on top of a 427 High Riser manifold.

rods, and cam with improved lubrication and failures stopped.

The 427's vastly improved oiling system made this engine a world-beater against Ferrari at Le Mans. In fact, the Side Oiler became the gold standard for big-block power. The Side Oiler was teamed with Medium Riser heads and Carroll Shelby's 427 Cobra in 1965. The 427 Side Oiler was a culmination of nice refinements learned from experience in racing. The FE dominated NASCAR in the 1960s, winning five manufacturers championships and five Daytona 500s.

By 1965–1967, the 427 was the best it had ever been and guaranteed to finish the race. The challenge today is finding an undamaged Side Oiler with standard bores you can build. An alternative is to purchase an aftermarket Robert Pond 427 block, which will hold even more power than the original.

The 427's handicap is bore size limitations. Because bore size reaches the limits of this block at 4.230 inches you can only bore it .030-inch oversize unless you intend to re-sleeve,

CHAPTER 1

which averages more than $100 per bore. Unique to the 427 is a forged-steel crankshaft, although nodular cast-iron cranks were installed in some for non-performance applications.

The 427 SOHC Cammer was conceived as a specialty off-road engine for NASCAR-sanctioned stock car racing. Ford built approximately 1,000 427 Cammer engines for stock car racers. When NASCAR said no to the SOHC, Ford was stuck with at least a thousand engines. Ford ended up selling these engines in the aftermarket just to unload them. It is unknown exactly how many 427 Cammers were built. However, their value remains extremely high on the rare occasion they come up for sale.

The 427 SOHC block is unique to the SOHC heads. This means that you can run a Cammer block with wedge heads. However, Cammer heads will not work on a standard 427 block due to lubrication drainback differences, unless an external oil drainback line is used.

The 428

Because the 427 was an expensive engine to produce, Ford had to look at what it would take to get a cost-effective FE to the luxury car market. Ford introduced the FE Series 428 in 1966 as a low-revving alternative to the 427. Although the 428 was 1 ci larger than the 427, its architecture was different. It used a nodular-iron crank along with a 3.980-inch stroke and a 4.130-inch bore. So close in size (427/428), yet so different in how they made power. The 427 likes to rev high, making its greatest horsepower and torque at 6,000 rpm. The 428, with a smaller bore and longer stroke, likes to make torque at lower RPM ranges to smoothly motivate heavy cars around town and onto the freeway.

Ford probably didn't understand at the time, but it was birthing a new era of hot Ford performance in its 428 that would make it a winner in NHRA Super Stock competition. One lone Ford dealer in Providence, Rhode Island, Bob Tasca, who was an avid drag racer, wondered about

Here is Ford's 390 FE big-block swapped into a 1960 Thunderbird, replacing the 352. The 390 was introduced in 1961 in 2V, 4V, and High Performance configurations (4V and 6V). The 1961–1962 390 High Performance V-8 was factory fitted with an aggressive mechanical lifter camshaft and cast-iron headers.

The defining feature of the 406 and 427 standalone FE engines was this bulletproof cross-bolted main cap design that made the skirted block indestructible. No other FE big-block had a cross-bolted main block except late-1962 406s and all 427s through the end of production in 1969.

The FE big-block enjoys great interchangeability. Although there are a lot of head casting numbers, there isn't much difference across the board in terms of port and valve sizing. One exception to this rule is 427 heads. They can vary a lot across Low, Medium, and High Rise types. Heads and manifold must match.

This 1963 Galaxie Lightweight was spotted at a car show with a 427 topped with rare Mickey Thompson hemispherical combustion chamber "hemi" cylinder heads. It makes you wonder why Ford didn't do a 427 with a hemi cylinder head. Note the use of a magneto. Also noteworthy is the special Mickey Thompson induction.

10 FORD BIG-BLOCK PARTS INTERCHANGE

GENERAL DATA AND SPECIFICATIONS

Of all the FE Series big-blocks produced, the 390 is most common. This is the 390 High Performance GT V-8 in a 1967 Mustang. Although Ford identified these as 390 High Performance V-8s, they were little more than Galaxie 390s with improved GT heads. They lacked the aggressiveness of the early 1961–1962 390 High Performance V-8. You can make a big difference in the 390 High Performance V-8 with a hot roller cam.

The 390 High Performance V-8 didn't change much for 1968. This one is fitted with Ford's Thermactor injection pump system (arrows), which infused fresh air into the exhaust ports to reduce emissions. Thermactor parts are very hard to come by these days. Many were removed and thrown away back in the day.

the potential of Ford's long-stroke 428 in NHRA Super Stock competition. Ford's 390 High Performance V-8 for 1967–1968 was decidedly lame; Tasca believed that it was an embarrassment to Ford's legacy of high-performance race cars. Tasca saw the Mustang's 390 Hi-Po as nothing more than a Galaxie 390 with a modest cylinder head upgrade, which impressed no one.

Tasca went to the Ford parts bin, grabbed a handful of 427 parts, and went to work building a high-performance 428 with 427 Low Riser heads and induction, hotter cam, and Holley carburetion. Then he went racing. The results were so impressive that Tasca decided to present the idea to Ford Corporate in Dearborn, Michigan. Tasca's 1967 Mustang with a high-performance 428 so impressed Ford management that it decided to press this engine into production for midyear 1968. Ford began with 50 standard 1968 Mustang fastbacks built in December of 1967 with the new FE Series 428 Cobra Jet built specifically for NHRA Super Stock drag racing.

They rolled off the Dearborn, Michigan, assembly line bone stock and were delivered to veteran NHRA Super Stock drag racers who would turn them into stunning performers as a bold threat to drag racers everywhere. In January 1968 at the NHRA Winternationals in Pomona, California, Ford unveiled these Wimbledon White 1968½ Cobra Jet Mustangs in NHRA Super Stock competition. No one was laughing in the chilly Southern California air. Avid Ford campaigners rolled out their Cobra Jet fastbacks and awed the crowd with lightning-quick pony cars. The key to performance was the 428's long stroke and a complement of 427 components. Mustang got its respect back.

The production 428 Cobra Jet arrived on April 1, 1968, with a thicker, heavier block and beefy main webs for strength. On top were little more than 427 Medium Riser heads, even though Ford called them Cobra Jet heads. All 1968 Cobra Jet engines were basically the same in Fords, Mercurys, and Shelbys with Ram-Air.

For 1969–1970, there were two FE Series Cobra Jet engines available: Cobra Jet and Super Cobra Jet. The Super Cobra Jet was more an all-out drag racing package with C7AE-B Le Mans rods and a small counterweight to counterbalance additional rod weight. The Super Cobra Jet's bottom end was electronically dynamically balanced for added measure to minimize destructive vibration. Super Cobra Jet units were also fitted with an external oil cooler and drag race gearing (3.91:1 or 4.30:1).

You can build your own Cobra Jet FE with off-the-shelf parts from the Ford parts bin or the aftermarket and make huge sums of power like Bob Tasca did a half-century ago. A 390 or 428 block can be fitted with a Scat stroker kit to achieve 430 to 450 ci with incredible stroke and the resulting torque. What's more, your big-cube FE stroker won't have to rev high to get good time slips because it's all about torque.

CHAPTER 1

Thunderbolt: NHRA World Beater

Ford went after the rest of Detroit muscle aggressively in NHRA Super Stock competition in the early 1960s with its lightweight 427 Galaxies. Despite Ford's best efforts, it couldn't catch General Motors and Chrysler with the lightweight fiberglass-bodied Galaxie super cars. This was when Ford went to work conceiving the smaller, lighter-weight Fairlane coupled with 427 FE power. It had to build at least 100 production 1964 Fairlanes to qualify for NHRA Super Stock competition. Ford built 49 4-speed cars and 51 with automatics.

Ford began to develop the Thunderbolt using a 1963 Fairlane development mule coupled with a 427-ci FE High Riser. Dearborn Steel Tubing built these cars, which rolled off the Dearborn, Michigan, assembly line as "K" serial numbered 289 High Performance intermediates. This has been confirmed with Ford documentation that includes all 100 vehicle identification numbers. These cars were shipped to Dearborn Steel Tubing and surgically modified to accommodate the rotund 427 big-block. Body structures were welded along the seams to provide strength.

Thunderbolt Fairlanes had all of the lightweight fiberglass body components including front bumper, Plexiglas side windows, and Econoline Van bucket seats. These cars were completely gutted including the deletion of radio, heater, window mechanicals, sun visors, and anything else that wasn't welded to the body. The 1964 Thunderbolt received structural modifications and suspension improvements that made them better able to tolerate the 427's brutal torque. High-beam headlamps were deleted to make way for cold-air induction.

The Thunderbolt remains the 427 FE's greatest calling card because it quickly became a clear demonstration of power, less weight, and the ability to trek the quarter-mile in short order. Although replica Thunderbolts are out there, only 100 of these cars were produced as "K" serialized 289 High Performance Fairlanes. They remain among the most highly valued muscle cars of the mid-20th Century. ■

Easily the most legendary 427 outside of Le Mans was Ford's limited-production lightweight 1964 Thunderbolt Fairlane sedan. The 427 Thunderbolt Fairlane stood drag racing on its ear when these beasts rolled into the staging lanes of dragstrips from coast to coast.

FT Series

The FE Series big-block has a tougher fraternal twin brother known as the FT big-block, which is a heavy-duty mill engineered for medium- and heavy-duty truck use. Displacing 330, 359, 360, 389, and 391, the FT was the definitive low-revving workhorse. The beauty of the FT is its interchangeability with the FE, including its steel crankshaft

The 428 FE big-block, introduced in 1966 in the 7-Liter Galaxies, found its way into the 1967 Shelby GT500. Not all 1967 Shelbys had the 428-8V. Some had dealer-installed 427-8Vs.

GENERAL DATA AND SPECIFICATIONS

Another 1967 Shelby GT500 with a 428-8V and black wrinkled Cobra Le Mans valvecovers.

This is a 1968 GT500KR with the 428 Cobra Jet with Ram-Air and a single Holley 4150. The 428 Cobra Jet was a midyear option introduced on April 1, 1968. This engine replaced the 428 Police Interceptor version that was standard in the non-KR models.

The 335-horse 428 Cobra Jet FE was introduced on April 1, 1968, with Ram-Air, which became optional in 1969–1970. The Cobra Jet gave the Mustang a renewed performance image in the wake of the rather lame 325-horse 390 High Performance V-8 in 1967.

Ford's 428 Cobra Jet got these finned cast-aluminum valvecovers early in the 1970 model year. They replaced stamped steel chrome valvecovers that were common from 1967 to 1969. This R-code 428 Cobra Jet is fitted with optional shaker Ram-Air.

and heavy-duty block with thicker main webs and cylinder walls. The downside to the FT block is the weight penalty. Blocks and cranks are heavier.

The MEL

The MEL (Mercury-Edsel-Lincoln) big-block, produced from 1958 to 1967, is Ford's most unusual big-block. It was conceived to replace the Lincoln Y-block of the 1950s. Produced in displacements of 383, 410, 430, and 462 ci, the MEL was available in the Mercury, Edsel, Lincoln, and even Ford Thunderbird. When this engine entered production at the beginning of the 1958 model year at Ford's new Lima, Ohio, engine plant, it wasn't officially known as the MEL. In fact, based on Ford documentation from the period the Mercury-Edsel-Lincoln (MEL) Division of Ford didn't exist until January 1958 when it was officially announced.

What makes the MEL an odd-duck big-block is its unusual combustion chamber and cylinder head design similar to Chevrolet's W Series 348/409-ci big-blocks. Instead of a wedge-shaped chamber in the cylinder head, the MEL used the top of the cylinder bore as a combustion chamber with a flat-surface cylinder head. Cylinder heads resemble those from a diesel with a flat deck. The block deck was milled at an angle to the cylinder bore to where the piston

CHAPTER 1

Engine Identification Tag Information

Beginning with the 1965 model year, Ford V-8 engines were equipped with identification tags from the factory. This tag includes displacement, model year, year and month of assembly, and the change level. The change level advanced only when a replacement part or upgrade was introduced. The change level addressed engineering changes, making it easier to identify engines. This information was more for Ford's use than the enthusiast's. The identification tag is attached to the intake manifold on the FE Series big-block V-8s. The tag is located at the ignition coil bracket of 429/460 engines. ■

Tag Code	Displacement (ci)	Carburetor	Warranty Plate Code	Ford Parts List No.
274	302	Autolite 2100	F	60.5
275	302	Autolite 2100	F	60.5
276	302	Autolite 2100	D, F	60.5
277	302	Autolite 2100	F	60.5
278	302	Autolite 2100	D	60.5
279	302	Autolite 2100	F	60.5
280	302	Autolite 2100	F	60.5
281	302	Autolite 2100	F	60.5
282	302	Autolite 2100	F	60.5
283	302	Autolite 4300	J	60.5
284	302	Autolite 4300	J	60.5
285	302	Autolite 2100	F	60.5
286	302	Autolite 2100	D	60.5
287	302	Autolite 2100	F	60.5
288	302	Autolite 2100	F	60.5
296	Boss 302	Holley 4160	G	60.5
299	Boss 302	Holley 4160	G	60.5
300	Boss 302	Holley 4160	G	60.5
310	390	Autolite 2100	Y	60.6
311	390	Autolite 2100	Y	60.6
312	390	Autolite 2100	Y	60.6
313	390	Autolite 4100	Z	60.6
314	390	Autolite 4100	Z	60.6
316	390	Autolite 2100	H, Y	60.6
317	390	Autolite 2100	X	60.6
318	390HP	Autolite 4100	S	60.6
319	390HP	Autolite 4100	S	60.6
321	390HP	Autolite 4100	S	60.6
322	390HP	Autolite 4100	S	60.6
324	390HP	Autolite 4100	S	60.6
341	390	Autolite 4100	Z	60.6
343	390	Autolite 4100	Z	60.6
348	390	Autolite 4100	P	60.6
349	390	Autolite 4100	P	60.6
350	427	Holley 4160	W	60.8
353	427	Holley 4160 x 2	R	60.8
357	390	Autolite 4100	W	60.6
359	427SOHC	Holley 4160	W	60.8
359	427SOHC	Holley 4160 x 2		60.8
360	427	Holley 4160	W	60.8
361	427	Holley 4160 x 2	R	60.8
362	427	Holley 4160 x 2	R	60.8
363	427SOHC	Holley 4160 x 2		60.8
364	427	Holley 4160	W	60.8
382	390HP	Autolite 4100	S	60.6
383	390HP	Autolite 4100	S	60.6
384	390HP	Autolite 4100	S	60.6
385	390HP	Autolite 4100	S	60.6
386	390HP	Autolite 4100	S	60.6
400	428	Autolite 4100	Q	60.9
401	428	Autolite 4100	Q	60.9
404	428	Autolite 4100	P	60.9
405	428	Autolite 4100	P	60.9
407	428CJ	Holley 4160	R	60.9
408	428CJ	Holley 4160	R	60.9
410	428	Autolite 4100	Q	60.9
418	428CJ	Holley 4160	R	60.9
419	428CJ	Holley 4160	R	60.9
420	428CJ	Holley 4160	R	60.9
421	428CJ	Holley 4160	R	60.9
422	428SCJ	Holley 4160	R	60.9
423	428SCJ	Holley 4160	R	60.9
424	428SCJ	Holley 4160	R	60.9
425	428SCJ	Holley 4160	R	60.9
426	428SCJ	Holley 4160	R	60.9
563	289HP	Autolite 4100	K	60.4
564	289HP	Autolite 4100	K	60.4
566	289	Autolite 4100	A	60.4
567	289	Autolite 4100	A	60.4
600	351C	Autolite 2100	H	60.5A

GENERAL DATA AND SPECIFICATIONS

Tag Code	Displacement (ci)	Carburetor	Warranty Plate Code	Ford Parts List No.	Tag Code	Displacement (ci)	Carburetor	Warranty Plate Code	Ford Parts List No.
601	351C	Autolite 2100	H	60.5A	816	429	Autolite 2100	N	60.9
602	351C	Autolite 2100	H	60.5A	816	429	Autolite 2100	K	60.9
604	351C	Autolite 2100	H	60.5A	816	429	Autolite 4300	N	60.9
606	351C	Autolite 2100	H	60.5A	817	429	Autolite 4300	N	60.9
608	351C	Autolite 4300	M	60.5A	818	429	Autolite 4300	N	60.9
609	351C	Autolite 4300	M	60.5A	819	429	Autolite 4300	N	60.9
610	351C	Autolite 2100	H	60.5A	820	Boss 429	Holley 4150	Z	60.9
611	351C	Autolite 2100	H	60.5A	821	429	Autolite 4300	N	60.9
612	351C	Autolite 4300	M	60.5A	822	429	Autolite 4300	N	60.9
613	351C	Autolite 4300	M	60.5A	824	429CJ	Rochester Q-Jet	C	60.9
614	351C	Autolite 2100	H	60.5A					
615	351C	Autolite 2100	H	60.5A	826	429CJ	Rochester Q-Jet	C	60.9
616	351C	Autolite 4300	M	60.5A					
617	351C	Autolite 4300	M	60.5A	828	429 Spec.	Autolite 4300	Z	60.9
620	351C CJ	Autolite 4300	Q	60.5A	829	429SCJ	Holley 4150	J	60.9
621	351C CJ	Autolite 4300	Q	60.5A	830	429SCJ	Holley 4150	J	60.9
625	Boss 351C	Autolite 4300D	R	60.5A	831	429SCJ	Holley 4150	J	60.9
630	351C	Autolite 4300	M	60.5A	832	429PI	Autolite 4300	P	60.9
632	351C	Autolite 2100	H	60.5A	833	429CJ	Rochester Q-Jet	C	60.9
809	429	Autolite 2100	K	60.9					
810	429	Autolite 2100	K	60.9	834	429CJ	Rochester Q-Jet	C	60.9
811	429	Autolite 4300	N	60.9	835	429SCJ	Holley 4150	J	60.9
813	429	Autolite 4300	N	60.9	836	429SCJ	Holley 4150	J	60.9
814	429	Autolite 4300	N	60.9	837	429SCJ	Holley 4150	J	60.9
815	429	Autolite 2100	K	60.9	877	460	Autolite 4300	A	60.9

dome determined compression ratio. The MEL had shaft-mounted rocker arms similar to those found in the FE/FT Series big-blocks.

The MEL employed an open valley with a stamped pan beneath the intake manifold similar to the Ford and Lincoln Y-block V-8s. Intake manifolds were not equipped with a cold-start heat feature. Down under, the MEL had a brute cast crank, heavy cast pistons, and large-shouldered connecting rods. Although Ford called this engine the "MEL," it was installed in the Thunderbird as well as a premium engine option (430 ci) in 1959–1960.

The Mercury-only 383-ci MEL engine was available from 1958 to 1960 sporting a 4.300-inch bore and 3.300-inch stroke. The 410 yielded a smaller 4.200-inch bore and longer 3.700-inch stroke. The larger 430-ci MEL, produced from 1958 to 1965, was available in the Lincoln, Lincoln Continental, Mercury, and Ford Thunderbird and had a 4.300-inch bore and 3.700-inch stroke. Ford fitted the 430 with three 2-barrel carburetion to conceive the Super Marauder.

The 430 was legendary for unwieldy amounts of torque. They were very popular with the powerboat crowd. Ford's 430-ci Thunderbirds stood racing on its ear when Holman and Moody took them to the racetrack. Ironically, the performance aftermarket never embraced the 383/410/430/462 MEL big-blocks, which called for a lot of private enterprise innovation in race shops around the country.

Ford took the MEL to 462 ci in 1966 with a 4.380-inch bore and 3.830-inch stroke to power big, heavy Lincolns. This was the MEL's last hurrah for the 1967 model year. The MEL was considered dated and in 1968, the lighter skirtless-block 385 Series 429/460-ci engine family replaced it.

The Super Duty

The new Ford V-8 engines had a banner year in 1958. This included the FE, FT, MEL, and Super Duty, or "SD," which displaced 401, 477, and 534 ci. The Super Duty 401/477/534

CHAPTER 1

engine was a heavy-duty, truck-only super-size V-8 with a production run from 1958 to 1982. It has nothing in common with the FE, FT, or MEL. Forget about this engine for your Mustang, Galaxie, or F-Series pickup.

The Super Duty is easily one of the largest and heaviest gasoline engines ever made. Some aspects of the Super Duty can be considered iconic, such as its early log-style induction system. It struggled with fuel distribution problems and cold-start issues. If you grew up around this engine you will remember lean off-idle intake backfire as the throttle was opened. They coughed and sputtered until they were warmed up.

What the Super Duty did share with the MEL was that same 90-degree V-8 with a 60-degree flat deck where the top of the wedge cylinder became the combustion chamber. Pistons had a large dome that took up space and provided compression. The Super Duty was quite the workhorse and did it well for a long time.

427 SOHC Cammer

Ford can be considered notorious for going way out on a limb with engineering innovations that excite the senses. The Single Overhead-Cam (SOHC) 427-ci FE big-block is one such example and easily the most memorable. However, it can be considered a significant corporate flop for Ford Motor Company.

Ford developed the 427 SOHC as a response to the beating it was taking in stock car racing. Chrysler's 426

About Ford Part Numbers

Ford part and casting numbers can be confusing, especially if you have not dealt with them before. There are actually two different part-numbering systems. The more common system, 1950–1998, applies to engines addressed in this book. Things changed in 1999 with a new numbering system. Here's how the 1950–1998 system works:

Typical Ford Part/Casting Number

C5ZZ - 9510 - K
Prefix - Basic Part Number - Suffix

The prefix tells you when the part was originally released for production, what car line it was released for, and what engineering group it came from. The prefix breaks down like this:

First Position (Decade)
B = 1950–1959
C = 1960–1969
D = 1970–1979
E = 1980–1989
F = 1990–1999

Second Position (Year of Decade)
Indicates the year the part was released by Engineering for production.

Third Position (Car Line)
A = Ford
D = Falcon
G = Comet, Montego, Cyclone
J = Marine and Industrial
K = Edsel
M = Mercury
O = Fairlane, Torino
S = Thunderbird
T = Ford Truck
V = Lincoln
W = Cougar
Z = Mustang

Fourth Position (Engineering Group)
A = Chassis
B = Body
E = Engine

However, regarding a service replacement part, the fourth position means division, as follows:

Z = Ford Division
Y = Lincoln-Mercury
X = Original Ford Muscle Parts Program
M = Ford Motorsport SVO or Ford Racing Performance Parts

Basic Part Number

The Basic Part or Casting Number is the same whether it is an engineering number or a service number. For example, "9510" is the basic number for all carburetors. A finished engine block would be "6015" as another example. Each engine part gets another basic part number.

GENERAL DATA AND SPECIFICATIONS

Hemi was beating everyone. Ford was determined to get back into the winner's circle. When Ford presented the 427 SOHC Cammer to NASCAR head honcho Bill France early in 1964 it was promptly rejected as too exotic for stock car racing. Ford continued to lobby for the 427 SOHC against NASCAR's pushback. Ford's own racing chief, Jacque Passino, stressed the importance of leveling the playing field. France continued to say no.

Despite NASCAR's continuing rejection, Ford continued with SOHC development hoping that attitudes would change in North Carolina. They didn't. Ford's development included relocation of spark plugs from the bottom of the chamber to the top, much like the 4.6L and 5.4L SOHC Modular V-8s of today, to ease access. Ford worked at developing a more racer-friendly SOHC racing

The monster mash 427-ci SOHC Cammer remains the most exotic muscle engine ever produced by a Detroit automaker in the 1960s. Originally produced for NASCAR use, the Cammer enabled Ford to put hemi heads on the FE. Ford learned a miserable lesson when NASCAR said no to the use of an overhead-cam V-8 in Ford stock cars. Ford wound up with at least 1,000 of these engines, which were sold on the aftermarket to racers and enthusiasts.

Suffix

The Suffix identifies the change level. "A" means original status of released part. "B" indicates at least one engineering change. The entire alphabet is used except for the letters "I" and "L," which could be mistaken for the number "1." When Ford goes through the entire alphabet, it starts over again at "AA," "AB," "AC," and so on.

It is important to understand that part, casting, engineering, and service numbers rarely match. The casting number is derived from the actual casting or part, and typically does not match the part, engineering, or service numbers. Unless the casting has been revised, the basic casting number does not change. It means the number you see in the casting will not match the part number in the Ford Master Parts Catalog. And if the catalog you are using is dated, as most are, expect even more changes in your Ford dealer's microfiche or computer when it comes to suffixes. When demand for a part falls below a predetermined level, Ford will discontinue or "N/R" ("Not Replaced") the part.

Date Code

Ford makes it easy to identify engine castings because it has three foolproof systems in place. First is the casting number, which identifies engineering level and when the engineering level originated. Second is the casting date code that is an alphanumeric code identifying the exact date that the item was cast at the foundry. When you compare the Ford part/casting number with the date code, it helps you determine the year of the date code. For example, a C5OE-12345-A casting number is likely going to coincide with the date code below of "5A26" meaning "1965 - January - 26." If this part has a D5AE-12345-A casting number the date code below would mean "1975 - January - 26." To determine a casting or assembly date, you have to first decipher the casting number.

A foundry logo is also cast into the piece that indicates where it was cast.

Finally, unless any machine work has been performed, a manufacturing date code is normally stamped into a machined surface that confirms when the component was manufactured. Casting and manufacture date codes look like this:

5A26
5 = 1965
A = January
26 = Day

If this code is cast into the piece, it indicates the date the piece was cast at the foundry. If the date code is stamped or inked, it indicates date of manufacture. When a cylinder block or deck is milled, the stamped manufacture date code is normally lost in the machining process.

Also expect to see foundry codes such as DIF (Dearborn Iron Foundry), CF (Cleveland Foundry), or WIF (Windsor Iron Foundry). There was also Michigan Casting. Some iron and aluminum castings were produced outside Ford. ∎

FORD BIG-BLOCK PARTS INTERCHANGE

CHAPTER 1

Ford Basic Part Numbers

Basic Part Number	Component/Group	Basic Part Number	Component/Group
1000–1250	Wheels, Hubs, Brake Drums	10654–10756	Battery
1350–1499	Spare Wheel/Tire Carrier	10838–10990	Instrument Panel and Related Parts
2001–2085	Brakes (Service Item)	11000–11388	Starter
2307–2438	Power Brakes	11450–11688	Lighting and Electrical
2442–2482	Brake Controls	12000–12390	Ignition System
2505–2900	Parking Brake	12402–12425	Spark Plugs
3000–3359	Front Suspension/Steering	13002–13248	Lighting (Front)
3500–3764	Steering Gear	13402–13796	Lighting (Rear)
4000–4296	Rear Axle	13839–13853	Lighting and Horns
4600–4859	Drive Shaft	14197–14689	Electrical Wiring
5000–5176	Frame	15000–15858	Accessories
5200–5299	Exhaust System	16000–16550	Front Fenders
5300–5499	Front Spring and Stabilizer Bar	16600–16699	Hood
5550–5832	Rear Springs	17005–17125	Ford Specific Tools
6000–6898	Engine	17248–17383	Speedometer and Tachometer
6905–6968	Transmission and Overdrive	17402–17666	Windshield Wiper and Washer
7000–7999	Manual and Automatic Transmission	17700–17730	Mirrors
8000–8499	Radiator	17736–17999	Bumpers
8500–8699	Water Pump and Cooling Fan	18000–18125	Shock Absorbers
9002–9256	Fuel Tank	18148–18249	Comfort/Convenience Accessories
9301–9420	Fuel Pump	18250–18699	Heater
9421–9499	Intake Manifold and Related Parts	18800	Radio and Related Accessories
9500–9599	Carburetor and Related Parts	18900	Speakers
9600–9699	Air Cleaner	19000	Fuel
9700–9999	Accelerator Linkage	19100	Fire Extinguisher
10000–10499	Alternator and Generator	19500–19585	Appearance Improvement
10500–10653	Voltage Regulator	19600–19980	Air Conditioning

Ford stuck its neck way out there with the 427-ci SOHC big-block. It rolled the dice on being able to run this engine in NASCAR competition and lost. Despite a lot of engineering time spent developing this engine, the best Ford could do was make these engines available to the racing industry and enthusiasts via the aftermarket and Ford dealer parts departments. (Photo Courtesy Barry Rabotnick)

engine. The following year, 1965, Ford went back to NASCAR seeking its consideration. NASCAR again said no.

Ford's 427 Cammer was easily the most technologically advanced engine of its time but in no way user friendly. It had a 7-foot-long timing chain and was very challenging to service and tune. It still is today. Racers developed gear-drive timing systems to eliminate the complexities of a chain system.

The 427 Cammer's output was astounding for its day: 616 hp at 7,000 rpm and 515 ft-lbs of torque at 3,800 rpm. Although it is less impressive by today's standards, more than 600 hp in 1965 was incredible. When NASCAR put an end to Ford's pursuit of the big track, Ford looked for a place to go with all the parts it had produced to create the Cammer. Ford investigated other motorsports venues, including drag racing, to peddle the Cammer and its many parts. Racers lined up to buy 427 SOHC parts, which filtered into the performance parts pipeline.

Ford's problem was the Cammer's genetic code. It was a steady high-RPM racing engine designed for the big NASCAR tracks, not the dragstrip. Although it made more than

GENERAL DATA AND SPECIFICATIONS

Ford Part Numbers 1999-On

Although this book deals primarily with the vintage Ford part numbering system, late model 385 Series big-block parts as well as vintage Ford V-8 parts show up in the new 1999-on Ford part numbering system. The new system works differently than the old one and takes some getting used to. The only real difference is the first four characters in the part number. The rest of it remains much the same. Instead of seeing part numbers such as C8AE-9510-A, you will see XL3E-9510-A. Here's how 1999-on Ford part numbers work.

Typical Ford Part/Casting Number

XL3E   -   9510   -   A
Prefix   -   Basic Part Number   -   Suffix

First Position (Model Year)
V = 1997   X = 1999
W = 1998   Y = 2000

1 through 9 = 2001–2009
A = 2010   C = 2012   E = 2014
B = 2011   D = 2013   F = 2015

The alphabet continues accordingly after 2015 with "G" for 2016 and so on. Again, Ford does not use the letter "I" or "L" because they are too easily confused with the number "1."

Second and Third Positions
For example, "R3" indicates Mustang. "L4" is Maverick. "R2" is Falcon, and so on.

Fourth Position
Engineering Department responsible for the part.

Basic Part Number

Same as prior to 1999. A cleaner numbering system, however, with driver-side and passenger-side specifics. Easier to follow and understand.

Suffix

Same as prior to 1999. Again, easier to follow and understand. ■

---

600 hp as Ford intended, the Cammer was capable of 2,500 hp. The downside to 2,500 hp was durability. The Cammer could make 2,500 hp with a blower on top; however, it could only do it a couple of times before racers ran over their crankshafts. The Cammer's weakness wasn't its heads, but instead a mile-long timing chain and a block that was never designed for the kind of power professional drag racers were seeking. The Cammer could hold a 7,000-rpm rev all day long. It was the abrupt nature of drag racing that made these engines vulnerable.

Had Ford been willing to develop the 427 SOHC further it could have enjoyed an extraordinary windfall of success in drag racing much as Chrysler did with the Hemi. However, it was not to be. Cammer blocks, heads, and similar components wound up flowing into the new and used parts markets; production ended with what Ford had on the shelf. On the rare occasion SOHC parts show up, the sale prices are reflected by rarity. Bill Coon Cammers produces 427 SOHC parts including heads and blocks, which makes this engine now available on a mass scale.

385 Series

When the MEL big-block became long in the tooth Ford reviewed its shortcomings and looked at building a lightweight big-block replacement at the Lima, Ohio, engine plant. The new 385 Series big-block in 429- and 460-ci displacements would be skirtless and resemble the small-block Ford architecturally. It would just be larger with a similar oiling system and main web structure.

The 385 Series engine is a fiercely rugged and reliable big-block sporting less weight, but it is long on torque. Even though the 385 was an intended luxury car powerplant, Ford went far with this engine as did drag racers. Drag racers took this mild-mannered big-block and made it psychotic where it could rev to 7,000 rpm without consequence.

The 460 with a 4.360-inch bore and 3.850-inch stroke was first on the scene for the 1968 Lincoln Continental followed by the lower displacement 429 with the same 4.360-inch bore and less stroke at 3.590 inches. Because these engines have the same bore size it makes more sense to build a 460 than it does a 429. There are also more 460 cores out there

CHAPTER 1

When Ford introduced the FE Series big-block in 1958, a distant cousin, the 383/410/430/462-ci MEL (Mercury-Edsel-Lincoln) big-block, joined it. This engine did not have a conventional combustion chamber. Instead, the MEL used the top of the cylinder as a wedge chamber like the 348/409-ci Chevrolets with a flat-surface cylinder head. The MEL was the 410 in the Edsel and the 383 in the Mercury. The MEL was also a Thunderbird option in 1959–1960. Note the fuel pump mounted on top of the timing cover, which is the quickest way to identify the MEL.

This is the MEL big-block from another angle. In the mid-1960s, MELs had the power steering pump driven directly off the crankshaft.

The MEL big-block was replaced by the 385 Series 429/460 big-block in 1968. Produced in the same plant as the MEL (Lima, Ohio), the 429/460 big-blocks remained a Ford mainstay well into the 1990s. For two years only, 1970–1971, Ford produced the 429-ci Cobra Jet for high-performance Mustang, Cougar, and intermediate applications. The premium option 429-ci Super Cobra Jet also produced in 1970–1971 was the only mechanical lifter 385 Series big-block ever produced.

than there are 429s. Both employ the same block.

The 429/460 has large 3.000-inch main journals with 2.500-inch rod journals. The 429/460 benefited from good Cleveland-style poly-angle valve wedge cylinder heads out of the box. In 1970, Ford topped the 429 with large-port cylinder heads to birth the Cobra Jet and Super Cobra Jet engines.

The Cobra Jet yielded a whopping 11.0:1 compression ratio. The mechanical tappet Super Cobra Jet pegged the needle at 11.5:1 compression. Compression was the key to power, much as it always has been. The 385's time as a factory high-performance V-8 (429-ci wedge) with a tremendous amount of horsepower and torque available was short lived at just two model years, 1970 and 1971.

The Cobra Jet was fitted with a Rochester Quadrajet carburetor with a spread-bore manifold. The more powerful Super Cobra Jet had the Holley 4150 with a Holley baseplate compatible manifold.

Boss 429

Ford Motor Company never gave up in its pursuit of a NASCAR-winning engine. When the 427 SOHC failed to endear NASCAR officials, Ford looked to its 385 Series big-block for hemi-chamber inspiration. The objective was to conceive a hemi-head 429 and go after Chrysler's 426-ci Hemi. Ford called its Hemi answer the Blue Crescent. During development, the Blue Crescent had iron hemispherical chamber cylinder heads and surely weighed a ton. Aluminum heads weren't far behind.

The Blue Crescent was a purpose-built racing engine developed for NASCAR competition, in particular the 1969 Torino Talladega and Mercury Cyclone Spoiler II race cars. Somewhere in all of that it became known as the Boss 429. To meet NASCAR homologation requirements, Ford had to produce a minimum of 500 street versions of the Boss 429 engine and a corresponding number of vehicles in which it would be raced.

Semon E. "Bunkie" Knudsen, Ford's short-term chief, came up with a way to get the most mileage out of the Boss 429 project. The decision was made to produce at least 500 Torino Talladegas with 428 Cobra Jets and at least 500 Boss 429 Mustangs. Mercury Cyclone Spoiler II street cars (Mercury's Talladega) were fitted with the 351W.

Although the Boss 429 was good for marketing mileage, it was an incredibly bad idea from a logistics and manufacturing standpoint. Producing Boss 429 Mustangs involved bucking and building these cars at Dearborn, then shipping them to Kar-Kraft in Brighton, Michigan, to be fitted with their Boss 429 powertrains. The Atlanta and Lorain assembly plants had to be shut down for a time to build the NASCAR-bodied long-nose Torino and Spoiler II street cars.

To add insult to injury, Ford and Mercury dealers couldn't give these

GENERAL DATA AND SPECIFICATIONS

Ford took another shot at NASCAR with the Boss 429 big-block in 1969–1970. Originally developed as the Ford Blue Crescent with cast-iron heads, Ford engineers refined the most exotic of the 385s giving it aluminum heads to reduce weight and enable more power. The downside to the street Boss 429 was its detuned reputation and poor performance, even though it did make 375 hp. The 1969 Boss 429s were fitted with hydraulic lifters. Realizing this engine's power shortcomings, Ford went to mechanical lifters and a more aggressive cam for 1970. This engine wanted to rev and did when built to NASCAR specifications.

cars away. The Boss 429 Mustang and 428 Cobra Jet Torino Talladegas didn't sell because they were impractical for the average buyer. Some sat on Ford dealer lots for years before they were sold. The Mustang's Boss 429 engines were detuned for the street and loaded down with the Thermactor emissions system, making them pigs compared to their NASCAR siblings. Few people wanted them.

The Boss 429 engine was another exotic offering from Ford. It was decidedly temperamental for so many reasons, which made it a less-than-adequate street engine. They sputtered and stalled. They had Cooper rings and O-ring seals instead of gaskets to keep combustion where it belonged within the dry deck.

Gross Horsepower/Torque versus SAE Net

Prior to the 1972 model year, manufacturers published horsepower and torque figures at the engine's crankshaft. Beginning in 1972, the Society of Automotive Engineers (SAE) changed horsepower and torque numbers from gross to net, which meant measuring power output with all accessories and related pieces installed and operating. In other words, SAE Net horsepower and torque is measured based as though the engine is installed in the vehicle. Gross horsepower and torque were measured at the crankshaft with the engine void of any accessories.

The 429 Cobra Jet for 1970–1971 with 360 hp on tap. Ram-Air was an option, as was the Super Cobra Jet with 375 hp. These were first to leave the traffic light, especially the solid lifter 429 Super Cobra Jet.

Gross horsepower and torque numbers weren't always honest either. Automakers raised numbers to sell more vehicles. They also reduced horsepower and torque numbers to satisfy regulating bodies and insurance companies. Power ratings depended largely on what was happening at the time. During the horsepower wars of the 1960s, automakers didn't always tell the truth about real, usable power. SAE Net quickly curbed gross numbers advertised by automakers, calculating real world power more accurately.

Ford FE Big-Block General Engine Specifications

Some engine specifications were unavailable.

Displacement (ci)	332	352
Horsepower	240 @ 4,600 rpm (2V) 1958 265 @ 4,600 rpm (4V) 1958 225 @ 4,400 rpm (2V) 1959	300 @ 4,600 rpm (4V) 1958–1959 360 @ 6,000 rpm (HP/4V) 1960 220 @ 4,300 rpm (2V) 1961–1962 250 @ 4,400 rpm (4V) 1965–1966
Torque	260 @ 2,800 rpm (2V) 1958 325 @ 2,200 rpm (2V) 1959	380 @ 2,800 rpm (4V) 1958–1959 336 @ 2,400 rpm (HP/4V) 1960 336 @ 2,600 rpm (2V) 1961–1962 352 @ 2,800 rpm (4V) 1965–1966
Carburetion	Holley 2300 2V	Holley 4160 4V (Early) Autolite 4100 4V (Typical)
Compression	9.5:1 1958 8.9:1 1959	9.6:1

CHAPTER 1

Displacement (ci)	332	352
Bore Size (inches)	4.000	4.000
Stroke (inches)	3.300	3.500
Crank Type	Nodular Iron	Nodular Iron
Crank Dimensions (inches)	2.7488 Main 2.4384 Rod	2.7488 Main 2.4384 Rod
Piston Type	Cast Aluminum	Cast Aluminum
Connecting Rod Length (inches)	6.540	6.540
Valve Size (inch)	2.020 Intake 1.550 Exhaust	2.020 Intake 1.550 Exhaust
Lifter Type	Mechanical (Early 1958) Hydraulic (Late 1958)	Mechanical (Early 1958) Hydraulic (Late 1958-on)
Rocker Arm Ratio	1.76:1	1.76:1
Rocker Arm Type	Shaft Mounted	Shaft Mounted
Engine Balance	Internal	Internal
Displacement (ci)	360 Ford Truck Only	361 Edsel Only
Horsepower	215 @ 4,100 rpm (1968–1971) 196 @ 4,000 rpm (1972–1976)	303 @ 4,600 rpm (1958–1959)
Torque	375 @ 2,600 rpm (1968–1971) 327 @ 2,400 rpm (1968–1976)	400 @ 2,800 rpm (1958) (4V) 390 @ 2,900 rpm (1959) (4V)
Carburetion	Autolite/Motorcraft 2100 Motorcraft 2150	Holley 4160 4V
Compression	8.4:1 (1968–1971) 8.0:1 (1972–1976)	10.5:1
Bore Size (inches)	4.050	4.050
Stroke (inches)	3.500	3.500
Crank Type	Nodular Iron	Nodular Iron
Piston Type	Cast Aluminum	Cast Aluminum
Connecting Rod Length (inches)	6.540	6.488
Valve Size (inches)	2.020 Intake 1.550 Exhaust	2.020 Intake 1.550 Exhaust
Lifter Type	Hydraulic	Hydraulic
Rocker Arm Ratio	1.76:1	1.76:1
Rocker Arm Type	Shaft Mounted	Shaft Mounted
Engine Balance	Internal	Internal
Displacement (ci)	390	406
Horsepower	265 @ 4,400 rpm (2V) 275 @ 4,400 rpm (PI) 315 @ 4,600 rpm (4V) 320 @ 4,600 rpm (HP/GT) 401 @ 6,000 rpm (HP/6V)	380 @ 5,800 rpm (4V) 405 @ 5,800 rpm (HP/6V)
Torque	401 @ 2,600 rpm (2V) 405 @ 2,600 rpm (PI) 427 @ 3,200 rpm (4V) 427 @ 3,200 rpm (HP/GT) 430 @ 3,500 rpm (HP/6V)	444 @ 3,400 rpm (4V) 448 @ 3,400 rpm (HP/6V)
Carburetion	Autolite 2100 Autolite 4100 Holley 2V x 3	Holley 4150 Holley 2300 x 3 (HP/6V)
Compression	9.6:1 (2V) 10.5:1 (4V) 11.0:1 (6V)	11.4:1
Bore Size (inches)	4.050	4.130
Stroke (inches)	3.780	3.780

GENERAL DATA AND SPECIFICATIONS

Displacement (ci)	390	406
Crank Type	Nodular Iron	Nodular Iron
Piston Type	Cast Aluminum	Cast Aluminum
Connecting Rod Length (inches)	6.488	6.488
Valve Size (inches)	2.020 Intake 1.550 Exhaust	2.020 Intake 1.550 Exhaust
Lifter Type	Mechanical (1961–1962 HP) Hydraulic (1961–1976)	Mechanical
Rocker Arm Ratio	1.76:1 Mechanical 1.73:1 Hydraulic	1.76:1 Mechanical
Rocker Arm Type	Shaft Mounted	Shaft Mounted
Engine Balance	Internal	Internal
Displacement (ci)	410	427
Horsepower	330 @ 4,600 rpm	410 @ 5,600 rpm (4V) 425 @ 6,000 rpm (8V) 616 @ 7,000 rpm (SOHC 4V) 657 @ 7,500 rpm (SOHC 8V)
Torque	444 @ 2,800 rpm	476 @ 3,400 rpm (4V) 480 @ 3,700 rpm (8V) 515 @ 3,800 rpm (SOHC 4V) 540 @ 3,700 rpm (SOHC 8V)
Carburetion	Autolite 4100	Holley 4160 (4V) Holley 4150 (8V)
Compression	10.5:1	11.5:1 (4V/8V) 12.5:1 (SOHC)
Bore Size (inches)	4.050	4.230
Stroke (inches)	3.980	3.780
Crank Type	Nodular Iron	Nodular Iron (1963–1964) Steel (1965–1968)
Piston Type	Cast Aluminum	Cast Aluminum
Connecting Rod Length (inches)	6.488	6.488
Valve Size (inches)	2.020 Intake 1.550 Exhaust	2.020 Intake (Early Low Riser) 1.650 Exhaust (Early Low Riser) 2.080 Intake (Late Low Riser) 1.650 Exhaust (Late Low Riser) 2.180 Intake (Medium/High Riser) 1.720 Exhaust (Medium/High Riser) 2.250 Intake (Tunnel Port) 1.720 Exhaust (Tunnel Port)
Lifter Type	Hydraulic	Mechanical (1963–1967) Hydraulic (1968)
Rocker Arm Ratio	1.73:1	1.76:1 Mechanical 1.73:1 Hydraulic
Rocker Arm Type	Shaft Mounted	Shaft Mounted
Engine Balance	External	Internal
Displacement (ci)	428	428 Cobra Jet
Horsepower	345 @ 4,600 rpm (4V) 355 @ 5,400 rpm (8V)	335 @ 5,200 rpm
Torque	362 @ 2,800 rpm (4V) 420 @ 3,200 rpm (8V)	440 @ 3,400 rpm
Carburetion	Autolite 4100 Holley 4150 x 2	Holley 4150
Compression	10.6:1 (1968–1969) 11.0:1 (1970)	10.5:1
Bore Size (inches)	4.130	4.130

Ford FE Big-Block General Engine Specifications CONTINUED

Displacement (ci)	428	428 Cobra Jet
Stroke (inches)	3.980	3.980
Crank Type	Nodular Iron	Nodular Iron
Piston Type	Cast Aluminum	Cast Aluminum (CJ) Forged Aluminum (SCJ)
Connecting Rod Length (inches)	6.488	6.488
Valve Size (inches)	2.080 Intake 1.650 Exhaust	2.080 Intake 1.650 Exhaust
Lifter Type	Hydraulic	Hydraulic
Rocker Arm Ratio	1.73:1	1.73:1
Rocker Arm Type	Shaft Mounted	Shaft Mounted
Engine Balance	External	External

Ford MEL Big-Block General Engine Specifications

Some engine specifications were unavailable. ■

Displacement (ci)	383	410
Horsepower	280 @ 4,600 rpm (2V) 312 @ 4,600 rpm (4V) 330 @ 4,600 rpm (4V)	345 @ 4,600 rpm
Torque	N/A	N/A
Carburetion	Holley	Holley
Compression	10.0:1	10.5:1
Bore Size (inches)	4.300	4.200
Stroke (inches)	3.300	3.700
Crank Type	Nodular Iron	Nodular Iron
Piston Type	Cast Aluminum	Cast Aluminum
Connecting Rod Length (inches)	6.600	6.600
Valve Size (inches)	2.150 Intake 1.780 Exhaust	2.150 Intake 1.780 Exhaust
Lifter Type	Hydraulic	Hydraulic
Rocker Arm Ratio	1.76:1	1.76:1
Rocker Arm Type	Shaft Mounted	Shaft Mounted
Engine Balance	External	External
Displacement (ci)	**430**	**462**
Horsepower	375 @ 4,800 rpm	340 @ 4,600 rpm
Torque	490 @ 3,100 rpm	485 @ 2,800 rpm
Carburetion	Carter	Carter
Compression	10.5:1	10.25:1
Bore Size (inches)	4.300	4.380
Stroke (inches)	3.700	3.380
Crank Type	Nodular Iron	Nodular Iron
Piston Type	Cast Aluminum	Cast Aluminum
Connecting Rod Length (inches)	6.600	6.600
Valve Size (inches)	2.080 Intake (5750062) 2.150 Intake (5750064) 1.780 Exhaust	2.020 Intake 1.660 Exhaust
Lifter Type	Hydraulic	Hydraulic
Rocker Arm Ratio	1.76:1	1.76:1
Rocker Arm Type	Shaft Mounted	Shaft Mounted
Engine Balance	External	External

GENERAL DATA AND SPECIFICATIONS

Ford 385 Series Big-Block General Engine Specifications

Some engine specifications were unavailable. ■

Displacement (ci)	429	460
Horsepower	320 @ 4,400 rpm (2V) 360 @ 4,600 rpm (4V) 360 @ 5,800 rpm (CJ) 375 @ 5,600 rpm (SCJ) 208 @ 4,400 rpm (4V) (1972 SAE Net) 202 @ 4,400 rpm (4V) (1973 SAE Net)	365 @ 4,600 rpm 224 @ 4,400 rpm (SAE Net)
Torque	460 @ 2,200 rpm (2V) 476 @ 2,800 rpm (4V)	500 @ 2,800 rpm 357 @ 2,800 rpm (SAE Net)
Carburetion	Rochester Quadrajet Holley 4150 (SCJ)	Autolite/Motorcraft 4300/4350
Compression	10.5:1 (2V) 11.0:1 (4V) 11.5:1 (CJ/SCJ) 8.0:1 (1972-on)	10.5:1 (1968–1971) 8.5:1 (1972-on)
Bore Size (inches)	4.360	4.360
Stroke (inches)	3.590	3.850
Crank Type	Nodular Iron	Nodular Iron
Piston Type	Cast Aluminum	Cast Aluminum
Connecting Rod Length (inches)	6.600	6.600
Valve Size (inches)	2.090 Intake 1.660 Exhaust	2.090 Intake 1.660 Exhaust
Lifter Type	Hydraulic Mechanical (SCJ)	Hydraulic
Rocker Arm Ratio	1.75:1	1.75:1
Rocker Arm Type	Bolt Fulcrum Stud Mounted (SCJ)	Bolt Fulcrum
Engine Balance	Internal	Internal (1968–1978 "2Y" Crank) External (1979-on "3Y" Crank)

Displacement (ci)	Boss 429
Horsepower	375 @ 5,200 rpm
Torque	450 @ 4,500 rpm
Carburetion	Holley 4150
Compression	10.5:1
Bore Size (inches)	4.360
Stroke (inches)	3.590
Crank Type	Steel
Piston Type	Forged
Connecting Rod Length (inches)	6.600

Displacement (ci)	Boss 429
Valve Size (inches)	2.250 Intake 1.720 Exhaust
Lifter Type	Hydraulic Lifter (1969) Mechanical Lifter (1970) Mechanical Lifter (Race) Mechanical Lifters (820-A and 820-T Engines after June 1, 1969)
Rocker Arm Ratio	1.73:1
Rocker Arm Type	Shaft-Mounted (Adjustable)
Engine Balance	Internal

CHAPTER 2

CYLINDER BLOCK

The very heart of any big-block Ford build is the cylinder block. Block selection contributes to the success or failure of an engine project. Whether you're building a mild 332 for a vintage Ford restoration or erecting a stump puller of a 460, it's important to know the difference between a good block and a bad one. Because Ford has long been infamous for engineering changes, you can count on a plethora of block castings in a single model year.

FE Series

Although there are few differences in FE Series blocks it is important to understand what these differences are in order to choose the correct block for your application. Those first production 332- and 352-ci FE blocks were manufactured for mechanical lifters only, which means there are no lifter oil galleys. In midyear 1958, Ford upgraded the 332 and 352 to hydraulic lifters, which means you may opt for mechanical or hydraulic lifters. One exception to this rule is the 1960 352 High Performance block, which is not drilled for hydraulic lifters.

Another area to watch for is the FE engine mount bolt holes prior to 1965. FE blocks prior to 1965 have two-bolt engine mounts. Since 1965 there are four–bolt-hole engine mounts of which three holes are used. This isn't a problem if you're planning to use a 1965 or later block in a pre-1965 vehicle. However, there will be issues when you try to install a pre-1965 FE in a post-1965 Ford vehicle. A custom adapter plate or some drilling and machining will be required. If you unearth a block with four engine-mount bolt holes, you've found an FT truck block.

Another very important change addresses FE cylinder head bolts beginning in 1961. From 1958 to 1960, all FE blocks were fitted with four 7/32-inch-long cylinder head bolts in all locations. Beginning in 1961 all FE blocks were equipped with two 7/8-inch-long head bolts along the outside of the block and four 19/32-inch-long bolts inside. Another change is late 1963-on FE blocks where an additional bolt hole for the alternator is incorporated into the block on the passenger's side.

In your search for a block, bore size is your first clue in block identification apart from oil galleys, casting numbers, and date codes. The 332 and 352 have 4.000-inch bores. The Edsel 361 was the first FE with a 4.050-inch bore followed by the 360, 390, and 410.

360/361/390/410

Aside from bore size, the 360/361/390/410 blocks with 4.050-inch bores don't differ much from the 332 and 352 in terms of main webs, pan rails, and block walls. The decidedly rare 410 Merc is little more than a 390 block with a 428 crank giving it a 3.980-inch stroke. Take that same 4.050-inch bore and give it the 352 crank and you have a 360 for trucks.

This 4.050-inch bore block varies in the 1961–1965 390 High Performance and Police Interceptor: C1AE-V, C2AE-BC, C2AE-BE, C2AE-BR, C2AE-BS, C3AE-KY, C3ME-B, C4AE-F, and C5AE-B. These special performance blocks have thicker main bearing caps and undrilled oil galleys for mechanical lifters. This means that only mechanical lifters can be used in this block.

406

The 406 was Ford's first real high-performance FE block; it was a result of Ford's racing ambitions. As

CYLINDER BLOCK

with any FE race block, the 406 was a thicker, heavier casting than the 332, 352, 361, and 390. Look for C2AE-J, C2AE-K, or C2AE-V. These blocks came from what was learned from the 390 High Performance engine in competition.

The 406 block didn't make it through 1962 without significant engineering changes. Although cross-bolted main caps are associated with the 427 they originated with the 406 late in 1962. Ford engineered improvements into the FE when the 390 and 406 engines rattled themselves apart at high RPM in stock car racing. Main bearing caps tended to work loose causing catastrophic engine failure. Ford went to cross-bolted main caps at number -2, -3, and -4 main bearings, which solved the problem.

Although the cross-bolted 406 block is easy to identify by measuring the bore, 4.130 inches, plus casting number and date code, they are not easy to find these days. Expect to pay a high price for the 406 C2AE-BD cross-bolt block.

427

The most desirable FE block in existence is the 427 because it sports the FE's largest bore at 4.230 inches, cross-bolted main caps, thicker main webs, and cylinder walls with a unique outside shape known as the cloverleaf. Although there have always been rumors that the 427 block contains high nickel content for strength, this has never been true, according to Jay Brown at FE Power. Thicker decks can take the 427 ultra-high-compression ratios. Drop a 428 crank (3.980-inch stroke) into the 427 block and you have a 454.

The 427 block's 4.230-inch bore pushes this block to its limits. Typically, you can only bore this block .030-inch oversize. After that, it must be sleeved. If you unearth a 427 block that has never been bored, expect to spend a lot to get it. Because Ford produced at least 24 different 427 block casting numbers, learning what you've found may be the greatest challenge.

Despite all of Ford's best efforts to bolster the 427's bottom end, in the early 1960s these engines continued to fail at high RPM at NASCAR tracks across the country. Ford engineers went to work investigating these failures and concluded that main and rod bearings tended to be oil starved at high RPM. Oil galleys could not keep up with the rigors of keeping a solid oil wedge at main and rod bearings.

Ford had to make a substantial investment in the 427's oiling system, which meant a complete block redesign. A large single oil galley was designed into the driver's side of the block with the relief valve at the rear of the block away from the oil pump. This engineering refinement became known as the Side Oiler. The Side Oiler had durability and the winner's circle finally arrived with this engine. Engines stayed together and racers finished races.

Although the Side Oiler upgrade improved durability significantly, Ford engineers still had challenges with the high-RPM 427. Cylinder wall failures continued despite cross-bolted main caps and oiling system improvements. The cylinder wall issue was corrected for 1966. When Ford had enough cylinder wall thickness, the 427 became unbeatable. It went to Le Mans and won four times straight.

In your search for a Side Oiler block, look for these casting numbers: C5AE-D, C5AE-H, C6AE-B, C6AE-C, and C6AE-D. If you desire hydraulic lifters, there were Side Oiler blocks drilled for this purpose: C8AE-A, C8AE-B, and C8AE-H. Some, but not all of these have ribbed sides and the Side Oiler oil galley plugs. The 427 industrial blocks also have ribbed sides, which can create confusion.

The basic FE block didn't change much throughout its 18-year production. This is what you can expect to see with 332, 352, 360, 361, and 390 blocks: The Edsel 361, Ford 360 and 390, and the Mercury 410 all have a larger 4.050-inch bore than the 332 and 352. What makes the 360, 361, and 390 different in terms of displacement is stroke within the 4.050-inch bore block. The 406 and 428 have a 4.130-inch bore. The 427 has the largest FE bore at 4.230 inches.

The FE is a tried-and-proven skirted Y-block design engineered to keep strength around the rotating mass down under. There's plenty of iron down there even with the standard FE blocks. This 390 block has studded main caps for durability.

FORD BIG-BLOCK PARTS INTERCHANGE

CHAPTER 2

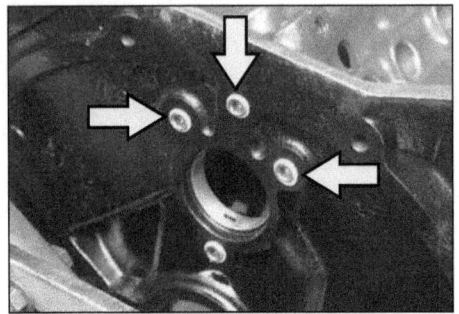

Hydraulic lifter FE blocks have three oil galleys around the cam journals, which supply the lifters with oil pressure. This is the most common block you will find out there. Very few are mechanical lifter blocks.

This is a mechanical lifter 427 block without the oil galleys found with hydraulic lifter FE blocks. Because this block lacks the lifter oil galleys, you cannot use hydraulic lifters.

Typical side shot of an FE block. The keys to identification are casting numbers and date codes. You will want to examine all block casting numbers and codes to be proof-positive that you have found the proper block for your application. Then, check cylinder bore and line bore dimensions and the deck for warpage. It's a good idea to Magna-flux the block to check for cracks.

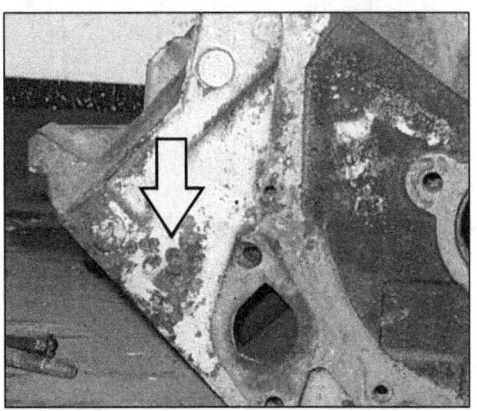

The FE block, head on. Most apparent here is the "352" found on the front of most FE blocks. The "352" doesn't mean you've found a 352 block. Bore size, casting number, and date code are positive indicators of block type.

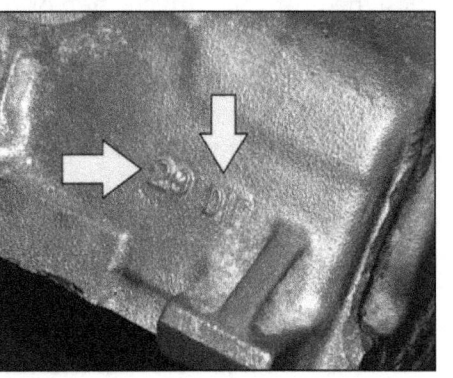

"DIF" indicates that this FE block was cast at the Dearborn Iron Foundry. The "29" is believed to be cavity or sand casting number 29.

This is the block's alphanumeric casting date code of "6H31" indicating August 31, 1966. A date code stamped into the block indicates the date the engine was manufactured at the Dearborn Engine Plant.

Ford produced industrial 427s for use outside of passenger cars and racing. This is a cheaper way to get into a 427 block and still enjoy the same benefits. Look for C5JE-D or C7JE-E, which were industrial blocks. Marine blocks were C6JE-B and C7JE-A.

428

The 428 block is one of the easier FE blocks to score and use for an engine building project. Casting numbers to look for are C6ME, C6ME-A, C7ME, C7ME-A, and C8ME, which are 428-4V and Police Interceptor blocks. Early production Cobra Jet blocks are C7ME-A and C7ME-C. Look for

The 406/427 cross-bolted bottom end employs thicker webbing in addition to the cross-bolted network of main journals.

CYLINDER BLOCK

These are the 406/427 FE cross-bolt main bearing caps. After they are seated and secured in the block, they offer incredible bottom-end strength. If you're building a 406/427, use ARP studs and cross-bolts for added security.

Cross-bolt main caps are shown here before the spacers and cross-bolts in a 427 block. Spacers and cross-bolts should be installed (but not tightened) before main cap bolts are tightened and torqued. Torque main cap bolts or studs first, then cross-bolts.

Spacers install between each main cap and block skirt (as shown). Bolts and spacers should be installed loosely, the main caps torqued in the proper order, and then the cross-bolts are torqued to Ford specifications. Never torque the cross-bolts first.

The completed bottom end of the 427 block demonstrates the strength that Ford engineered into the cross-bolted 406/427 High Performance engines. This was the first phase of producing an indestructible racing engine. Despite cross-bolted main caps, the 427 struggled with failure after failure. Ford had to redesign the 427's oil system.

Ford engineers learned that the 427's main and rod bearings suffered from poor lubrication at high RPM. The 427's oiling system had to be completely redesigned with a single oil galley on the driver's side with a relief valve in the back of the block just below the side galley. This revision was known as the Side Oiler, which kept the main and rod bearings supplied with a good oil wedge under extreme conditions.

C8ME as well with the thicker main webs. Not all 428 and 428 Cobra Jet blocks will have casting numbers. The service part number for all 1966–1970 428 blocks is C6AZ-6010-F.

The quickest way to identify a 428 block is to look inside the center freeze plug hole for "428" in the casting. However, not all of them will have this number. Also, not all FE/FT blocks had the casting number after 1966 according to the 428 Cobra Jet Registry. In fact, these casting numbers ultimately returned in the 1970s when FE blocks were cast at the new, but now defunct, Michigan Casting Center (MCC) in Flat Rock, Michigan, not the Dearborn facility. The "MCC" FE/FT blocks no longer had the familiar "352" at the front of the block, but instead a "105."

Another way to identify 428 blocks is at the back of the block where you will see a "C" or an "A" in many of these blocks, but not all of them. Most FT truck blocks had heavier main webs (like the 428 Cobra Jet's), which can add to the confusion.

None of the other FE blocks are cast the same way as the 428. If you stumble upon a C6ME-A block you've found a 428 mechanical lifter block void of lifter oil galleys. The C6ME-A block is also the Police Interceptor block. Keep this in mind when you're scouting for a 428 or 428 Cobra Jet block. Adding to the confusion is a C6ME-A casting number on hydraulic lifter blocks meaning you need to be looking for the presence of lifter galleys either way. Look for C6ME, C6AE-F, and C7ME-A.

Key points to observe when you're looking for a high-performance 428 block are thicker main webs, ribs, and main bearing caps. Through the years, I've seen 428 blocks with provisions for cross-bolted main caps. Cross-bolt main cap provisions have been seen on one side of the block, but not the other, which has to do with sand castings at the Dearborn

CHAPTER 2

New FE Blocks

New FE blocks are available from Robert Pond Motorsports and Bear Block Motors.

Robert Pond Motorsports

Robert Pond Motorsports produces what is undoubtedly the best FE block in the marketplace. Because Pond has a tremendous amount of FE racing experience, he has taken what he has learned in racing, manufacturing, and from Ford, and infused this knowledge into the production of both iron and aluminum FE blocks.

The Robert Pond 427 Ford FE aluminum engine block is much stronger than the original cast-iron Ford block with better casting technology and greater attention to detail. The Pond engine block is designed with siamesed cylinders for strength. The block deck is 3/4 inch thick. Main saddles are extremely rigid with redesigned billet steel main caps along with special ARP bolts and studs. This aluminum casting is heat-treated to T356. Pond's engine block Brinnell tests at greater than 225.

The Pond 427 Side Oiler block is cast in a tightly controlled domestic foundry that specializes in low-porosity parts for mining operations and steel mills. In short, an environment where there is zero tolerance for error. Robert Pond Motorsports specifically engineered tooling for these FE Pond blocks for the 427. What's more, Pond has advanced CNC machining cells engineered to make sure every machining phase is spot on, ensuring you receive the precision you've paid for.

Racers running the Pond aluminum engine block are running higher than 1,300 hp without consequence. According to Robert Pond, these lightweight aluminum blocks are 100 percent stronger than the original cast-iron Ford block. The aluminum engine block has spun ductile iron cylinder sleeves that Brinnell-test out at 280, which is remarkable whether you're building a street FE or all-out racer.

The Pond block's oiling system is similar to the Side Oiler 427. It has been modified to be a priority oiling system, meaning crankshaft main bearings get oil under pressure first, with the lifters being last. Robert Pond comments how important this is because the original FE Side Oiler block was designed the other way around.

The cool thing about the Pond FE block is its status as a drop-in replacement for the original 427 FE Side Oiler. Everything from the original Side Oiler is a perfect fit. What you get on the outside is an FE block casting that defies detection including the Ford casting number and date code. The aluminum block can have a maximum bore size of 4.310 inches with a 4.375-inch stroke crank. This can net you more than 500 ci. The FE cast-iron Side Oiler block yields a maximum bore of 4.400 inches.

If you're one of the fortunate few who gets to build a 427 SOHC Cammer, Robert Pond Motorsports can help there too. The Pond 427 SOHC FE Ford block gets its inspiration from the original Side Oiler block, combining the technical superiority of Ford's Indy small-block cylinder heads, dual overhead cams, and the displacement of the high-revving 427 High Riser FE.

Pond's SOHC Ford blocks are manufactured in both aluminum and cast

This is the Robert Pond Motorsports 427 SOHC Cammer block in high-grade aluminum. On the outside, it is authentic in appearance including Ford casting numbers and date codes. Inside, it sports extensive improvements that give it extraordinary strength. The Pond block comes from extensive drag experience over a lifetime. Its quality is unbeatable; this is the best FE block in the business.

Down under, the Pond FE Cammer block shows off its integrity with steel interference-fit main caps with ARP studs and hidden dowel pins. These caps will not move.

Robert Pond also does an iron FE Cammer block with all the same features as the aluminum blocks. Pond FE blocks are available for both wedge and SOHC engines.

CYLINDER BLOCK

iron, which gives you options. The basics are the same as the Pond FE wedge block, except weight is 2 to 3 pounds greater because there's more iron mid-block due to the absence of lifter galleys and bores. Deck height is 10.170 inches instead of 10.155. Oil drainback passages are in the back of the block that a wedge FE would not have.

Bear Block Motors

Another FE block option is the 427 Side Oiler block from Bear Block Motors in aluminum and cast iron along with corresponding high-tech cylinder heads. This enables you to build a new FE big-block without the tiresome search for used castings. The Bear Block FE iron and aluminum blocks are authentic in detail including Ford casting numbers and date codes. Paint them and it's challenging to tell the difference.

What makes the Bear Block Motors 427 block better is improved technology and a high-standard casting technique. The Bear Block FE 427 block is cast with high tensile diesel-grade iron with a thick .750-inch deck to handle higher compression ratios. Siamesed cylinder walls allow you to bore to 4.440 inches. Out of the box, bores are 4.245 inches, to be finish honed to 4.250 inches. An optional 4.150-inch bore will be available for the 428 in time according to Bear Block Motors. Cross-bolted main caps are a perfect interference fit amid the block skirts without spacers. Locating dowels in the main saddles lock the forged- and heat-treated 8620 steel main caps in place.

The bottom end includes thicker main webs and pan rails for superior strength. What's more, these redesigned FE blocks accept both FE and Cleveland main bearings, which gives you a wider choice of high-performance bearings. Water jackets are cast solid right up to the bottom of the lower core plugs to maximize cylinder strength and support. You may use standard ARP FE head bolts or studs. Main oil gallery passages are larger than the factory originals for increased oil volume. These Bear Block FE iron blocks tip the scales at 250 pounds. In addition to these nice features, cross-valley ribs provide extraordinary strength where it is needed the most. Find us an original factory 427 block with this kind of support. Lifter bores are oil galley fed for hydraulic lifters.

If weight is a concern for you, Bear Block Motors is producing an aluminum FE block that weighs just 125 pounds for only $1,200 more than the iron. Made from virgin high-density aluminum using the best casting technique in the world, the Bear Block aluminum 427 is a dry-sleeve block and sports centrifugally spun, high tensile strength, nodular-iron flanged sleeves. Maximum bore is 4.320 inches, with decks finished to 10.155 inches. All this block needs is finish honing and you are good to go. ∎

The 427 Side Oiler iron block from Bear Block Motors is a faithful reproduction of the original C8AE-H block from Ford. It has the hydraulic lifter provision.

What makes the Bear Block Motors 427 better than the Ford original is modern casting technology and quality, which delivers an outstanding diesel-grade iron casting.

Underneath are steel interference-fit cross-bolted main caps void of spacers and adjusters. They are a perfect, committed fit to each block.

The Bear Block Motors 427 Side Oiler is drilled for hydraulic lifters, which gives you the option of solids or hydraulics. Note the 66-427 in the casting, as on those original Side Oilers. These are huge oil galleys offering generous oil flow.

This is the 427 SOHC Cammer Side Oiler block. What makes this block SOHC-specific is the oil drainback passage (arrow) for the hemispherical heads. You can run wedge heads on an SOHC block. However, you cannot run SOHC heads on a wedge block.

One question FE enthusiasts have is about oil galley passages at the crank journals. Not all line up with the main bearing inserts. This one does.

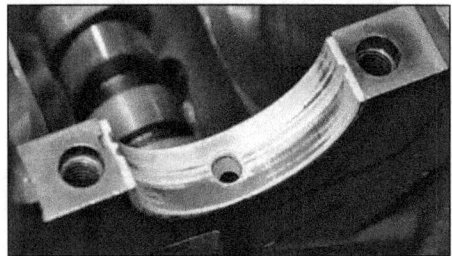

This FE main bearing oil hole doesn't line up with the oil galley, which looks like a manufacturing error. However, according to Jay Brown at FE Power, "The oil holes are actually lined up with the cam bearings, not the mains. This misalignment is by design. Ford released a memo on this in the early 1960s, reassuring mechanics that this was not a problem and was by design."

Foundry and nothing to do with performance or durability.

Another strong clue with FE big-blocks is the cooling passage size, which became progressively larger as displacement increased during the 1960s. In time, the oft-seen "352" at the front of the block (driver's side) vanished and a "105" appeared on the front of FE blocks. FE blocks, including the 360, 361, 390, 406, 410, and 427, had the "352," which doesn't mean you've found a 352 block.

FE Series block casting numbers are located on the passenger's side of the block just below the deck. Expect to see six-digit casting numbers prior to 1960 and the more familiar Ford alphanumeric casting number from 1960-on.

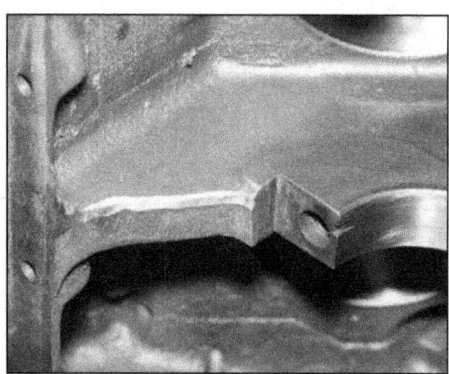

Another good tip is to grind off stress risers (ragged edges) throughout the block casting to minimize the risk of cracking. Do this during basic block prep and machining. Then, do a thorough block cleaning to remove any metal particles on the surfaces and in oil galleys. While you're at it, chase all bolt hole threads with a tap or thread chaser.

This is an early FE block with a six-digit casting number on the passenger's side of the block just below the deck along with the corresponding date code.

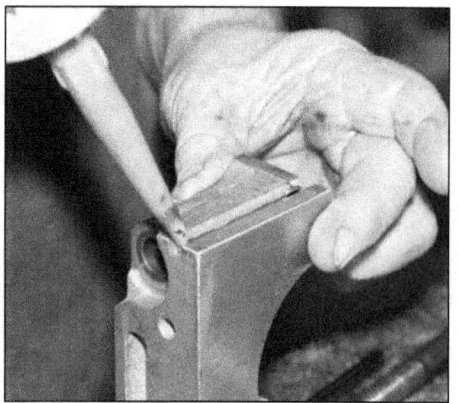

FE big-blocks tend to be leakers, but they don't have to be. Rear main seals require extraordinary care during assembly. Side seals call for Permatex The Right Stuff on both sides of each seal prior to installing pins. Crank seals call for The Right Stuff between the seal and block/cap, but never on the crank side of the seal. Main seal lips should point toward the crankshaft, never toward the outside. Finally, seal lips and crank must be bathed in plenty of engine assembly lube or SAE 30-weight engine oil.

CYLINDER BLOCK

FE Big-Block Engine Block Information

Displacement/Year	Part/Casting Number (6015)	Bore Size (inches)	Other Information
332 ci 1958	EDC	4.000	Solid Lifter Block
332 ci 1958	575063	4.000	Hydraulic Lifter Block
332 ci 1958–59	5751091	4.000	Hydraulic Lifter Block
332 ci 1959	B9AE-B	4.000	Hydraulic Lifter Block
352 ci 1958	EDC	4.000	Solid Lifter Block
352 ci 1958	575063	4.000	Hydraulic Lifter Block
352 ci 1958–59	5751091	4.000	Hydraulic Lifter Block
352 ci 1959–60	B9AE-B	4.000	Hydraulic Lifter Block
352 ci 1960	EDC-B	4.000	Solid Lifter Block
352 ci 1960	EDC-C	4.000	Solid Lifter Block
352 ci 1961–62	C1AE-G	4.000	Hydraulic Lifter Block
352 ci 1963	C3AE-A	4.000	Hydraulic Lifter Block
352 ci 1963	C3AE-F	4.000	Hydraulic Lifter Block
352 ci 1964	C3AE-G	4.000	Hydraulic Lifter Block
352 ci 1964	C4AE-A	4.000	Hydraulic Lifter Block
352 ci 1965	C5AE-C	4.000	Hydraulic Lifter Block
352 ci 1966	C6TE-C	4.000	Hydraulic Lifter Truck Block
352 ci 1966	C6TE-L	4.000	Hydraulic Lifter Truck Block
352 ci 1966–67	C6ME-A	4.000	Hydraulic Lifter Block
352 ci 1967	C7AE	4.000	Hydraulic Lifter Block
360 ci 1968–76	C6ME	4.050	Hydraulic Lifter Truck Block
360 ci 1968–76	C6ME-A	4.050	Hydraulic Lifter Truck Block
360 ci 1968–76	C8AE-A	4.050	Hydraulic Lifter Truck Block
360 ci 1968–76	C8AE-C	4.050	Hydraulic Lifter Truck Block
360 ci 1968–76	C8AE-E	4.050	Hydraulic Lifter Truck Block
360 ci 1968–76	D3TE	4.050	Hydraulic Lifter Truck Block/Heavy Duty
360 ci 1973–76	D3TE-1	4.050	Hydraulic Lifter Truck Block
360 ci 1973–76	D3TE-AC	4.050	Hydraulic Lifter Truck Block/Heavy Duty
360 ci 1973–76	D3TE-HA	4.050	Hydraulic Lifter Truck Block/Heavy Duty
360 ci 1974–76	D4TE-AC	4.050	Hydraulic Lifter Truck Block/Heavy Duty
360 ci 1968–76	D7TE-BA	4.050	Service Block
361 ci 1958–59 Edsel Only	EDC	4.050	Solid Lifter Block
390 ci 1961–62	C1AE-C	4.050	Hydraulic Lifter Block
390 ci 1961–62	C1AE-G	4.050	Hydraulic Lifter Block
390 ci 1961	C1AE-V	4.050	Solid Lifter Block
390 ci 1962	C2AE-BC	4.050	Solid Lifter Block
390 ci 1962	C2AE-BE	4.050	Solid Lifter Block
390 ci 1962	C2AE-BR	4.050	Solid Lifter Block
390 ci 1962	C2AE-BS	4.050	Solid Lifter Block

Bold indicates high-performance applications.

FE Big-Block Engine Block Information *continued*

Displacement/Year	Part/Casting Number (6015)	Bore Size (inches)	Other Information
390 ci 1962	C2SE	4.050	Hydraulic Lifter Block
390 ci 1962	C3SE-A	4.050	Hydraulic Lifter Block
390 ci 1963 Police Interceptor	C3ME-B	4.050	Solid Lifter Block
390 ci 1963 Police Interceptor	C3AE-KY	4.050	Solid Lifter Block
390 ci 1963	C3AE-AY	4.050	Hydraulic Lifter Block
390 ci 1964	C4AE-D		Hydraulic Lifter Block
390 ci 1964 Police Interceptor	C4AE-F	4.050	Solid Lifter Block
390 ci 1964	C4AE-D		
390 ci 1965	C5AE-A	4.050	Hydraulic Lifter Block
390 ci 1965 Police Interceptor	C5AE-B	4.050	Solid Lifter Block
390 ci 1966	C6ME-A	4.050	Hydraulic Lifter Block
390 ci 1968	C8AE-A	4.050	Hydraulic Lifter Block
390 ci 1968	C8AE-C	4.050	Hydraulic Lifter Block
390 ci 1968	C8AE-E	4.050	Hydraulic Lifter Block
390 ci 1973	D3TE	4.050	Hydraulic Lifter Truck Block
390 ci 1973	D3TE-AC	4.050	Hydraulic Lifter Truck Block
390 ci 1973	D3TE-HA	4.050	Hydraulic Lifter Truck Block
390 ci 1974	D4TE-AC	4.050	Hydraulic Lifter Truck Block
390 ci 1976	D7TE-BA	4.050	Service Block
406 ci 1962	C2AE-J	4.130	Solid Lifter Block
406 ci 1962	C2AE-K	4.130	Solid Lifter Block
406 ci 1962	C2AE-V	4.130	Solid Lifter Block
406 ci 1962–63	C2AE-BD	4.130	Solid Lifter Block, Cross-Bolted Main Caps
406 ci 1963	C3AE-D	4.130	Solid Lifter Block, can be converted to cross-bolted mains
406 ci 1963	C3AE-V	4.130	Solid Lifter Block, can be converted to cross-bolted mains
410 ci 1966–67	C6ME	4.050	
410 ci 1966–67	C6ME-A	4.050	
427 ci 1963	C3AE-M	4.230	
427 ci 1963	C3AE-AB	4.230	
427 ci 1963	C3AE-Z	4.230	
427 ci 1964	C4AE	4.230	
427 ci 1964	C4AE-A	4.230	
427 ci 1965	C5AE-A	4.230	
427 ci 1965	C5AE-E	4.230	
427 ci 1965	C5AE-D	4.230	

Bold indicates high-performance applications.

CYLINDER BLOCK

Displacement/Year	Part/Casting Number (6015)	Bore Size (inches)	Other Information
427 ci 1965–66	C5AE-H	4.230	Side Oiler
427 ci 1965–66	C6AE-B	4.230	Side Oiler
427 ci 1966	C6AE-C	4.230	Side Oiler
427 ci 1966–67	C6AE-D	4.230	Side Oiler
427 ci 1967	C7AE-A	4.230	Side Oiler
427 ci 1965–66	C5JE-D	4.230	Industrial
427 ci 1965–66	C6JE-B	4.230	Marine Use
427 ci 1965–66	C7JE-E	4.230	Industrial
427 ci 1965–66	C7JE-A	4.230	Marine Use
427 ci 1968	C8AE-A	4.230	Hydraulic Lifter Block Side Oiler
427 ci 1968	C8AE-B	4.230	Hydraulic Lifter Block Side Oiler
427 ci 1968	C8AE-H	4.230	Hydraulic Lifter Block Side Oiler
428 ci 1966–67	C6AE-A	4.130	
428 ci 1966 Police Interceptor	C6AE-B	4.130	Solid Lifter Block
428 ci 1966 Police Interceptor	C6AE-F	4.130	Solid Lifter Block
428 ci 1966–68	C6ME	4.130	
428 ci 1966–68	C6ME-A	4.130	
428 ci 1967–68	C7ME	4.130	
428 ci 1967–68	C7ME-A	4.130	
428 ci 1968–70 Cobra Jet	C8ME	4.130	Thicker Main Webs

Bold indicates high-performance applications.

429/460

The 429/460 block is hardy in its most basic form. Heavy main webs and thick cylinder walls make the 429/460 block virtually indestructible. This means that you can build a brute 429/460 and have little concern when you infuse a lot of power into this block. The 429 and 460 are completely interchangeable because both have 4.360-inch bores. The only difference in these engines is stroke. Drop a 460 crank into a 429 block and you have a 460, and vice versa. Aftermarket stroker

The 429/460-ci 385 Series big-block is the most interchangeable block Ford has ever created; you can load it up any way you wish. This is a 1979 D9TE-AB truck block. It can be adapted to any application imaginable and is as rugged as it gets. **You can stroke this block to nearly 500 ci or go with the 429 crank for 429 ci.**

CHAPTER 2

The nice thing about the 429/460 block is how easy it is to find and build. This is another D9TE truck block sporting ARP bolts (even better with studs and a stud girdle) and two-bolt main caps. Most 385 blocks can be converted to four-bolt main caps by any qualified machine shop. Billet four-bolt main caps for the 429/460 are available from Milodon and Summit Racing Equipment.

Block casting numbers on the 385 Series block can be found on the passenger-side rear of the block by the starter. This is a D1VE-6015-A2B 429/460-ci block.

kits allow you to huff as much as 500 ci into this block.

The 429/460 block is identifiable by the casting number, C8VE, D0VE, and D1VE-A. You can also expect to see truck blocks with D7TE, D8TE, D9TE, and so on. All 1970 Super Cobra Jet blocks had four-bolt mains (three center mains) as did 1971-on Cobra Jet and Super Cobra Jet blocks. There are also Police Interceptor 429 blocks with four-bolt mains even though this

These extra-thick two-bolt main caps contain tremendous amounts of power. With ARP bolts or studs and a stud girdle, they can withstand more than 600 hp.

This is the D0VE-A 429/460 block, which has thicker main webbing and was produced in two- and four-bolt–main configurations. There may to be some confusion because it resembles the Boss 429 block in the main web area.

Here's a D9TE truck block with the two-piece rear main seal. The key to leak prevention is staggering the seal ends away from main cap and block parting lines, plus the use of The Right Stuff between seal halves and block/cap. The seal lip must be pointed toward the crankcase or you can count on oil leakage.

Any of the 460 truck blocks are a good bet for a build project. This is the D9TE truck block, with the "T" meaning truck. Any of these blocks from the 1970s through the 1990s will work quite well in terms of durability. These blocks will handle outrageous amounts of power and stay together because they employ nice, thick main webs and cylinder walls.

This is the 385 Series bellhousing bolt pattern, which remained virtually the same throughout this engine's production life. The 400-ci Cleveland small-block has this same bellhousing bolt pattern. Some early 400 Clevelands (1971) had both small-block and 385 Series bellhousing bolt patterns.

36   FORD BIG-BLOCK PARTS INTERCHANGE

CYLINDER BLOCK

This is the D0VE-A block with four-bolt main caps. The D0VE-A block, whether it has two- or four-bolt mains, has thicker main webs and provisions for four-bolt main caps. What confuses people is the endless debate over Cobra Jet (CJ) versus a standard 429/460 block. Ford cast CJ in the valleys of D0VE-A blocks, but not all D0VE-A blocks were Cobra Jets. Suffice it to say that a D0VE-A block with its thick main webs is a good bet as long as it has not been bored beyond .040 inch oversize.

can get very confusing. Not all Police Interceptor blocks had four-bolt mains. Even with two-bolt mains, a 385 Series block is engineered to stay together under grueling conditions.

Boss 429

Ford's legendary Boss 429 has its own distinctive four-bolt main block (four of the mains are four-bolt) specific to the Boss 429. Look for the "HP 429" on the front of the Boss 429 block. This is a high-nickel block developed exclusively for NASCAR with a unique Boss 429-specific oiling system similar to the FE 427 Side Oiler with quad oil galleys mid-block. There's no other 385 Series block like it.

Here's a D0VE-A block with CJ cast in the valley. It is not known why some D0VE-A blocks were CJs and others were not. It is known that these blocks consistently have thicker main webs. The block casting date is "1F15" meaning June 15, 1971, at the "DIF" (not visible here) or Dearborn Iron Foundry.

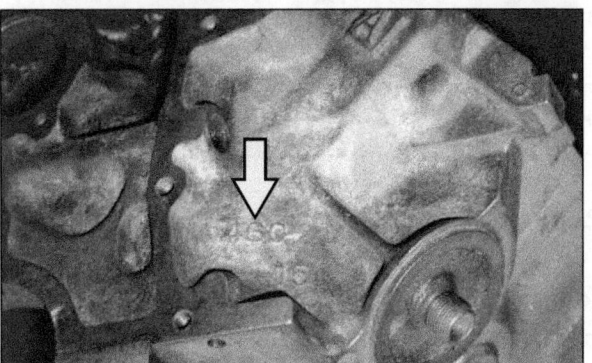

The front of a 460 block with "460" cast into the iron. The 460 is meaningless from an engine build standpoint because the 429/460 block will accommodate the 429 or 460 crank, rods, and pistons.

You can convert any 429/460 block to four-bolt main caps with a four-bolt main cap kit. This one is from JGM Performance Engineering. However, Milodon also offers a complete kit (PN MIL-11450) available from Summit Racing Equipment.

JGM Performance Engineering begins four-bolt main conversion by chasing main bolt threads to achieve a precise torque reading and a precision fit.

ARP main studs are screwed into the block. Studs offer greater stability than bolts. Studs aren't seated fully, but instead are threaded just shy of bottoming out. Threads should be lubricated lightly with SAE 30-weight oil. Avoid filling the bottom of the hole with oil. You risk hydrolocking and block cracking.

FORD BIG-BLOCK PARTS INTERCHANGE

385 Series Big-Block Engine Block Information

Displacement/Year	Casting Number (6010)	Bore Size (inches)	Other Information
429/460 ci 1968–70	C8VE-F	4.360	
429/460 ci 1968–70	C8VY-A	4.360	
429/460 ci 1969–70	C9VY-A	4.360	
429/460 ci 1969–70	C9VE-B	4.360	
429/460 ci 1970–71	D0SZ-A	4.360	
429 ci 1970–71 Cobra Jet, Super Cobra Jet, Police Interceptor	D0OE-B	4.360	
429/460 ci 1971-on	D1VZ	4.360	
429/460 ci 1971-on	D1VE	4.360	
429/460 ci 1971-on	D1ZE-AZ	4.360	
429/460 ci 1975-on	D5TE	4.360	Truck Block
460 ci 1976-on	D6TE	4.360	Truck Block
460 ci 1977-on	D7TE	4.360	Truck Block
460 ci 1978-on	D8TE	4.360	Truck Block
460 ci 1979-on	D9TE	4.360	Truck Block
429 ci Boss 429	C9AE-E	4.360	Boss 429 Block HP429
429 ci Boss 429	C9AE-E	4.360	Boss 429 Service Block 460 A

Bold indicates high-performance applications.

Main caps are positioned as shown and the block main saddles are scribed for machining. A mill is used to machine the main saddles for precision fit.

Main caps are checked for proper alignment and fit before line honing takes place.

With main caps torqued to specifications, the line bore is honed to proper sizing. Line bore must be bored/honed any time you replace main caps.

The quickest way to identify a Boss 429 block aside from four-bolt mains (mains 1 to 4) is the "S" code in the lifter valley and the four oil galleys surrounding the cam journals. The Boss 429 service replacement block will have a "460" and an "A" cast in the front of the block instead of "HP429." Expect to see variations out there with both "429" and "460."

Where four-bolt main conversion gets tricky is when you use aftermarket splayed-bolt caps. This requires precision machining by a seasoned machinist. JGM Performance Engineering has set up this block and cap for drilling and tapping. The same procedure applies if you are using four-bolt main caps from another 429/460 block: line boring/honing, mock-up, drilling, and then tapping for ARP hardware.

CYLINDER BLOCK

The Boss 429 block is clearly a stand-alone piece from mainstream 385 Series blocks. Quick identification includes screw-in freeze plugs and four-bolt main caps at cap numbers 1 to 4. This is a C9AE-E service replacement Boss 429 block, which will not have the same markings as the original factory Boss 429 block.

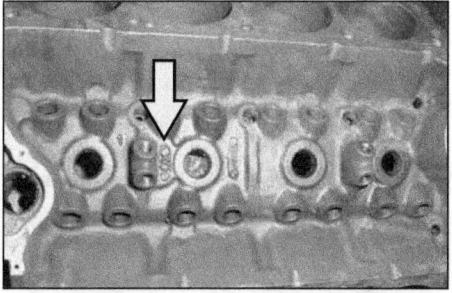

The Boss 429's valley (arrow) differs from the 429/460 block due to thicker walls around the lifters and drainbacks. This is an S block.

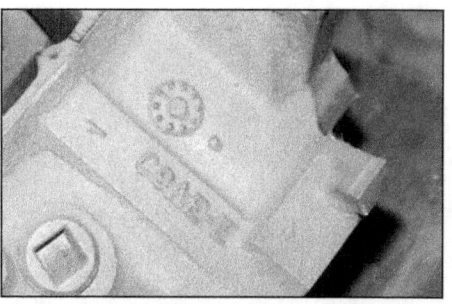

The C9AE-E block casting number identifies this block as a Boss 429 service replacement. Note the screw-in freeze plugs unique to the Boss 429 block. No other factory 429 block had screw-in freeze plugs or four-bolt main caps in four positions.

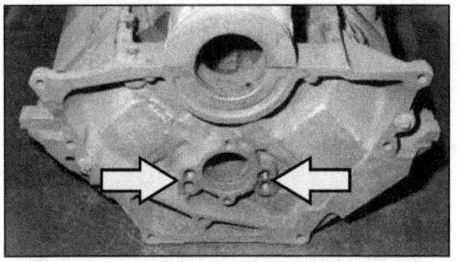

Oil galleys are what differentiate the Boss 429 block from the rest. Look for these quad galleys (arrows) on both sides of the cam bore.

The Boss 429 service replacement block isn't marked the same as the production Boss block. This block has a "460" and an "A" cast into the front of the block (arrow), yet this is clearly a Boss 429 block.

The MEL

Ford's most unusual big-block is not easily forgotten with its deck angle 10 degrees off the bore axis. The top of the cylinder bore is also the wedge combustion chamber.

Combustion chamber shape/design is determined by piston dome shape, not the cylinder head. The MEL's cylinder head deck is flat like a diesel engine with an intake and exhaust valve. What makes it different than the diesel is a spark plug instead of a pre-chamber or injector. The logic then was that you could control compression and combustion nuances better by changing the shape of the piston crown instead of the cylinder head. This was an idea that didn't live long.

The MEL block shares some characteristics with the FE Series block. However, the MEL block is bolstered in ways similar to those in big luxury cars. This is a thick, heavy, old-school block. Main bearing journals are 2.900 inches, with rod journals checking in at 2.600 inches. I'm talking huge journals around a large, heavy nodular-iron crankshaft with sizable counterweights.

The quickest way to identify an MEL block is the casting number and date code located on the passenger's side of the block just below the deck. Bore size is another good method of identification.

Ford's MEL big-block is easily the most unusual big-block Ford has ever made with its odd-angle deck some 10-degree off-bore square. The tops of the bores act as combustion chambers, hence the deck angle. The piston dome controls chamber size.

The driver's side of the MEL block shows accessory mounting pads and engine mount bolt holes.

CHAPTER 2

The driver-side front of the block shows the water pump passage and freeze plug. The block part number is stamped in the front of the block.

The MEL block's lifter valley is similar to the FE and 385 Series engines with three oil galleys down the middle.

Sleeve and Save It

Blocks that have been bored to their limits or suffer from damaged cylinder walls don't have to be scrapped. JGM Performance Engineering saves precious blocks all the time with a cylinder re-sleeve, whether it's one bore or eight. The average cost is $100 per bore.

Steel cylinder sleeves are placed in a deep freeze to shrink them. The bores in the block are re-bored to slightly larger than the bore's beginning measurement. Next, the blocks are heated and then the sleeves are installed. When the temperatures settle, the cylinders are cleaned up and honed. ■

Block sleeving begins with the replacement sleeve, which is placed in a deep freeze where it shrinks to proper size for installation with .001 inch of pinch.

Adhesive is applied to existing cylinder walls to secure the cylinder sleeve.

The replacement sleeve is sized to block deck dimensions prior to installation.

JGM Performance Engineering bores the block for .001 inch of interference fit when the sleeve is installed.

The sleeve is driven into the cylinder bore and seated against the base of the bore. The final machine work will include milling the decks and putting a taper at the top of the bore.

40   FORD BIG-BLOCK PARTS INTERCHANGE

CYLINDER BLOCK

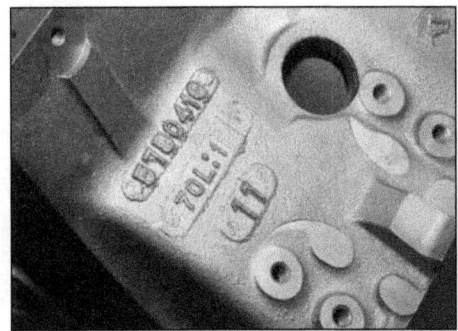

The block casting number and date code are cast into the block along with the cavity number. Prior to 1960, casting numbers were six digits. From 1960-on, you will see the more conventional Ford alphanumeric casting number.

The MEL block's bottom end is cast like Fort Knox with the thickest main webs of any Ford block. Lubrication is generous. Main bearing caps are wedged in nice and tight for rigidity as they are on the FE block.

The number-5 main cap is similar to the FE's rear main cap with side seals as well as the crank rear main seal. These had rope seals originally. Rope seals may be the only option today. Check with Fel Pro Gaskets for a rubber-reinforced rear main seal.

The MEL's block deck is unlike any Ford block deck out there. Notice the 10-degree off-bore angle with the wedge combustion chamber located at the top of the block instead of the cylinder head.

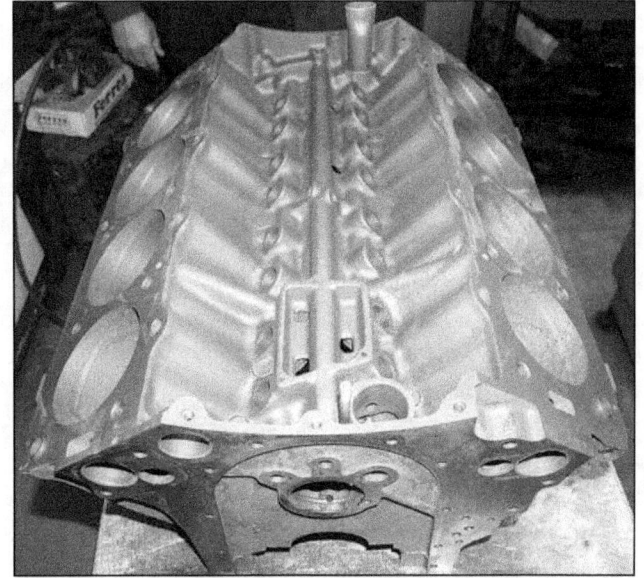

The MEL block head-on is clearly different than other Ford V-8s of the period. Note the 10-degree off-angle bores. (Photo Courtesy Dave Stribling)

The MEL's bellhousing bolt pattern is like the FE pattern of the day. There is one oil galley parallel with the cam journals.

FE and MEL blocks inverted side by side. The MEL block (right) is more rugged and designed for big, heavy, luxury cars. Shown here is an FE 427 block (left) and the 430-ci block (right). (Photo Courtesy Dave Stribling)

CHAPTER 2

MEL-Series Big-Block Engine Block Information

Displacement/Year	Part/Casting Number (6010)	Bore Size (inches)	Other Information
430 ci 1958–59	B85-6010-A 5752000	4.300	Edsel/Lincoln
410 ci 1958	B8EY-6010-B B8KE-6010-B B8KY-6010-B	4.200	Edsel
430 ci 1958	PB8M-6010-A PB8M-6010-B	4.300	
383 ci 1959	B9ME-6010-D	4.300	Mercury
430 ci 1960	C0ME-6010-A	4.300	Lincoln, Thunderbird
430 ci 1961	C1VE-6010-A	4.300	Lincoln
430 ci 1961	C1VE-6010-D	4.300	Lincoln
430 ci 1961	C1VE-6010-F	4.300	Lincoln
430 ci 1961	C1VY-6010-F	4.300	Lincoln
430 ci 1962	C2VY-6010-A	4.300	Lincoln
430 ci 1962	C2VY-6010-B	4.300	Lincoln
430 ci 1964	C4VE-6010-A C4VY-6010-A	4.300	Lincoln
462 ci 1966–68	C6VE-6010-A C6VY-6010-A	4.380	Lincoln

Checking Cylinder Wall Thickness

Cylinder wall thickness should be the first thing an engine builder checks once a block is cleaned up for machine work, whether it is a standard-bore block or a block bored to its limits. This process is known as sonic checking. Every machine shop has its own approach to sonic checking a block. Common practice is to check cylinder walls at four points in the top, middle, and bottom. ∎

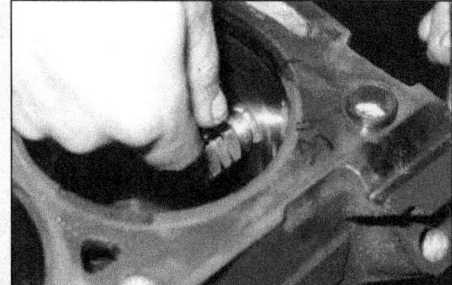

Sonic checking an FE block for cylinder wall thickness. It is extremely important to check both bore size and wall thickness whenever you're buying a block. Because casting irregularities are common with older castings, wall thickness is crucial.

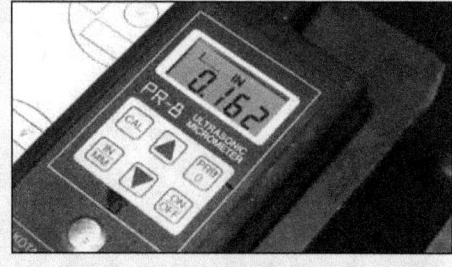

Ultrasonic Micrometer confirms that a .162-inch-thick cylinder wall is on this particular bore.

Ryan Peart of JGM Performance Engineering checks FE cylinder wall thickness to confirm a block is suitable for a build.

CHAPTER 3

ROTATING ASSEMBLY

Ford's family of big-block V-8 engines includes a variety of castings and forgings engineered to meet the needs of performance and restoration enthusiasts. Three basic engine families are addressed here: the FE (Ford-Edsel) and FT (Ford Truck), the 385, and the MEL (Mercury-Edsel-Lincoln). All three big-block engine families have been adapted to high-performance use with a lot of good factory and aftermarket bottom-end parts out there for your engine-building project.

Because Ford is notorious for engineering changes and refinements, you can count on a series of improvements across the bottom ends of the FE/FT and 385 Series engines. Count on finding castings and forgings that you haven't seen before or that people say never existed. Experimental pieces went out the back door at Ford; they end up at swap meets and online auctions all the time. The MEL didn't change much at all through its 10-year production life. The same can be said for the 385, which was a bulletproof big-block from the start in 1968.

When you can't get the displacement desired from factory pieces, the aftermarket offers a variety of stroker kits engineered to take your big-block to more than 500 ci. Reproduction blocks are also available that allow you to go beyond 500 ci.

FE/FT Rotating Assembly

The FE/FT engines employ both nodular-iron and forged-steel crankshafts. The FE uses mostly nodular-iron (cast-iron) cranks. The exception is the 406 and 427 high-performance engines, which were fitted with both iron and steel depending upon application. A close sibling of the FE is the FT heavy-duty truck-only engine, which uses a steel crankshaft and shares the same stroke as the FE. This makes it possible to machine and adapt the cheaper FT steel crank to an FE.

The real beauty of the FE/FT engines is interchangeability across the blocks and bottom ends. All FE/FT cranks have 2.7488-inch main and 2.4384-inch rod journals. This means you can turn your FE into nearly any displacement imaginable. One snag is the internal versus external balancing issues of the 410 and 428 engines. These engines are externally balanced while all other FE engines are internally balanced. The 428 Super Cobra Jet requires methodical dynamic balancing due to its heavier Le Mans connecting rods and add-on counterweight.

There are two FE connecting rod sizes: the long rod at 6.540 inches and the short rod at 6.488 inches. There are four FE strokes: 3.300, 3.500, 3.780, and 3.980 inches. Displacement also comes from four bore sizes. The short FE rod is the most common at 6.488 inches for the 390, 406, 410, 427, and 428. The long rod was associated with the low-displacement 332, 352, 360, and 361. The long rod was also specific to the 330 FT.

The short 3.330- and 3.350-inch strokes belong to the low-displacement 332, 352, 360, and 361. Greater strokes of 3.780 and 3.980 inches belong to the 390, 406, 410, 427, and 428.

332/352/360/361

The low-displacement 332/352/360/361 FE engines employ the shortest strokes at 3.300 and 3.500 inches. The 332, which was introduced first, has a stroke of 3.300 inches with 3 known crank castings. The 352, 360, and 361 at 3.500 inches, employed a variety of crank castings. The 352 had 14 known crank castings throughout its production life. The 360, which was truck only, used 2 known crank castings.

CHAPTER 3

Your search for bottom-end components should begin with knowing both what you need and what you've found. The adrenaline rush of finding the proper crank for your application can turn bitter in a hurry when you discover it has been ground beyond a serviceable size and is a throwaway. Confirm condition in detail, including journal dimensions and condition, before putting your money down.

FE crankshafts were produced in nodular iron and forged steel, and are easily identified by their casting/forging numbers. This is a 3.780-inch stroke nodular-iron crank for the 390/406/427.

The 3.780-inch stroke 427 forged-steel crankshaft was produced in at least two ways. According to John Vermeersch of Total Performance, early 427 steel cranks had press-in C-clip plugs (arrow) in the journals. Ford abandoned them for screw-in plugs.

If you're seeking a forged-steel crank for your 332/352/360/361 project, look to the FT parts shelf from the 330MD or 361. All FT medium/heavy-duty truck engines, such as the 410 and 428 FE, were externally balanced. This calls for specialized balancing procedures your builder needs to be aware of if you opt for an FT crank in your FE. The FT crankshaft has a longer crank snoot in front at 1.750 inches in contrast to the FE's 1.375 inches. This requires a qualified machinist who can cut the shaft down to 1.375 inches for your FE; then, drill and tap for the dampener.

390/406/410/427/428

The 390 FE crank, aside from the 3.780-inch stroke, is the same visually as the 332, 352, 360, and 361. It is nodular iron and internally balanced. Some 16 known 390 cranks

This is the 427's steel crank with screw-in journal plugs (arrows), which are more secure. These plugs must be removed during crankshaft machining and cleaning. During the cleaning process, pay very close attention to any minute debris that can do engine damage.

A closer look at the screw-in crank journal plugs in the 427 steel crank. It is unknown when Ford went to these screw-in plugs.

The FE's thrust bearing is located in the number-3 main journal position. Here, crankshaft endplay is checked on an FE 390. Endplay is .004 to .010 inch. If you're going racing, make it closer to .010 inch.

FE and FT engines employ a crank spacer located between the harmonic dampener and timing cover. This spacer fits inside the crankshaft's front main seal. It should be lubricated generously with assembly lube to avoid seal damage.

ROTATING ASSEMBLY

were produced from 1961 to 1976. If you're up for a steel crank for your 390, there's always the 427 crank or the 391 FT crankshaft to choose from. There are two basic strokes here: 3.780 and 3.980 inches.

The 428 nodular-iron crankshaft offers the greatest stroke of any FE, which means you can stroke your FE to the maximum factory stroke regardless of bore size including the 332, 352, 360, and 361. Of course, this wouldn't make much sense considering the large-bore blocks available. The 406 and 427 were fitted with

FE 332/352/360/361/390 Crankshaft Identification

Displacement/Year	Casting Number	Stroke (inches)	Other Information
332 ci 1958	EDC	3.30	
332 ci 1959	5752421	3.30	
332 ci 1958–59	C0AE-C	3.30	Service Replacement
352 ci 1958 (Also 330MD FT)	EDD	3.50	
352 ci 1959	5752420	3.50	
352 ci 1960	**C0AE-A**	3.50	Heavier Counterweights (without grooved journals)
352 ci 1960	**C0AE-D**	3.50	Heavier Counterweights (without grooved journals)
352 ci 1960–62	C0AE-B	3.50	
352 ci 1963	C3AE-A	3.50	
352 ci 1964	C4AE-A	3.50	
352 ci 1964 (Also 330MD FT)	C4AE-E	3.50	
352 ci 1965	C5AE-A	3.50	
352 ci 1965	C5AE-B	3.50	
352 ci 1966–67 (Also 330MD FT)	C6AE-B	3.50	
352 ci 1966–67 (Also 330MD FT)	C6AE-D	3.50	
361 ci 1958	EDD	3.50	Same as 352 ci Engine
361 ci 1959	5752420	3.50	Same as 352 ci Engine
360 ci 1968–76 (Also 330MD FT)	2T	3.50	
360 ci 1968–76 (Also 330MD FT)	2TA	3.50	
390 ci 1961–62	C1AE-A	3.78	
390 ci 1961	**C1AE-D**	3.78	Heavier Counterweights (with grooved journals)
390 ci 1961	**C1AE-H**	3.78	Heavier Counterweights (with grooved journals)
390 ci 1962	**C2AE-B**	3.78	Heavier Counterweights (with grooved journals)
390 ci 1963	C3AE-B	3.78	
390 ci 1963	C3AE-C	3.78	
390 ci 1963	C3AE-E	3.78	
390 ci 1964–65 Police Interceptor	**C4AE-C**	3.78	
390 ci 1964–65 Police Interceptor	**C4AE-D**	3.78	
390 ci 1965	C5AE-C	3.78	
390 ci 1966	C6AE-A	3.78	
390 ci 1966	C6AE-C	3.78	
390 ci 1966	C6JE-J	3.78	Marine Use/Reverse Rotation
390 ci 1966–73 Car & Truck	2U	3.78	
390 ci 1973–76 Pickup Truck	3U	3.78	
390 ci 1973–76 Pickup Truck	2UA	3.78	

Bold indicates high-performance application.

CHAPTER 3

FE 406/410/427/428 Crankshaft Identification

Displacement/ Year	Casting Number	Stroke (inches)	Other Information
406 ci 1962–63	C2AE-D	3.78	
406 ci 1963	C3AE-D	3.78	
427 ci 1963	C3AE-G	3.78	Cast Crank
427 ci 1963	C3AE-U	3.78	Cast Crank
427 ci 1964	C4AE-B	3.78	Cast Crank
427 ci 1964	C4AE-H	3.78	Forged Steel/Cross-Drilled
427 ci 1964	C4AE-AJ	3.78	Forged Steel
427 ci 1965	C5AE-C	3.78	Forged Steel/Cross-Drilled
427 ci 1965	C5JE-A	3.78	Cast Crank/Marine
427 ci 1965	C5JE-B	3.78	Cast Crank/Marine/Reverse Rotation
427 ci 1966	C6JE-B	3.78	Cast Crank/Marine
427 ci 1966	C6JE-C	3.78	Cast Crank/Marine
427 ci 1966	C6JE-D	3.78	Cast Crank/Marine/Reverse Rotation
427 ci 1968	C8AE-A	3.78	Cast Crank
427 ci 1968	C8AE-B	3.78	Cast Crank
427 ci 1969	C9AE-A	3.78	Forged Steel/NASCAR
410/428 ci 1966–67	C6ME	3.98	Cast Crank
428 ci 1968–69 PI and Cobra Jet	IU	3.98	Cast Crank
428 ci 1969–70 PI and Cobra Jet	IUB or A	3.98	Cast Crank
428 ci 1969 Super Cobra Jet	IUA	3.98	Cast Crank
428 ci 1969 Super Cobra Jet	B (Also IUA)	3.98	Cast Crank

Bold indicates high-performance application.

FT 330HD/361/391 Crankshaft Identification

Displacement	Forging Number	Stroke (inches)	Other Information
330/361 ci HD	C4TE-A	3.50	Forged Steel
330/361 ci HD	C4TE-AF	3.50	Forged Steel
330/361 ci HD	C6TE-B	3.50	Forged Steel/Large Shaft
330/361 ci HD	C6TE-D	3.50	Forged Steel
330/361 ci HD	C7TE-A	3.50	Forged Steel
330/361 ci HD	D2TE-A	3.50	Forged Steel
330/361 ci HD	D2TE-AA	3.50	Forged Steel
391 ci HD	C4TE-B	3.78	Forged Steel
391 ci HD	C4TE-G	3.78	Forged Steel
391 ci HD	C6TE-C	3.78	Forged Steel
391 ci HD	C6TE-E	3.78	Forged Steel
391 ci HD	C7TE-B	3.78	Forged Steel
391 ci HD	D2TE-EA	3.78	Forged Steel

nodular-iron or steel cranks, depending upon application. Ford never produced a forged-steel crank for the 428. All were nodular iron and tolerated the extremes of NHRA Super Stock drag racing without failure. They require methodical preparation if you're planning high-RPM operation.

FE Connecting Rods

Although Ford produced a plethora of connecting rod forgings for the FE and FT engines, it is easy to understand them and choose one. There are four basic connecting rods to be aware of: Basic, High Performance, Le Mans, and NASCAR.

Low-displacement FE engines got the "long" 6.540-inch rod, which I have already mentioned. There is the beefy C0AE-A long rod with a wide beam and 3/8-inch bolts, and the even better C1AE-B 6.540-inch "long" rod with a wider beam and larger 13/32-inch bolts for the 352 High Performance engines, which are scarce and a nice upgrade for a 332/352 in your quest for power. There's also the 6.540-inch "long" C1AE-A or C7TE-A truck rod for the low-displacement FE/FT engines.

The most common FE rod is

ROTATING ASSEMBLY

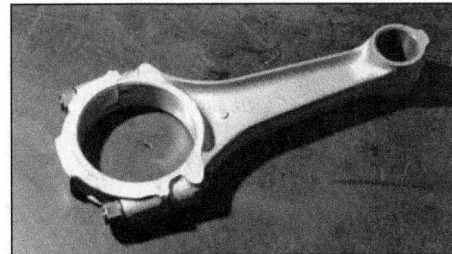

The C6AE-C connecting rod is one of the FE's short connecting rods at 6.488 inches center to center with 3/8-inch rod bolts. Expect to see this rod in 360 and 390 engines. These are durable rods; you can weave strength into them via shot peening and ARP bolts. They can take 400 to 500 hp if properly prepared and fitted with 3/8-inch ARP bolts.

This is the C6AE-E rod for the 427 Le Mans and 428 Super Cobra Jet with 7/16-inch cap screw bolts. On top is a Speed Pro coated and forged-aluminum flat-top piston. Aside from the NASCAR rod, the C6AE-E Le Mans rod is the most durable factory rod available.

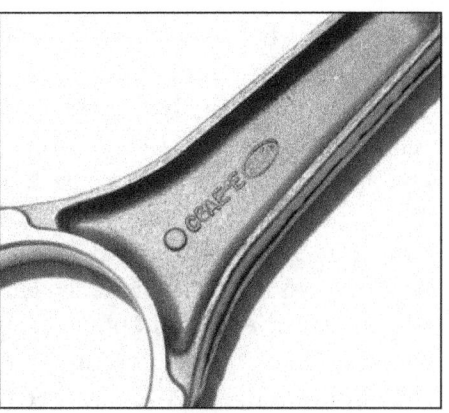

A closer look at the Le Mans rod reveals its thicker main beam leading to a heavier large end and cap screw bolts.

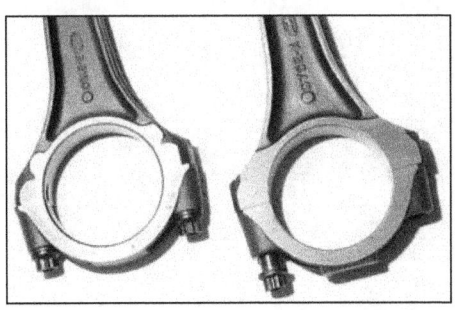

Closer inspection of the Le Mans rod (left) and NASCAR rod (right) demonstrate huge differences in these factory high-performance FE rods. The NASCAR rod is an all-out race rod; it is unnecessary for the street or even a weekend racer.

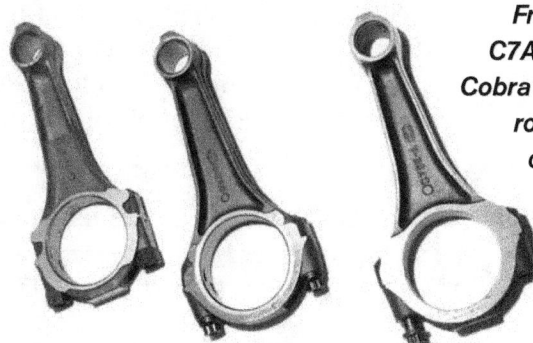

From left to right are three FE rods: C7AE-B 390, C6AE-E Le Mans/Super Cobra Jet, and C7OE-A NASCAR. These rods are the short 6.488-inch piece common to everything beyond the 332/352/361 FE and 330 FT engines. The long 6.540-inch FE/FT rods are specific to the 332/352/361 FE and 330 FT engines.

This set of 427 Le Mans/428 Super Cobra Jet rods is being checked for distortion. Rods must be checked for twist and other signs of fatigue. These rods have been around for a long time unless they're new old stock (NOS) fresh out of Ford packaging. Any set of used rods should be checked for fatigue issues.

This fixture is used to check for rod twist. No more than .012 inch of twist is allowable from pin to rod bearing bore.

Rods must also be checked for bend. No more than .004 inch is allowable. Checking rod dimension is crucial to engine life regardless of your game plan. Not enough engine builders check rod trueness. Yours should.

FORD BIG-BLOCK PARTS INTERCHANGE

the "short" 6.488-inch rod used in higher displacement applications. At a glance, it is virtually impossible to tell the difference between a short FE rod and a long one unless you look at the forging number or measure the rod center to center. The difference in these rods is .052 inch, which isn't much more than a spark plug gap.

The first high-performance FE short rod was the C1AE-E rod used in the 390 Police Interceptor in 1961–1962. At least five revised short rods were employed in the 390 and 406 High Performance engines. Of these rods, the best to use is the C2AE-D with 3/8-inch bolts for high-performance street and weekend racing applications. Regardless of which FE rod you choose, it should be reconditioned, shot peened for strength, and fitted with ARP bolts. This is as good as it gets with the basic FE short rod.

The C5AE-B 427 Le Mans rod is the first of the Le Mans rods, which is fitted with 7/16-inch cap screw bolts. This is the first FE cap screw connecting rod. What's more, it is heavier by 70 grams than the 390/406 High Performance/Police Interceptor connecting rods. With each revision of the Le Mans rod came a new Ford forging number along with corresponding strength.

The Le Mans rod was originally a 427 piece. In due course, it was used in the 428 Super Cobra Jet for 1969–1970. The 428's longer stroke made it necessary to employ cap screws with shorter bolt heads to clear the 428 block. Keep this in mind if you're using 427 Le Mans rods in a 428.

Also important to consider is rod weight. The 427 Le Mans rod is heavier because there's more bolt head. One more thing: The 410/428 is externally balanced versus the 427's internally balanced status.

The most rare FE rod is the NASCAR rod, which sports a lot of meat at the large end. You won't need this rod in a street or even a mild weekend racing engine. What's more, the NASCAR rod has its own crankshaft with wider journals (by .080 inch) than a standard production FE high-performance crankshaft.

FE Connecting Rod Identification

Displacement/Year	Forging Number	Other Information (inches)
332/352/361 ci 1958	EDC	Long Rod/6.540
332/352/361 ci 1959–60	EDC-A	Long Rod/6.540
352/360 ci 1960–78	C1AE-A	Long Rod/6.540
330 ci MD/330 ci HD 1967–78	C1AE-A	Long Rod/6.540 Truck Rod
352 ci 1960	**C0AE-A**	Long Rod/6.540 Early 1960 with 3/8-inch bolts
352 ci 1960	**C1AE-B**	Long Rod/6.540 Late 1960 with 13/32-inch bolts
330 ci/330 ci MD 1967-78	C7TE-A	Long Rod/6.540 Truck Rod
390 ci 1961–62	C1AE-C	Short Rod/6.488
390 ci 1963–65	C3AE-A	Short Rod/6.488
330/361/391 ci HD	C3AE-A	Short Rod/6.488
390 ci 1961	C1AE-E	Short Rod/6.488
390 ci 1961	C1AE-F	Short Rod/6.488
390 ci 1961–62	C1AE-G	Short Rod/6.488
390/406 ci 1962–63	C2AE-B	Short Rod/6.488 **Also Police Interceptor**
390/406 ci 1962–65	C2AE-D	Short Rod/6.488 **Also Police Interceptor**
427 ci 1963–65	C3AE-C	Short Rod/6.488
427 ci 1963–65	C3AE-C	Short Rod/6.488
427 ci 1963–65	C3AE-F	Short Rod/6.488
427 ci 1965	C5AE-B	Short Rod/6.488 **Le Mans Rod**
427 ci 1965–66	C5AE-C	Short Rod/6.488 **Le Mans Rod**
427 ci 1965–67	C5AE-D	Short Rod/6.488 **Le Mans Rod**
427 ci/428 ci SCJ	C6AE-E	Short Rod/6.488
427 ci 1967–70	C7OE-A	Short Rod/6.488 **NASCAR Rod**
428 ci 1966–70	C6AE-D	Short Rod/6.488 **Also 1968 427 Hi-Po**
428 ci 1966–70	C7AE-B	Short Rod/6.488 **Also 1968 427 Hi-Po**

Bold indicates high-performance application.

ROTATING ASSEMBLY

FE Pistons

All FE pistons, with the exception of the 427, were factory fitted with cast-aluminum pistons. All had free-floating wrist pins with a clip on each side. The 427 was the only FE engine factory fitted with forged-aluminum pistons.

The 332- and 352-ci FE engines had 4.000-inch bores with flat-top cast-aluminum pistons equipped with valve reliefs (eyebrows) to clear valves during overlap. Compression height on the 352 was .100 inch less than the smaller 332 due to the .200-inch-longer stroke of the 352. Pistons of the 332 and 352 are not interchangeable.

The 360, 361, 390 and 410 pistons had larger 4.050-inch bores, which made them different blocks than the 332 and 352. Piston interchangeability across the 360, 361, 390, and 410 is challenging due to compression height and crankshaft counterweight clearance concerns. As with the 332 and 352, this cross-section of FE engines had flat-top pistons with valve reliefs. Compression has often been controlled by dish (negative dome) size. The 406 and 428 engines had a 4.130-inch bore with flat-top pistons. Where the 406 and 428 differ are valve reliefs and piston dish. The 406 has a flat-top piston.

FE Flywheels, Flexplates, Dampeners

When you're selecting a flywheel, flexplate, or harmonic dampener for your FE big-block, it is important to understand what is compatible and what isn't. Because FE engines are both internally and externally balanced, flywheels, flexplates, and harmonic dampeners must be compatible with the engine's internals. This means these bolt-on rotating parts must be dynamically balanced with the crank, rods, and pistons if the engine is externally balanced.

The 410 and 428 are externally balanced, as are the FT truck engines. You must have a counterweighted flywheel/flexplate and harmonic dampener with the 410, 428, and FT truck engines. The counterweighting is visible with each.

Internally balanced FE engines may have flywheel, flexplate, and harmonic dampener balanced separately from the crank, rods, and pistons even though they can also be balanced together.

You may ask why the 410 and 428 are externally balanced. External balancing is necessary because there's no room in the FE block for the size of counterweights these engines would need to balance out the rod and piston mass. This calls for adding the counterweight mass outside the engine at the flywheel/flexplate and harmonic dampener.

Each type of FE engine calls for a different type of flywheel/flexplate or harmonic dampener. When you're building a 410 or 428, or perhaps one of the FT engines, you have to go back to balancing school. The 410 and 428 are counterweighted at the flywheel/flexplate. However, the 330, 361, and 391 truck crank calls

There are at least two FE harmonic dampener variations. Early FE engines have a harmonic dampener/pulley combination (left). Later versions have a bolt-on pulley. Prior to 1970, FE engines have a three-bolt pulley (right). Keep this in mind when you're shopping for harmonic dampeners.

FE engines have this harmonic dampener spacer, which is located between the dampener and timing cover. It slides into the front main seal and calls for a lot of engine assembly lube/engine oil during installation to prevent seal damage and leakage. This is a pre-1970 three-bolt dampener.

This is an FE pulley package for use with a lot of accessories including power steering, air conditioning, and Thermactor emissions.

An early 427 receives the wide dampener with a single integral crank pulley.

FORD BIG-BLOCK PARTS INTERCHANGE

CHAPTER 3

This FE 390 stroker has an aftermarket three-bolt harmonic dampener with ARP bolt crank and bolt-on pulley. Note the bolt-on two-screw timing indicator. There are at least three known FE timing pointers.

This is an early FE 427 with the extended timing pointer; you will find timing marks on the pulley.

FE Quick Tip

Don't forget FE internal versus external balancing. The 332, 360, 361, 390, 406, and 427 are all internally balanced. The 410/428-ci engines introduced in 1966 were externally balanced with external balance weights. All FT truck engines were externally balanced as well.

for counterweighting the harmonic dampener as well. That said, the best advice is to blueprint the bottom end, dynamically balancing your FE/FT at both ends of the crank.

When you order a flywheel/flexplate and harmonic dampener, always keep externally/internally balanced in mind. This means never installing a 410/428 flywheel/flexplate on a 390, as one example, or a neutral balance flywheel/flexplate/dampener on a 410/428. Pay very close attention to these parts when you're amassing a bottom-end assembly.

And one more thing, FE harmonic dampeners from 1958 to 1969 are designed for a three-bolt drive pulley. From 1970 to 1976, they are four-bolts.

429/460 Rotating Assembly

Because the 385 Series big-blocks are a straightforward engine family with two displacements, crankshaft choices are quite limited. This also makes selection easy. Unless you're building a box stocker you're going to want the most displacement possible at 460 ci. All 429/460 engines were fitted with 2Y or 3Y nodular-iron crankshafts. The exception to this statement is the Boss 429, which was fitted with a forged-steel crankshaft marked with Ford forging numbers for NASCAR competition including street versions.

The 385 Series engines included two displacements as well as two strokes: 3.590 and 3.850 inches. Crankshafts are easily identified because they are marked accordingly. The 429 cranks are marked 4U and

An early 428 Cobra Jet flexplate (left) versus later (right). Both flexplates are two-piece units; however, they vary greatly in terms of weight and strength. Because these are 410/428 parts, each has a counterweight because these FE engines are externally balanced. This means you cannot use the 410/428 harmonic dampener, flexplate, or flywheel on a 332/352/360/361/390/406/427 FE.

This is the 385 Series 429/460 harmonic dampener (D2VE-AA) with a four-bolt pulley provision.

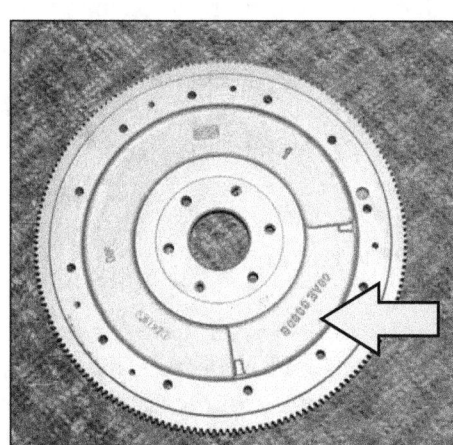

The 410/428 flywheel is counterweighted because these engines are externally balanced. The C6AE casting number indicates origination in the 1966 model year on the 410/428. This flywheel was cast "2K19" indicating October 19, 1972, which makes it a service replacement.

ROTATING ASSEMBLY

A closer look at the 410/428 flywheel and the cast-in counterweight. The key to identification is the Ford casting number, date code, and the counterweight cast into the flywheel. Flexplates will have a welded-on counterweight.

The 429/460 crankshaft is easy to identify. This is a 2Y crank, which means 460 with a 3.850-inch stroke. A 4U or 4UA is a 429 crank with a 3.590-inch stroke. Later 460 engine crankshafts are 3Y. A 3Y crankshaft is a 1979-on 460, which is externally balanced. Boss 429 steel cranks are identified by a Ford forging number of C9AE-A, C9AE-B, or C9AE-C.

Chamfer the oil galleys at main and rod journals to improve oil flow. This is an Eagle stroker crank, which is already chamfered.

The 429/460 crank snout void of a timing set and cover. The 429/460 engine is not a skirted block, which leaves the main caps out in the open as on this 429.

The 429/460 block can be stroked to more than 500 ci with an Eagle stroker kit. Here, Marvin McAfee of MCE Engines in Los Angeles prepares a steel Eagle crank for installation. He will check counterweight-to-block clearances in a mock-up before final assembly.

Although Ford 2Y and 3Y cranks are plentiful, the aftermarket offers you stroke and displacement. Eagle, Scat, and a host of others can pump 500 ci into your Ford block. This is a Ford Performance race block with room for 600 ci.

4UA. The 460 cranks are 2Y, 2YA, 2YAB, and 2YABC prior to 1979. After 1978, they are marked 3Y. It is also important to note that not all 3Y crankshafts are marked.

What makes the 3Y different than the 2Y or even the 4U is internal versus external balancing. The 2Y and 4U are internally balanced. The 3Y is externally balanced. This means that 460 engines from 1979-on are externally balanced and must be treated accordingly. Flywheel/flexplate and harmonic dampener must be compatible with the crankshaft.

429/460 Connecting Rods

The 385 Series big-block was originally conceived as a big luxury car engine with all the proper bones to be both luxury and high-performance. The 429 and 460 employ the same connecting rod, which is 6.650 inches center to center. The one exception is the Boss 429 rod, which is 6.549 inches center to center. There is,

429/460 Crankshaft Identification

Displacement/ Year	Casting /Forging Number	Stroke (inches)	Other Information
429 ci 1968–78	4U, 4UA	3.59	Cast Crank
429 ci 1970–71 Cobra Jet/Super Cobra Jet	4U, 4UA	3.59	Cast Crank/Brinell Test Mark
429 ci 1969–70 Boss 429	C9AE-A or C9AE-B	3.59	Forged Steel
429 ci 1969–70 Boss 429	C9AE-C	3.59	Forged Steel
460 ci 1968–78	2Y, 2YA, 2YAB, 2YABC	3.85	Cast Crank
460 ci 1979+	3Y	3.85	Cast Crank

Bold indicates high-performance application.

429/460 Connecting Rod Identification

Displacement/Year	Forging Number	Other Information
429/460 ci 1968+	C8VE-A	
429 ci 1970–71 Cobra Jet/ Super Cobra Jet	D0OE-A	
429 ci 1969–70 Boss 429	C9AE-A	"S" Rod
429 ci 1969–70 Boss 429	C9AE-B	"T" Rod
429 ci 1969–70 Boss 429	C9AX-A	Early NASCAR
429 ci 1969–70 Boss 429	C9AX-B	NASCAR
429/460 ci 1976+ Truck Rod	D6VE-AA	Substitute for D0OE-A

Bold indicates high-performance application.

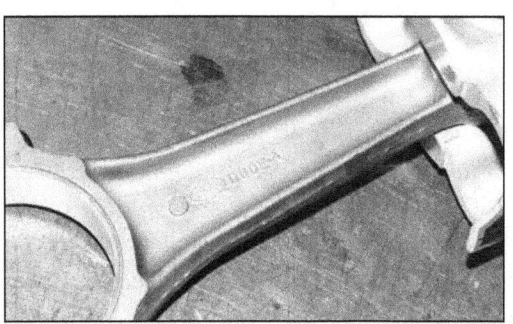

The 429/460 rod varies little across the 385's production life. This is the D0OE-A Cobra Jet/ Super Cobra Jet connecting rod, 6.605 inches center to center. Like the FE, all this rod needs is de-stressing, shot peening, and ARP bolts to make it capable of withstanding 400 to 500 hp. The D6VE-AA truck rod is a drop-in replacement for the D0AE-A connecting rod. The C8VE-A connecting rod is the least desirable because it doesn't have as much metal at the large end as the D6VE-AA rod.

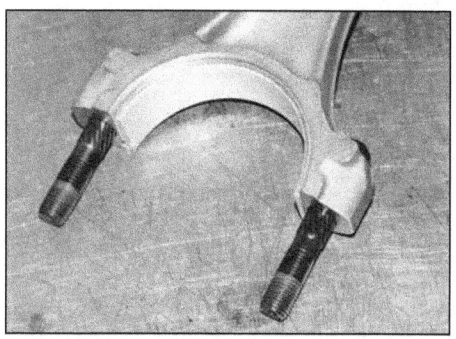

ARP rod bolts give the 385 rod unequalled strength, assuming they are given a cleaning up and shot peening. When you de-stress and shot peen this rod, it infuses strength and reduces the risk of failure.

C9AE-B rod caps are universal to most 429/460 connecting rods. Expect to see this cap on most 385 Series connecting rods.

however, a difference in rod strength. The Boss 429 rod, in both lengths, is a heavy-duty race rod. What's more, the Boss 429 rod was produced in at least four forgings.

For the rest of you building 429/460 engines there are basically three rod forgings: the original C8VE-A rod, the D0OE-A Cobra Jet/ Super Cobra Jet, and the D6VE-AA replacement for the D0OE-A rod. The D0AE-A and D6VE-AA rods are the best pieces for high-performance street and weekend racing applications. As with other desirable factory connecting rod forgings, all you have to do with these rods is recondition, shot peen, and fit them with ARP bolts. They will withstand 400 to 500 hp on average, although you should opt for a good aftermarket rod if you decide to pump the power to more than 400.

ROTATING ASSEMBLY

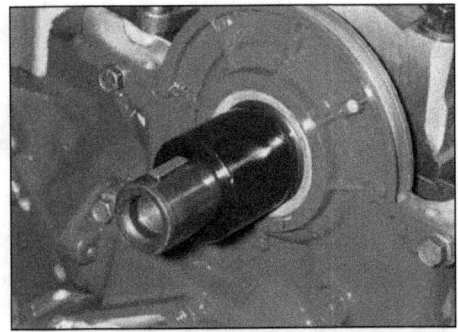

Like the FE big-blocks, the 429/460 385 Series engines get this crank spacer that inserts into the front main seal and butts up against the crank timing sprocket. There are two types of spacers: the 1968–1978 internal balance (shown) and the 1979-on spacer with a counterweight for external balance.

This is a stroker of more than 500 ci from a 460 block with steel crank and high-performance I-beam rods. It is remarkable how much power you can get from a stock block and additional displacement.

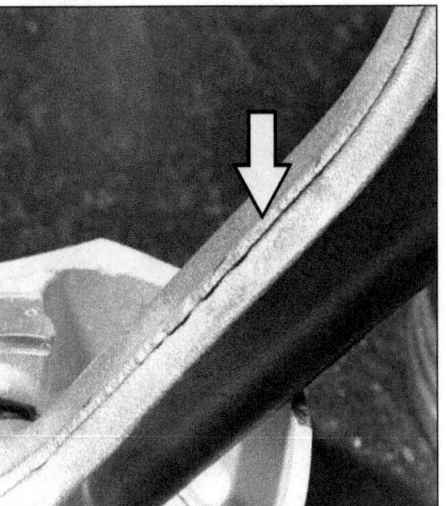

De-stressing stock 385 Series connecting rods involves removing stress risers (arrow), then shot peening the rod for additional strength. This is connecting rod blueprinting, which involves a lot of detail work to breathe strength into stock rods.

429/460 Flywheel/Flexplate/Harmonic Dampener

In your search for a harmonic dampener, flywheel, or flexplate for a 429/460, keep internal versus external balancing in mind. All 429-ci engines were internally balanced. All 460-ci engines were internally balanced prior to 1979. All 460-ci engines since 1979 are externally balanced. Prior to 1979, 460-ci engines have a spacer between the harmonic dampener and crank. Since 1979, this spacer includes a counterweight. This means all 429/460 harmonic

The D0OE-A connecting rod is common to the 429 Cobra Jet and Super Cobra Jet. Recondition this rod and fit it with ARP bolts and it's good for 400 to 500 hp.

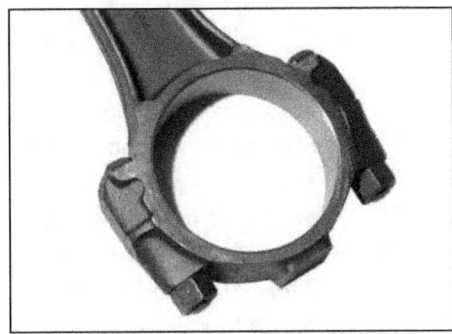

There's plenty of material here at the large end of the D0AE-A rod. This is the stock rod you want. If you can't find a D0AE-A rod, look for a D6VE-AA truck rod.

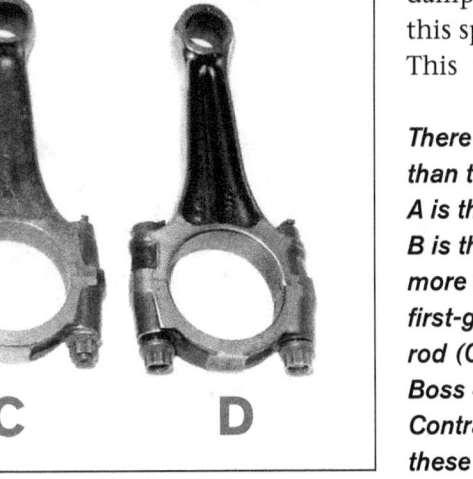

There are more Boss 429 rod options than there are regular 429/460 rods. A is the Boss 429 T rod (C9AE-B). B is the S rod (C9AE-A), which has more steel at the large end. C is the first-generation Boss 429 NASCAR rod (C9AX-B). And D is the revised Boss 429 NASCAR rod (C9AX-B). Contrary to popular belief, none of these rods has cap screws.

CHAPTER 3

Both piston and connecting rod dimensions determine deck height. Piston selection becomes easier when you consult with manufacturers and provide them with detailed information. Cylinder head gasket thickness also determines compression ratio.

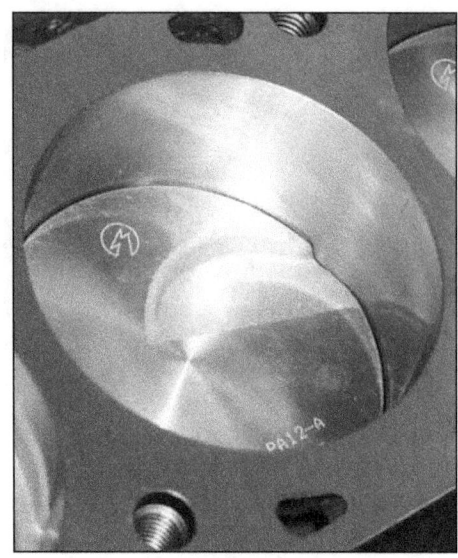

The 385 Series big-block piston employs this large intake valve relief.

Crankshaft counterweight clearances must be checked in an assembly mock-up before even thinking of final assembly. Replacement oil pumps don't always clear the crank. Aftermarket cranks don't always clear the oil pump. Take your mock-up even further with a pump pick-up and pan fit check.

If you intend to push horsepower beyond 450 to 500, seriously consider the switch to a good aftermarket H-beam rod such as one from Eagle (left). There are also excellent budget-priced I-beam rods that offer improved strength over stock rods without breaking your budget. On the right is a stock D0OE rod.

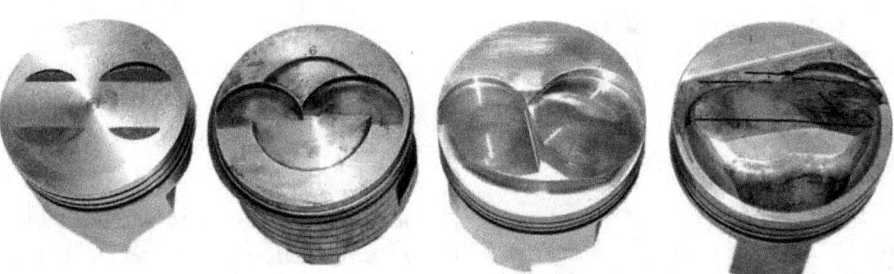

Pistons alone don't determine compression. Shown here are a variety of Ford big-block pistons. Deck and compression height, combustion chamber size, and head gasket thickness also contribute to compression ratio.

dampeners are interchangeable depending upon vehicle application. All dampeners are zero balance. The spacer with a counterweight is separate from the harmonic dampener.

Another important issue is 1968–1969 harmonic dampeners versus 1970–1978 dampeners. From 1968 to 1969, 429/460 dampeners have three-bolt pulleys similar to all other Ford V-8s of the period. From 1970 to 1978, they have four-bolt pulleys. From 1979-on, all 460 dampeners have four-bolt pulleys.

Internally balanced 460-ci engines (1968–1978 with 2Y cranks) will have a zero-balance flywheel/flexplate void of a balance weight. Externally balanced 460-ci engines (1979-on with 3Y cranks) will have a balance weight welded to the flywheel/flexplate.

MEL Rotating Assembly

If you're building an MEL (Mercury-Edsel-Lincoln) fat block there is a choice of three strokes

ROTATING ASSEMBLY

MEL Crankshaft Identification

Displacement/Year	Part Number/Casting Number	Stroke (inches)	Other Information
410/430 ci 1958–60	B8E-6303-A	3.700	
383 ci 1958–59	EDF-6303-A	3.300	
430 ci 1961	C1VE	3.700	
430 ci 1962	C2VY-A	3.700	
430 ci 1963–65	C3VY-A	3.700	
462 ci 1966–68	C6VY-A	3.830	

The MEL's EDJ nodular-iron crankshaft is identified by markings such as these prior to 1960. From 1960-on, a Ford alphanumeric number was used.

This is the Ford oval in an MEL crankshaft. Expect to see a variety of markings in the MEL crank including a cavity number.

This is an MEL 430 EDC crankshaft with journal dimensions inscribed by the builder. These crankshafts were well known for their indestructible demeanor back in the day thanks to nodular-iron construction. You will want to do all the usual hot-rodding tricks, including chamfering the oil holes and cleaning up the radii.

and a multitude of nodular-iron crankshafts. This is undoubtedly the heaviest crankshaft you will ever pick up and set on a bench with 3.300-, 3.700-, and 3.830-inch strokes. The Mercury 383 ci is a standalone crank at 3.300 inches in stroke. The 410 and 430, which are more popular, possess a 3.700-inch stroke. The behemoth 462 tips the scales at 3.830 inches of stroke. The MEL main journal size is 2.8994 to 2.9002 inches. Rod journals are 2.5992 to 2.6000.

MEL Connecting Rods

The MEL connecting rod didn't change dimensionally over the production life of this engine. Ford produced at least six connecting rods for the MEL.

The MEL connecting rod is a broad-shouldered forging that is very wide at the large end; it tapers to the small end with a .975-inch wrist pin. All MEL connecting rods were 6.600 inches center to center.

CHAPTER 3

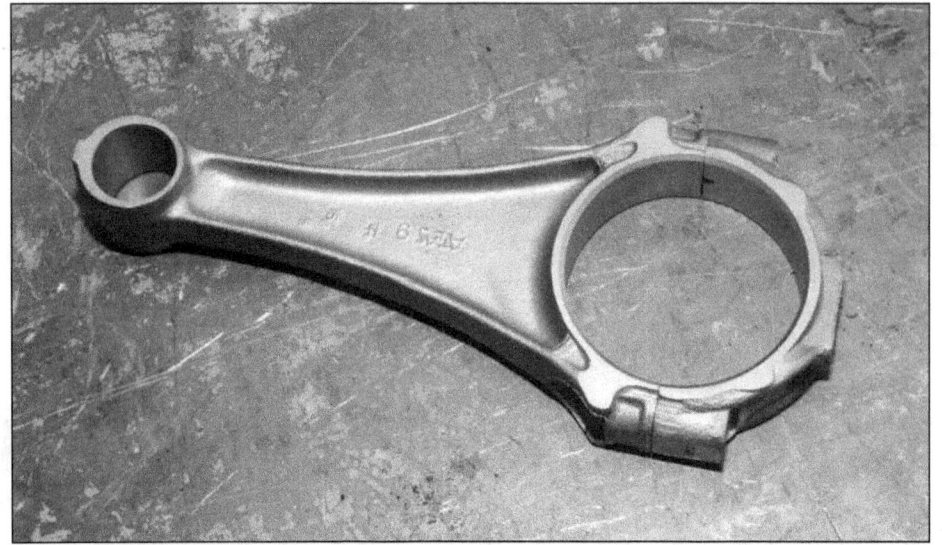

The MEL connecting rod is a brute piece with a wide I-beam ready to shoulder the load. As with the FE and 385 engines, these rods can withstand 400 to 500 hp with sufficient prep. There are also aftermarket rods available for the MEL.

MEL Connecting Rod Identification

Displacement/Year	Forging Number/Part Number	Other information
383/430 ci 1958	EDG-6200-A	Before 7AP
383/430 ci 1958	EDF-6200-A	
410 ci 1958–59	B8S-6200-A/5750737	
383/430 ci 1958–59	B8S-6200-A/5750737	After 7AP
383/430 ci 1960–61	C0ME-6200-A	
430/462 ci 1961–68	C1VE-6200-A	
430/462 ci 1963–68	C3VY-6200-A	

MEL Pistons

The MEL has a sizable assortment of pistons from the factory, not to mention the aftermarket, which offers even more. The objective with the MEL piston was to control with greater precision how the fuel/air mix was ignited in the chamber. It can be considered the beginning of a high-swirl chamber.

The piston's unique dome shape thrust the air/fuel mixture into a turbulent swirl, then, nearing the top of the compression stroke, wedged the mix into that tight area between the flat and the raised dome. In theory, this would create turbulence at the spark plug right at the point of ignition. It was a tricky learning curve for Ford because the head and piston relationship had to be reviewed and revised several times.

Some MEL builders have mistakenly gone to flat-top pistons, which erodes both performance and smoothness. The perception is that a flat-top will improve performance when, in fact, it will do exactly the opposite. The MEL's unique piston dome shape, as designed by Ford's best engineers, is what makes this engine tick. Piston dome design makes or breaks the success of a MEL build. This is why you must look to the expertise of Wiseco and Egge Machine for piston selection. These folks have a long history with the MEL. They know what works and what doesn't.

Early MEL cylinder heads had perfectly flat deck surfaces, leaving chamber shape to piston design alone. The piston's high dome or wedge is there to literally form the combustion chamber's shape. When you go to a flat-top piston, you take the factory's intended chamber shape and function away.

MEL pistons vary significantly, depending upon cylinder head type and engine displacement. Ford went through a huge learning curve with the MEL due to performance issues rooted in detonation and rough running. Wiseco and Egge Machine offer a selection of custom pistons for the MEL. It is extremely important to be detailed in your communications when ordering pistons for the MEL.

CHAPTER 4

LUBRICATION

Ford big-block lubrication systems don't vary much from engine type to engine type. They're all controlled pressure via a gerotor pump and a relief valve into a network of oil galleys that begin at the main bearing journals, rod journals, up to the cam journals, and ultimately the valvetrain on top.

Your big-block's oil pump is driven off the distributor gear via a hex shaft, which is driven by the camshaft. Within the pump are two rotors (inner and outer) that wind around each other, hence the term *gerotor*. In their rotary relationship, the inner rotor drives the outer rotor. As the inner rotor hauls the outer rotor around in a 360-degree cavity, the two conspire to move oil under pressure through the cavity to the engine's oil galleys. A spring-loaded pressure relief valve in the pump (or in both block and pump with a 427 Side Oiler) unseats when pressure becomes excessive, venting excess pressure back to the pan.

FE Oiling System

Although oiling systems are categorized by engine type, all are basically the same. For any FE engine build you're going to want a high-volume oil pump. It's just good engine life insurance. There are

The FE's oiling system begins at this external oil filter adapter mount, which is typical of all FE/FT big-blocks. There's also an optional external oil cooler mount (not shown here) with provisions for oil lines common to the 428 Super Cobra Jet and the 427.

When you're building an FE big-block, opt for a high-volume oil pump. All oil pumps should be inspected and blueprinted prior to installation. Blueprinting is the checking of clearances and the pressure relief valve for proper function. Never install an oil pump straight out of the box.

There are a lot of opinions regarding oil galley plugs. These oil galley plugs in the FE valley are pressed in and tanged. This works for most rebuilds. If you are building an FE for high-performance use, opt for screw-in oil galley plugs in all locations.

FORD BIG-BLOCK PARTS INTERCHANGE

CHAPTER 4

There has been long discussion among FE builders concerning oil galley alignment at the main journals. Jay Brown of FE Power has confirmed that this is the norm with FE engine blocks. Some are in perfect alignment; others are not.

Here's another misaligned main journal oil galley. Again, this is not a cause for concern unless the galley is completely covered by the bearing shell. These galleys are generally centered on the cam bearings. They tend to vary at the main bearings. Some are in perfect alignment; others are not.

Mark Jeffrey of Trans Am Racing prefers to open up these main bearings to improve oil flow to the main bearings. Here, Mark has chamfered the oil galley (arrow).

three basic types of FE oiling systems: mechanical lifter, hydraulic lifter, and the Side Oiler. The mechanical lifter block isn't much different than the hydraulic lifter block with the exception being the absence of oil galleys running the length of the block with the lifter bores. The mechanical lifter block doesn't have a provision for hydraulic lifters.

The Side Oiler block is completely different from the center/top oiler in terms of oil distribution and control with a main bearing focused oil galley running down the driver's side of the block with an oil pressure relief valve at the back of the driver's side. The Side Oiler was conceived to deliver generous amounts of oil under pressure to the main bearings. There are two pressure relief valves in the Side Oiler, with one in the pump and one at the back of the block on the driver's side. Some builders choose to eliminate the block relief valve while others don't.

One concern with the FE is keeping plenty of oil in the sump to keep everything lubricated at high RPM. This is why high-performance applications have deeper sumps with at least a 6- to 7-quart (or greater) capacity. Barry Rabotnick at Survival Motorsports suggests a Melling M57HV high-volume pump for an FE engine along with a good blueprinting to ensure durability. Inlet and outlet are deburred along with the checking of tolerances. He adds that pump rotor clearances should be .001 to .003 inch at the most. Anything greater than .003 inch creates pressure concerns at lower RPM.

The factory Ford oil pump drive shaft is 1/4 inch in diameter. Toss your stock pump shaft and opt for an

FE blocks machined for hydraulic lifters will look like this: two oil galleys down the entire length of the block on each side of the cam (arrows). Mechanical lifter blocks will not have these galleys.

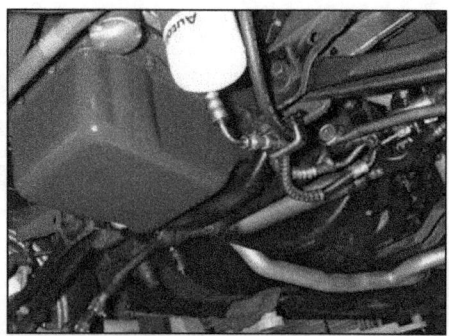

This is a typical FE front sump pan for Ford and Mercury compact and intermediates. Pan depths and sump positioning vary, depending upon application.

A Milodon high-volume oil pump for racing applications is shown on a 427 Side Oiler. This is one of John Vermeersch's Side Oilers at Total Performance.

LUBRICATION

ARP shaft, even for a stock application. The ARP shaft is much stronger than stock and can stand up to the rigors of racing.

There are basically two types of FE oil filter adapter mounts: the cast-aluminum oil filter mount with

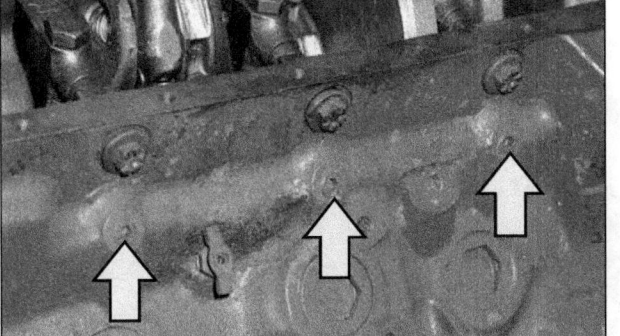

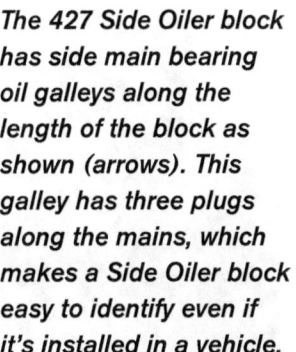

The 427 Side Oiler block has side main bearing oil galleys along the length of the block as shown (arrows). This galley has three plugs along the mains, which makes a Side Oiler block easy to identify even if it's installed in a vehicle.

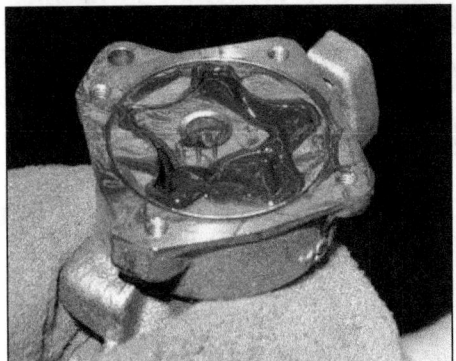

Pump inspection and blueprinting is an extremely important step in your FE build. Disassemble the oil pump and be sure to take note of the rotor index marks, which must be installed in proper alignment. Check tolerances. Before you button it up, fill the cavity with engine assembly lube for a good wet start-up.

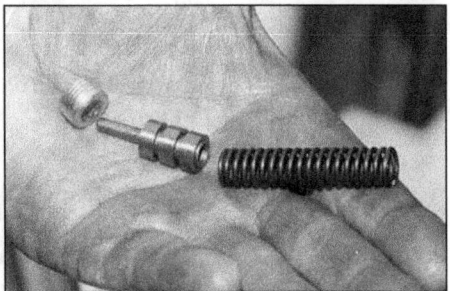

A Side Oiler block is easily identified by where the oil pressure relief valve is installed and the side galley ends.

The 427 Side Oiler's pressure relief valve consists of the piston, spring, and oil galley plug. Spring pressure determines maximum pressure.

The Side Oiler's pressure relief valve is installed spring first, followed by the piston and galley plug. The piston pin is pointed toward the galley plug. Always use a thread sealer on the galley plug.

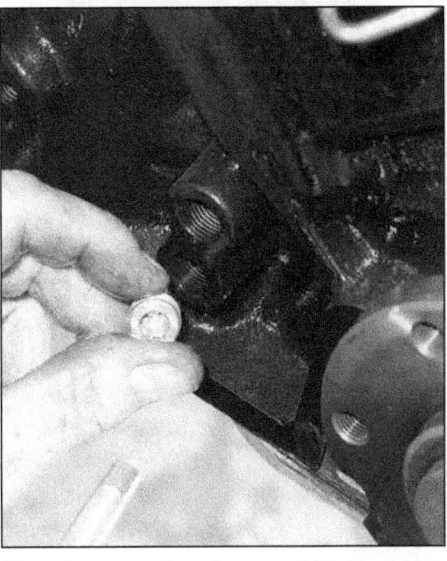

The piston and spring are installed. This is the oil galley plug. When you examine the back of a Side Oiler block, note the two galley plugs. One is the side galley for which the Side Oiler is known. The bottom plug gives the impression that it has two galleys. The bottom plug is for the oil pressure regulator, which is in the block on a Side Oiler.

Opening the pump pick-up passage from each end improves the oil volume in all FE blocks. This galley is approximately 1/2 inch in diameter. You will want to enlarge it in small steps when the block is bare. Chamfer these passages while you're at it to minimize fluid turbulence. JGM Performance Engineering performs this step to increase volume along with a high-volume pump.

FORD BIG-BLOCK PARTS INTERCHANGE 59

CHAPTER 4

A pick-up passage is drilled from the other end to increase volume along with the oil filter. This is a simple modification your machine shop can make during the machining process.

This is the oil cooler adapter for the 428 Super Cobra Jet. However, it can be applied to any FE engine. Because these tend to be rare they're also expensive. Look to the aftermarket for an oil cooler/filter adapter to save money. (Photo courtesy Barry Rabotnick)

This is another FE durability trick practiced by JGM Performance Engineering. Oil galleys at the rocker arm shafts are drilled and tapped for restrictors to reduce oil volume on top where it isn't as necessary and keeping oil down under where it is needed.

Restrictors are installed in each FE cylinder head to reduce oil flow at the valvetrain. This is a good and viable oil control procedure that's easy to perform. Always make sure all metal debris has been removed prior to engine assembly.

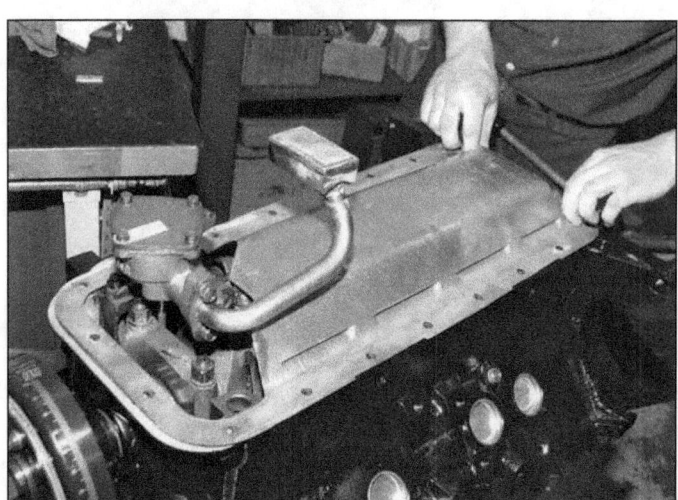

The windage tray is installed to prevent oil from being pulled out of the sump at high RPM. This windage tray is for the Cobra T-pan. Gaskets must be installed between the pan rails and windage tray, then between the windage tray and pan.

A high-volume oil pump is shown here with a Milodon pick-up for a Cobra T-pan. This pick-up can be used on any high-performance pan as long as it's within 1/8 to 1/4 inch of the pan sump bottom.

LUBRICATION

The cast-aluminum Cobra T-pan is a road-race pan. These baffles keep oil around the pickup in hard cornering. A drag race pan, by contrast, is deeper and keeps oil around the pick-up during hard acceleration. GE Glyptal is painted over the cast aluminum to prevent leakage and keep any tiny cast fragments from getting into the oil.

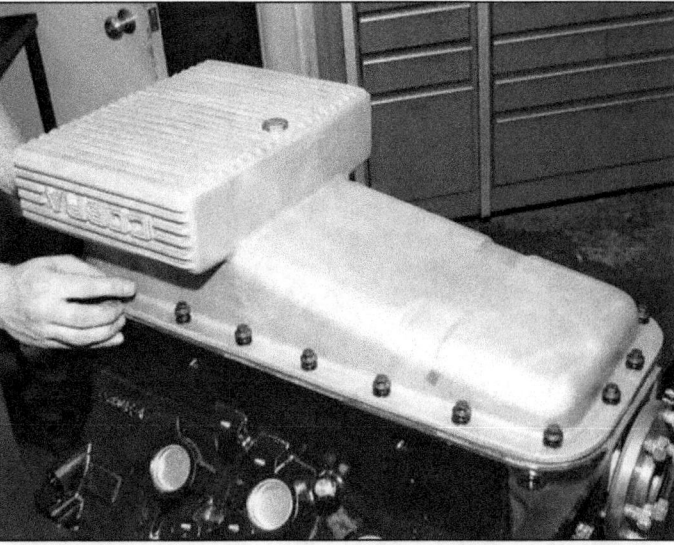

The only issue you may have with the Cobra T-pan in some applications is chassis clearance. For example, some aftermarket steering racks will not clear this pan.

a provision for the sending unit and the oil cooler adapter produced for the 428 Super Cobra Jet and other high-performance FE applications, including the 427. Unless you're performing a concours restoration you won't need the stock Super Cobra Jet oil cooler adapter because the aftermarket offers a wealth of adapters for the FE.

An external oil cooler/filter adapter is shown installed on an FE block. Check with Summit Racing Equipment for availability. These are more affordable than an original Ford oil cooler adapter.

429/460 Oiling System

The 429/460 oiling system is modeled after the 289/302-ci small-block Ford V-8. Oil filter and cam-driven gerotor pump are located at the driver-side front of the engine block. Oil is drawn from the pan via a gerotor pump equipped with an internal relief valve. The pump is located in a front sump pan. Deep-sump pans are available for drag racing applications. There are also dual-sump aftermarket 385 Series race pans and pick-ups for Fox body Mustangs.

the cam journals and the galleys (arrows) traveling the length of the block. Oil is pressure-fed up the pushrods to rocker arms and valves.

The 429/460 385 Series big-block has almost the same oiling system as a small-block Ford V-8. Oil is picked up in the pan and routed to a screw-on oil filter on the driver's side of the block. Oil travels to the main journals and then up to

Oil filter location on the 429/460 block. Oil is drawn from the pick-up to the pump (top arrow) through the filter to the main journals (right arrow).

FORD BIG-BLOCK PARTS INTERCHANGE

CHAPTER 4

The 429/460 oil pump is mounted in a similar fashion to the small-block Ford V-8. This is a high-volume pump on a 429 Super Cobra Jet.

This is a high-performance, high-volume race pump being installed on a 385 Series Ford Racing block. The pump has been blueprinted and the ARP bolts safety wired for durability.

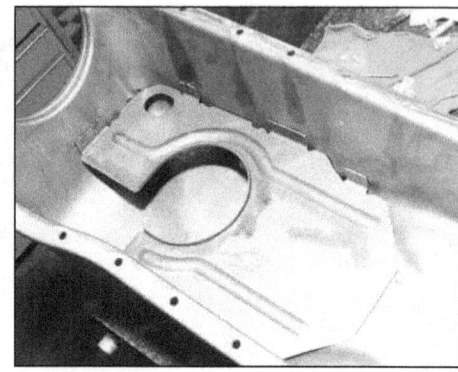

The 429 Super Cobra Jet oil pan is baffled to prevent oil pump cavitation. You should complement the baffled pan with a windage tray.

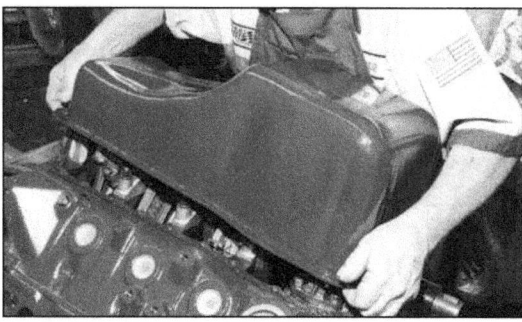

This is a typical 429/460 pan profile with front sump. However, this one is baffled to prevent oil slosh and keep oil in the sump. Aftermarket pans are also available that enable you to install a 429/460 in almost anything, including the 1979–1993 Fox-Body Mustang.

The MEL's oil pump and pick-up system is much the same as found on the FE and 385 Series big-blocks. It is a gerotor design with an internal pressure relief valve. The MEL oil pump can get tricky in vehicles with vacuum-operated windshield wipers; these have a vacuum pump incorporated into the oil pump. The vacuum pump is a piggyback vane pump blended into the bottom of the oil pump.

MEL Oiling System

The MEL big-block oiling system isn't much different than that of the FE with an internal gerotor cam-driven oil pump and external oil filter adapter located at the driver-side front of the block. The MEL is a center/top oiler much like its FE cousin sporting hydraulic lifter bores. One exception is the MEL oil pump piggybacked with a vacuum pump for vacuum-operated accessories on certain models. When you're shopping for oil pumps, be mindful of this vacuum pump.

This is the MEL oil pan with the anti-slosh feature welded into the pan. The baffle keeps oil where it belongs: at the sump. Like the FE, the MEL is a skirted block with a flat pan rail for 360 degrees.

CHAPTER 5

CYLINDER HEADS

Ford's family of big-block engines encompasses a wide variety of cylinder heads and applications. Ford engineers stayed busy focusing on engineering changes that drive enthusiasts crazy. Most of these engineering changes are hard to see on the surface, but each had a purpose. Few of these changes have any effect on power. Port size variation is something having little, if any, effect because ports are generally too large or too small, depending upon which engine family you are addressing.

FE Series port sizing is befuddling because there's very little difference in port size across the board unless you're talking 427 cylinder heads. The 385 Series big-block employs four basic cylinder heads even though there are a number of casting/part number differences. The MEL was a low-revving luxury car engine. However, it achieved fame in powerboat cruising and racing. Despite both factors, Ford produced one basic cylinder head for the MEL with slight variations.

The real beauty of Ford big-block heads is easy identification and broad selection in each engine family.

FE Series

A big plus for FE big-block buffs is a plethora of factory head castings, with the added bonus of OEM-style head castings from Blue Thunder, Robert Pond, Bear Block Motors, Survival Motorsports, and Edelbrock that give an FE build a stock demeanor without revealing what's inside. These manufacturers offer more choices than ever and that means unprecedented power gains.

FE cylinder heads have 10 head bolt holes and 4 rocker arm pedestal attachment bolt points. Each end sports 3/8-inch threaded bolt holes for accessories. What makes the FE cylinder head odd is that it shares the valvecover with the intake manifold. That makes the FE head narrow compared to the 385 and MEL series heads. All valves are on a common plane of 13 degrees in relation to the block deck. Combustion chambers range in size from 58 to 88 cc, depending upon which head you're thinking of.

Most FE cylinder heads have the smaller chambers at 58 to 74 cc. High-performance cylinder heads such as the 427's traditionally have larger 77- to 88-cc chambers, with compression regulated by piston dome configuration. Exhaust port passages jut way out from the valvecovers as they do on a Pontiac or Oldsmobile cylinder head.

It is well known that mass-production FE cylinder heads don't vary much across all castings. Port sizing across FE production history

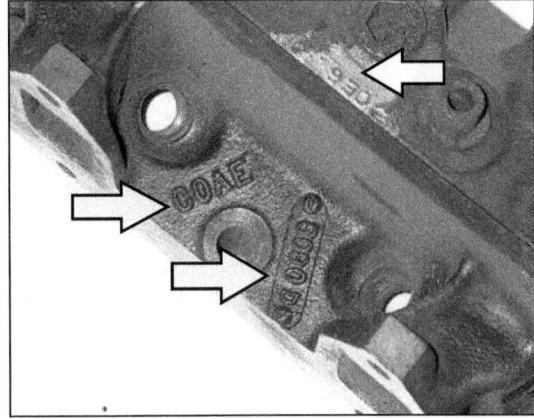

FE cylinder heads are identifiable by their casting number and date code. This is a C0AE-6090-D cylinder head for 1960 352 and 1961–1962 390. The casting number (bottom arrows) is almost never the same as the Ford part number. The alphanumeric casting date code of "0E6" (top arrow) indicates the exact date the part was cast: May 6, 1960.

CHAPTER 5

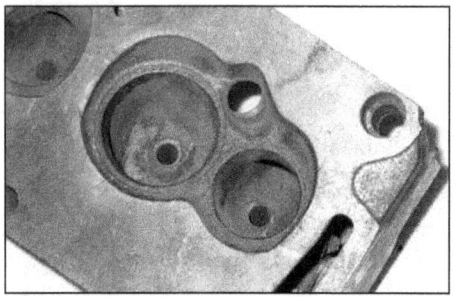

The C0AE-D cylinder head has these terrific 59- to 62-cc chambers, which offer great quench. One issue could be valve shrouding, which can be improved with the talents of a seasoned cylinder head porter. Valve sizing is 2.020/1.550-inch intake/exhaust. This is considered one of the best FE heads Ford ever produced due to its smaller chambers.

This is the 1967–1969 390 GT head, C7AE-A, with 2.020/1.550-inch intake/exhaust valves, 2.340 x 1.340-inch intake port sizing, and 1.840 x 1.340-inch exhaust. Chamber sizing is 67 to 70 cc.

The casting date code on this C7AE-A head is "6H24." That translates to August 24, 1966.

Here's a C8AE-H (top arrow) 390 Thermactor cylinder head cast on September 27, 1968 (bottom arrow). In dyno testing at JGM Performance Engineering, a 390 stroked to 431 ci with these heads managed 450 hp with comparable torque without port work.

The C8AE-H head has 67- to 70-cc chambers making it comparable to dozens of other FE head castings out there. Although Ford called this casting the GT head, it is challenging to see the difference between it and garden-variety FE castings. Valve, port, and chamber sizing are the same.

Viewed from above, it's easy to see that the C8AE-H 390 GT High Performance head sports the same 2.340 x 1.340-inch intake ports as the rest of the FE lineup. This is why head selection isn't that critical if you're building an engine for cruising or even weekend racing. It is best if you avoid the Thermactor head unless you're performing a matching-numbers concours restoration. Thermactor exhaust ports are restrictive.

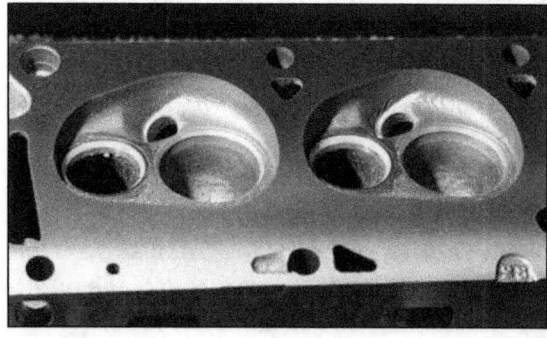

A pair of 1967–1969 390 GT combustion chambers fitted with hardened steel exhaust valveseats for use with unleaded fuels. Hardened exhaust valveseats are mandatory for any big-block if you want real longevity.

varies little despite dozens of part and casting numbers. For example, the GT High Performance cylinder head doesn't have enough of a port/valve size difference to be worth its distinction. It is basically the same head found on Galaxies and pickup trucks with only minute variations.

If you're searching for noticeable horsepower gains, the 427 Medium Riser/428 Cobra Jet head is your best

CYLINDER HEADS

A valve job should include 16 new stainless steel valves. Much depends upon the condition of the existing valves and that dictates whether you reuse or replace them. Face and stem condition should determine your decision. There are two ways to approach valveguides. Bronze guides are the most economical. However, you should replace all 16 guides and start fresh in the interest of durability, budget permitting. A standard three-angle valve job will work for most builds. If flow is crucial to your build, opt for a multi-angle valve and seat. Multi-angle valve jobs cost more because there's more set-up time.

The FE valvetrain receives its lubrication from the network of block oil galleys to this transition point in the cylinder head. From here, oil travels through a galley to the number-2 rocker arm shaft pedestal (driver's side) or the number-3 pedestal (passenger's side).

To expedite return oil flow from the top end, Ford added this stamped steel drain channel, which captures oil coming off the rocker arm assembly. It also keeps excessive amounts of oil from overwhelming the valve seals. The drain channel doesn't always clear aftermarket rocker arms. You can trim the channel for fit or eliminate it entirely.

When you opt for new valves, hardened exhaust seats, and new guides, you're building a new cylinder head casting. If guides are outside your budget, bronze liners are a suitable alternative. Bronze guides are liners that go inside the existing guides.

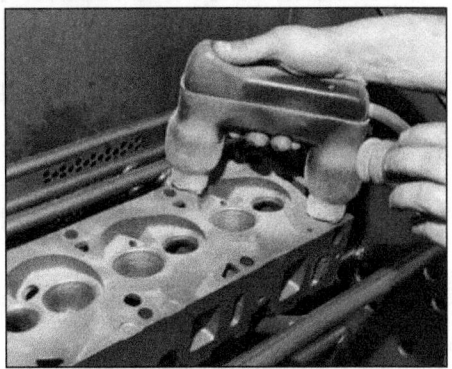

Before committing any time or money to a cylinder head casting, have it Magnafluxed to check for cracks, along with a detailed inspection to check for other flaws.

option in a factory iron head. You will find that dyno room port and bowl work makes a significant difference in FE power. Boosting compression, while keeping available pump gas in mind, is the quickest way to FE power. Compression should never go beyond 10.0:1 unless you can come up with a suitable cam profile designed to control dynamic compression.

The 332/352/360/361/390 and 410 all have 2.020-inch intake and 1.550-inch exhaust valves. Differences lie mainly in combustion chamber and port dimensions, with combustion chamber sizing having a direct effect on compression ratio. Huge differences exist when you examine the 427 cylinder head grouping. For street and weekend racing you're not going to need any more than the 427 Medium Riser casting. For all-out racing the 427 High Riser head is the best choice in a factory casting. The 427 Low Riser head isn't really any different than most FE heads of the era.

What made those first FE 332/352 cylinder heads distinctive were their machined combustion chambers, which went away when Ford started looking at cost. This is when Ford went to "as-cast" FE chambers. FE cylinder heads didn't change much after that. The beauty of the FE big-block head family is selection and interchangeability. The negative is the absence of choice. There's just not much difference in FE cylinder head castings; the exceptions are the 427 Medium Riser, High Riser, and Tunnel Port heads along with the 428 Cobra Jet head (which is basically the 427 Low Riser).

FORD BIG-BLOCK PARTS INTERCHANGE

FE Cylinder Head Identification

Some cylinder head castings may not be listed. ■

Displacement/Year	Casting Number	Chamber Size (cc)	Valve Size (inches)	Port Size (inches)
332/352 ci 1958	EDC or EDC-E	69 to 72	2.02 Intake 1.55 Exhaust	2.34 x 1.34 Intake 1.84 x 1.28 Exhaust
332/352 ci 1958	5752142	70 to 74	2.02 Intake 1.55 Exhaust	2.34 x 1.34 Intake 1.84 x 1.28 Exhaust
361 ci 1958–59 Edsel	5752142	70 to 74	2.02 Intake 1.55 Exhaust	2.34 x 1.34 Intake 1.84 x 1.28 Exhaust
332/352 ci 1959	5752143	70 to 74	2.02 Intake 1.55 Exhaust	2.34 x 1.34 Intake 1.84 x 1.28 Exhaust
361 ci 1959 Edsel	5752143	70 to 74	2.02 Intake 1.55 Exhaust	2.34 x 1.34 Intake 1.84 x 1.28 Exhaust
352 ci 1960	C0AE-C	73 to 76	2.02 Intake 1.55 Exhaust	2.34 x 1.34 Intake 1.84 x 1.28 Exhaust
352 ci 1960	**C0AE-D**	**59 to 62**	2.02 Intake 1.55 Exhaust	2.34 x 1.34 Intake 1.84 x 1.28 Exhaust
352/390 ci 1961–63	C1AE-A	71 to 74	2.02 Intake 1.55 Exhaust	2.34 x 1.34 Intake 1.84 x 1.28 Exhaust
352/390 ci 1961	C1SE-A	71 to 74	2.02 Intake 1.55 Exhaust	2.34 x 1.34 Intake 1.84 x 1.28 Exhaust
390 ci 1962–63	**C2SE-A**	**65 to 68**	2.02 Intake 1.55 Exhaust	2.34 x 1.34 Intake 1.84 x 1.28 Exhaust
406 ci 1962–63	**C2SE-B**	**64 to 67**	2.02 Intake 1.55 Exhaust	2.34 x 1.34 Intake 1.84 x 1.28 Exhaust
406 ci 1962–63	**C2SE-C**	**64 to 67**	2.02 Intake 1.55 Exhaust	2.34 x 1.34 Intake 1.84 x 1.28 Exhaust
406 ci 1963	**C3AE-C**	**64 to 67**	2.02 Intake 1.55 Exhaust	2.34 x 1.34 Intake 1.84 x 1.28 Exhaust
427 ci Low-Riser 1963	**C3AE-D**	**64 to 67**	2.08 Intake 1.64 Exhaust	2.34 x 1.34 Intake 1.84 x 1.28 Exhaust
427 ci Low-Riser 1963	**C3AE-G**	**73 to 76**	2.08 Intake 1.64 Exhaust	2.34 x 1.34 Intake 1.84 x 1.28 Exhaust
427 ci Low-Riser 1963	**C3AE-H**	**73 to 76**	**2.08 Intake 1.64 Exhaust**	2.34 x 1.34 Intake 1.84 x 1.28 Exhaust
427 ci Low-Riser 1963	**C3AE-J**	**73 to 76**	2.08 Intake 1.64 Exhaust	2.34 x 1.34 Intake 1.84 x 1.28 Exhaust
427 ci High-Riser 1963	**C3AE-K**	**73 to 76**	2.18 Intake 1.72 Exhaust	2.78 x 1.38 Intake 1.86 x 1.30 Exhaust
427 ci High-Riser 1964–65	**C4AE-F**	**73 to 76**	2.18 Intake 1.72 Exhaust	2.78 x 1.38 Intake 1.86 x 1.30 Exhaust
427 ci Medium-Riser 1965–67	**C5AE-F C5AE-R**	**88 to 91**	2.18 Intake 1.72 Exhaust	2.06 x 1.38 Intake 1.78 x 1.30 Exhaust

Bold Indicates high-performance application or change in valve/port size.

CYLINDER HEADS

Displacement/Year	Casting Number	Chamber Size (cc)	Valve Size (inches)	Port Size (inches)
427 ci Medium-Riser 1965–1967 (Canadian) Aluminum	**SK35369**	88 to 91	2.18 Intake 1.72 Exhaust	2.06 x 1.38 Intake 1.78 x 1.30 Exhaust
427 ci Medium-Riser 1965–67 Aluminum	**C5AE-H**	88-91	2.18 Intake 1.72 Exhaust	2.06 x 1.38 Intake 1.78 x 1.30 Exhaust
427 ci Medium-Riser 1966–67 Aluminum	**C6AE-F**	88 to 91	2.18 Intake 1.72 Exhaust	2.06 x 1.38 Intake 1.78 x 1.30 Exhaust
427 ci Medium-Riser 1965–67 Aluminum	**XE**	88 to 91	2.18 Intake 1.72 Exhaust	2.06 x 1.38 Intake 1.78 x 1.30 Exhaust
352/390/410/428 ci 1966	C6TE-B	71 to 74	2.02 Intake 1.55 Exhaust	2.34 x 1.34 Intake 1.84 x 1.34 Exhaust
352/390/410/428 ci 1966	C6TE-G	71 to 74	2.02 Intake 1.55 Exhaust	2.34 x 1.34 Intake 1.84 x 1.34 Exhaust
352/390/410/428 ci 1966	C6AE-K	71 to 74	2.02 Intake 1.55 Exhaust	2.34 x 1.34 Intake 1.84 x 1.34 Exhaust
352/390/410/428 ci 1966–67	C6AE-A C6AE-AA	71 to 74	2.02 Intake 1.55 Exhaust	2.34 x 1.34 Intake 1.84 x 1.34 Exhaust
352/390/410/428 ci 1966–67 (w/Thermactor)	C6AE-D	71 to 74	2.02 Intake 1.55 Exhaust	2.34 x 1.34 Intake 1.84 x 1.34 Exhaust
352 ci 1966–67	C6AE-R	71 to 74	2.02 Intake 1.55 Exhaust	2.34 x 1.34 Intake 1.84 x 1.34 Exhaust
352/390 ci 1966	C6AE-J	71 to 74	2.02 Intake 1.55 Exhaust	2.34 x 1.34 Intake 1.84 x 1.34 Exhaust
352/390 ci 1966	C6AE-RVL	71 to 74	2.02 Intake 1.55 Exhaust	2.34 x 1.34 Intake 1.84 x 1.34 Exhaust
352/390 ci 1966	C6AE-AB	71 to 74	2.02 Intake 1.55 Exhaust	2.34 x 1.34 Intake 1.84 x 1.34 Exhaust
390 ci 1966–68	C6AE-L	67 to 70	2.02 Intake 1.55 Exhaust	2.34 x 1.34 Intake 1.84 x 1.34 Exhaust
390 ci 1966–68	C6AE-U	67 to 70	2.02 Intake 1.55 Exhaust	2.34 x 1.34 Intake 1.84 x 1.34 Exhaust
390 ci 1966–68	C6OE-R	67 to 70	2.02 Intake 1.55 Exhaust	2.34 x 1.34 Intake 1.84 x 1.34 Exhaust
390 ci 1966–68 (w/Thermactor)	C6OE-H	71 to 74	2.02 Intake 1.55 Exhaust	2.34 x 1.34 Intake 1.84 x 1.34 Exhaust
390 ci 1966–68 (w/Thermactor)	**C6OE-AB**	67 to 70	2.02 Intake 1.55 Exhaust	2.34 x 1.34 Intake 1.84 x 1.34 Exhaust

Bold Indicates high-performance application or change in valve/port size.

FE Cylinder Head Identification CONTINUED

Displacement/Year	Casting Number	Chamber Size (cc)	Valve Size (inches)	Port Size (inches)
390 ci 1966–68	C6OE-Y	67 to 70	2.02 Intake 1.55 Exhaust	2.34 x 1.34 Intake 1.84 x 1.34 Exhaust
390 ci 1966–68	C6OE-AC	67 to 70	2.02 Intake 1.55 Exhaust	2.34 x 1.34 Intake 1.84 x 1.34 Exhaust
390 ci 1966–68 (w/Thermactor)	C6OE-AA	67 to 70	2.02 Intake 1.55 Exhaust	2.34 x 1.34 Intake 1.84 x 1.34 Exhaust
390 ci 1966–68 (w/Thermactor)	C7AE-A	67 to 70	2.02 Intake 1.55 Exhaust	2.34 x 1.34 Intake 1.84 x 1.34 Exhaust
352/390/410/428 ci 1967	C7AE-A	71 to 74	2.02 Intake 1.55 Exhaust	2.34 x 1.34 Intake 1.84 x 1.34 Exhaust
427 ci Tunnel Port **1967**	**C7OE-K**	**88 to 91**	**2.25 Intake** **1.72 Exhaust**	**2.17 x 2.34 Intake** **1.78 x 1.30 Exhaust**
427 ci Tunnel Port **1967**	**C8AX-A**	**88 to 91**	**2.25 Intake** **1.72 Exhaust**	**2.17 x 2.34 Intake** **1.78 x 1.30 Exhaust**
360/390/428 ci 1968 (w/Thermactor)	C8AE-A	67 to 70	2.02 Intake 1.55 Exhaust	2.34 x 1.34 Intake 1.84 x 1.34 Exhaust
360/390/428 ci 1968 (w/Thermactor)	C8AE-B	67 to 70	2.02 Intake 1.55 Exhaust	2.34 x 1.34 Intake 1.84 x 1.34 Exhaust
360/390/428 ci 1968 (w/Thermactor)	C8AE-H	67 to 70	2.02 Intake 1.55 Exhaust	2.34 x 1.34 Intake 1.84 x 1.34 Exhaust
390 ci 1968 (w/Thermactor)	C8OE-A	67 to 70	2.02 Intake 1.55 Exhaust	2.34 x 1.34 Intake 1.84 x 1.34 Exhaust
390 ci 1968	C8OE-B	67 to 70	2.02 Intake 1.55 Exhaust	2.34 x 1.34 Intake 1.84 x 1.34 Exhaust
390 ci 1969	C8OE-F	68 to 71	2.02 Intake 1.55 Exhaust	2.34 x 1.34 Intake 1.84 x 1.34 Exhaust
390 ci 1969	C8OE-XX	68 to 71	2.02 Intake 1.55 Exhaust	2.34 x 1.34 Intake 1.84 x 1.34 Exhaust
428 ci 1968–70 (w/Thermactor)	C8AE-F	68 to 71	2.02 Intake 1.55 Exhaust	2.34 x 1.34 Intake 1.84 x 1.34 Exhaust
427 ci Low-Riser **1968 (w/Thermactor)**	**C8AE-J**	**73 to 76**	**2.08 Intake** **1.65 Exhaust**	**2.34 x 1.34 Intake** **1.84 x 1.34 Exhaust**
427 ci Low-Riser **1968 (w/Thermactor)**	**C8AE-N**	**73 to 76**	**2.08 Intake** **1.65 Exhaust**	**2.34 x 1.34 Intake** **1.84 x 1.34 Exhaust**
427 ci Low-Riser **1968 (w/Thermactor)**	**C8WE-A**	**73 to 76**	**2.08 Intake** **1.65 Exhaust**	**2.34 x 1.34 Intake** **1.84 x 1.34 Exhaust**
428 ci Cobra Jet **1968 (w/Thermactor)**	**C8OE-H**	**73 to 76**	**2.08 Intake** **1.65 Exhaust**	**2.34 x 1.34 Intake** **1.84 x 1.34 Exhaust**
428 ci Cobra Jet **1968–70** **(w/Thermactor)**	**C8OE-N**	**73 to 76**	**2.08 Intake** **1.65 Exhaust**	**2.34 x 1.34 Intake** **1.84 x 1.34 Exhaust**

Bold Indicates high-performance application or change in valve/port size.

CYLINDER HEADS

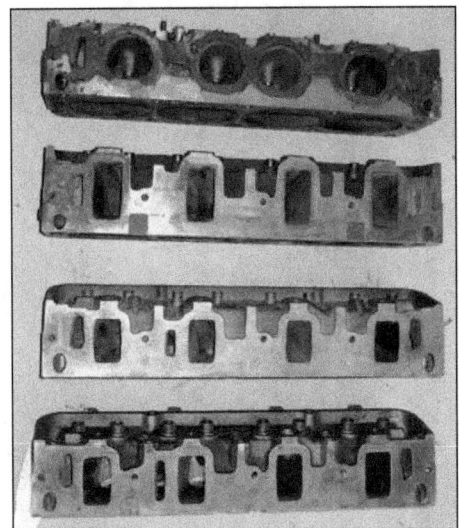

From top to bottom are the intake sides of four FE cylinder heads: 427 Tunnel Port, High Riser, Medium Riser, and 428 Cobra Jet. (Photo Courtesy Barry Rabotnick)

Four FE performance cylinder heads, chamber side, from top to bottom: 427 Tunnel Port, High Riser, Medium Riser, and the 428 Cobra Jet. The High Riser sports a 73- to 76-cc chamber with 2.180/1.720-inch intake/exhaust valves, 2.780 x 1.380–inch intake, and 1.780 x 1.300–inch exhaust ports. The Medium Riser is the best all-around head with 88- to 91-cc chambers with 2.180/1.720-inch intake/exhaust valves, 2.780 x 1.380–inch intake, and 1.780 x 1.300-inch exhaust ports. The 428 Cobra Jet head has 73- to 76-cc chambers with 2.080 x 1.650–inch intake/exhaust valves, 2.340 x 1.340 intake, and 1.840 x 1.340–inch exhaust ports. Finally, the Low Riser head (not pictured) has 2.080/1.640-inch intake/exhaust valves, 2.340 x 1.340-inch intake, and 1.840 x 1.280-inch exhaust ports. (Photo Courtesy Barry Rabotnick)

On the exhaust side are four FE examples, from top to bottom: 428 Cobra Jet, Medium Riser, High Riser, and the 427 Tunnel Port. The intent of each head is clear; the Tunnel Port is a pure high-performance race head. The Low Riser is not shown. (Photo Courtesy Barry Rabotnick)

You must also watch combustion chamber size and piston profile when you're shopping cylinder heads. It is easy to mismatch and wind up with either too much compression or not enough, which leads to unnecessary expense. For example, not all 427 heads bolt onto all FE engine blocks. Because the 427 has huge 4.230-inch cylinder bores, Ford was able to step up the 427 to larger valves. If you're going to bolt 427 heads on your 390 block, the 427's valves may not clear the smaller diameter cylinder walls, especially if you've copped a set of Tunnel Port heads, which very few would ever consider bolting onto a 390 block. A competent machine shop may be able to machine valve reliefs in the block deck depending on your application. It is best to keep 427 heads on 427 blocks or face the complications of mixing them up.

In your search for FE cylinder heads, be mindful of exhaust port configurations. You must have compatible exhaust manifolds/headers. There are three basic exhaust configurations with FE/FT cylinder heads: 16-bolt (four bolt holes at each port), 14-bolt (four bolt holes outer and three bolt holes inner), and 8-bolt (two bolt holes at each port). The

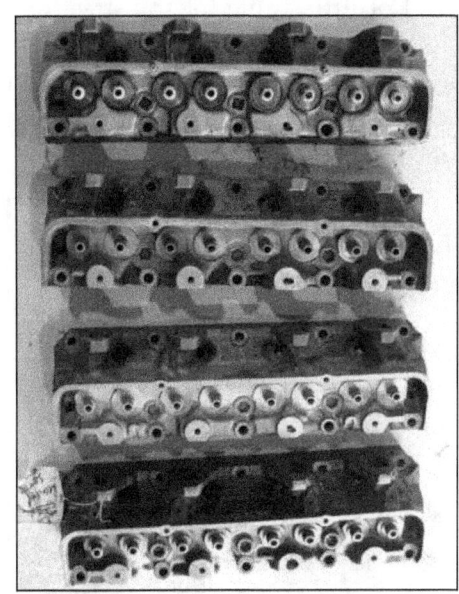

From top to bottom are the same four FE performance heads: 427 Tunnel Port, High Riser, Medium Riser, and the 428 Cobra Jet. The High Riser's casting numbers are C3AE-K and C4AE-F. Medium Riser casting numbers are C5AE-F, C5AE-H (aluminum), C5AE-R, SK-35369 (Canadian), C6AE-F, and XE (aluminum). Expect to see several XE iron and aluminum castings in your search. You will see XE followed by any number of digits. (Photo Courtesy Barry Rabotnick)

cylinder heads with 16 bolt holes are specific to the 428 Cobra Jet in the Mustang, Cougar, Fairlane, Cyclone, and Comet due to shock tower clearance issues. The 14–bolt-hole 390 GT head is more common. The 8-bolt FE heads are easily the most common cylinder head found in most Ford passenger cars and trucks.

All Low, Medium, and High Riser cylinder heads are 427 castings. The best all-around FE cylinder head is the 427 Medium-Riser. This head delivers a good balance of street and strip performance. The 427 High Riser head is a standalone casting engineered for racing only, even though some have applied it to street use. This casting is a high-RPM piece and of little value for the street due to its tall ports and smaller chambers (translated higher compression and the need for race gas). The High Riser head does its best work at high RPM,

The 1966–1969 390 High Performance head (left) is often mistaken for the 428 Cobra Jet casting (right). However, the Cobra Jet head has larger intake ports and both intake and exhaust valves. The same holds true for the C8AE-J, C8AE-N, and C8WE-H 427 Low Riser heads of the period.

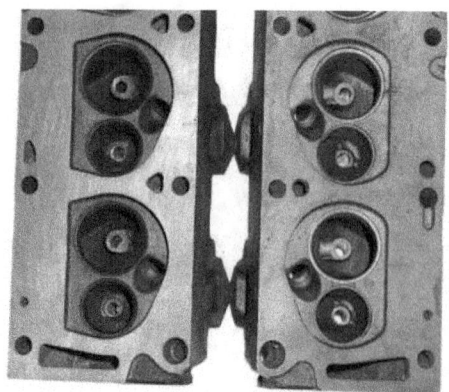

The 1961–1962 389 High Performance head (left) and the 428 Cobra Jet (right) with identical shovel-shape chamber sizing. The 390 Hi-Po's 65- to 68-cc chamber mirrors the 428 CJ's larger 73- to 76-cc chambers. Close inspection reveals the 428's larger chambers with less valve shrouding.

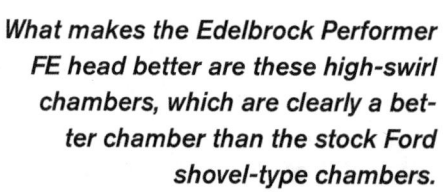

The Edelbrock 390/428 Performer RPM series for FE engines is based on the 427 Medium Riser and 428 Cobra Jet heads, which includes 16-bolt exhaust flanges for compact and intermediate Ford and Mercury.

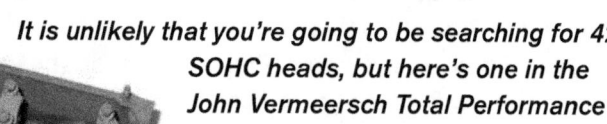

What makes the Edelbrock Performer FE head better are these high-swirl chambers, which are clearly a better chamber than the stock Ford shovel-type chambers.

The 428's larger exhaust ports (right) offer improved scavenging. The early 390 High Performance exhaust ports are more stifling. Also note the four-bolt exhaust ports on the CJ head, which are necessary on Ford/Mercury compact and intermediate models. This is known as the 16-bolt head. On the left is the 8-bolt head.

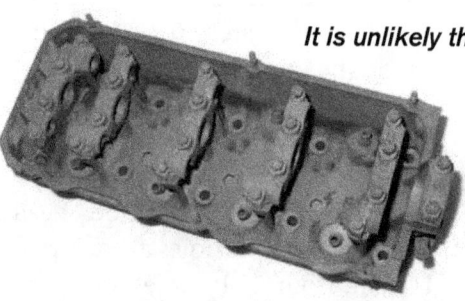

It is unlikely that you're going to be searching for 427 SOHC heads, but here's one in the John Vermeersch Total Performance inventory: C5AE-6090-E. These are heavy iron castings that make the 427 SOHC the heaviest FE big-block ever made. Early 427 SOHC heads had spark plugs positioned on the exhaust side. Ford improved spark plug positioning by moving them to the intake side of the head for easier access. Tip penetration is virtually the same.

CYLINDER HEADS

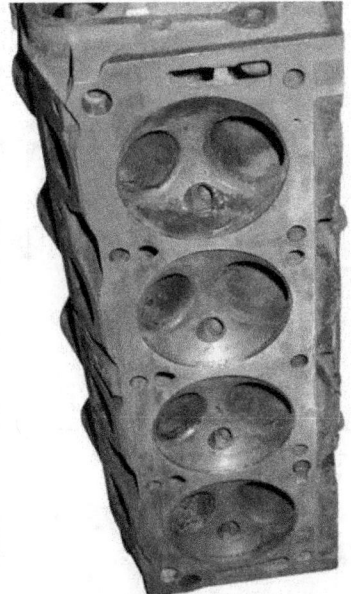

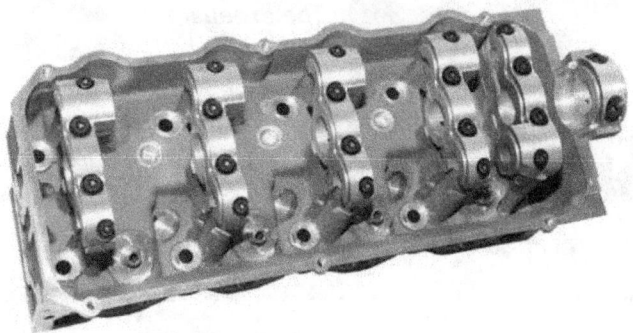

The 427 SOHC's hemispherical cross-flow chambers made it an optimum competitor for the Chrysler Hemi. The 427 SOHC head is a Tunnel Port design originally conceived for NASCAR competition. It wound up in drag racing after being rejected by NASCAR. There were at least two basic SOHC heads. The early head had spark plugs positioned on the exhaust side. The more familiar limited-production head had spark plugs positioned on the intake side. This is the C5AE-6090-E head casting.

Robert Pond Motorsports offers this incredible cast-aluminum 427 SOHC Cammer cylinder head for those who like life on the edge. These 427 SOHC cylinder heads are a direct replacement for the original SOHC head. The only visual difference is that Pond added five additional bolt holes to the exhaust flanges for better gasket seal.

The Pond SOHC heads as-shipped are CNC-ported. Flow is about 15 percent better than the original SOHC iron heads, with 2.350-inch intake and 1.900-inch exhaust valves. Flow is 393-cfm intake at .700-inch lift and 270-cfm exhaust at .700-inch lift.

FE Thermactor emissions heads are identifiable by the manifold ports at each exhaust port. When Thermactor is not employed, these ports are plugged (arrow).

This is the intake side of a C5AE-H Medium Riser aluminum cylinder head casting. These were produced in limited numbers for Ford's GT40 racing program in the mid-1960s. Legend has it some were custom installed in new 427 Cobras.

Ford produced a limited number of experimental 427 Medium Riser aluminum heads. Here's one set found at JGM Performance Engineering, bolted to a 427 Side Oiler. These are C5AE-H limited-production aluminum castings produced for the GT40 program in the mid-1960s for the Le Mans racing program.

FORD BIG-BLOCK PARTS INTERCHANGE

CHAPTER 5

The exhaust side of the C5AE-6090-H aluminum head with eight-bolt exhaust ports.

The C5AE-6090-H head has 427 Medium Riser 88- to 91-cc combustion chambers with 2.180/1.720-inch intake/exhaust valves.

Reproduction 427 Medium-Riser Heads

If you've had your fill of old FE castings, the aftermarket yields a wealth of FE-specific cylinder heads for your engine-building project. Robert Pond Motorsports offers a variety of both FE wedge and SOHC head castings. Robert Pond offers two cylinder heads, Stage 1 and Stage 2, for FE builders.

Robert Pond Motorsports Stage 1 FE cylinder heads are based on the original 427 Ford SK-35369 prototype cylinder head and have the special SK part number. These cylinder heads have 2.250-inch intake and 1.730-inch exhaust valves. They sport much thicker decks and spring pad areas than the original SK Ford heads. These cylinder heads, as cast, make an excellent street head. They are used on the Robert Pond 427 crate engines, which make more than 600 hp on pump gas.

Stage 2 Robert Pond SK cylinder heads are great street or race heads with 2.250-inch intake and 1.730 exhaust valves. What makes these heads different than Stage 1 is CNC porting. The intake ports flow about 15 percent better than the Stage 1 and will support more than 750 hp on pump gas, which is remarkable. They come with Pond's standard hydraulic roller crate engine, cam spring, and steel retainers.

Where Pond really gets noticed is the availability of SOHC 427 Cammer cylinder heads, which are a direct replacement for the original Ford SOHC castings. The only visual difference is the five additional bolt holes to the exhaust flange for better gasket seal. These heads, as shipped, are CNC ported. Flow is about 15 percent better than the stock Ford Cammer ports. With 2.350-inch intake and 1.900-inch exhaust valves, these heads flow very well. At 28 inches of water, the flow numbers are 393-cfm intake at .700-inch lift and 270-cfm exhaust at .700-inch lift. The Pond SOHC heads offer a thicker deck than the original Ford heads with a 1/2-inch-thick deck and thicker cam towers. These heads come bare from Pond fitted with 11/32-inch guides and 119-cc chambers and seats.

Blue Thunder is another excellent aftermarket cylinder head casting, which is available from Survival Motorsports according to Barry Rabotnick: The Blue Thunder FE head brings racing features into a streetable cylinder head package for high-displacement big-blocks. Blue Thunder is what you want when you're reaching for 6,500 rpm and higher. The Blue Thunder FE head comes bare, void of valveguides, which are packaged separately with the head.

The Blue Thunder cylinder head is based externally on the 428 Cobra Jet head casting with a 16-bolt exhaust port bolt pattern for virtually any Ford imaginable. These heads are either Medium or High Riser depending upon your needs. These heads are a class act with a rocker system designed for different mount types. According to Rabotnick, the popular Medium Riser casting from Blue Thunder uses a Cobra Jet/Low Riser-size port floor set in the Medium Riser position, on par with a raised port head.

Bear Block Motors (BBM) also offers a new FE cylinder head for 390, 427, and 428 big-blocks with 2.150/1.650- or 2.200/1.650-inch intake/exhaust valves with the lightweight 11/32-inch stems. Combustion chambers are engineered for optimum quench. High-swirl/high-quench chambers allow for more aggressive ignition timing with today's more unforgiving pump gas. These heads flow 35 to 50 more CFM than current aftermarket FE heads and with 3 to 5 degrees less timing. Also available are CNC-ported FE aluminum heads with 2.250/1.710-inch valves, which calls for a 4.230-inch minimum bore size.

CYLINDER HEADS

This close-up of the C5AE-H 427 aluminum head shows that it is obviously an experimental casting with "PROCESS FD[1]." Earlier castings show "PROCESS FB."

Instead of an alphanumeric date code on these rare Ford FE aluminum heads, the actual casting date is cast into the block. Here, "1-8-65" means January 8, 1965.

The BBM FE heads feature outstanding casting quality with a stock appearance, factory-installed TIME-SERT threaded inserts, manganese bronze valveguides, hardened high-grade ductile iron interlocked valveseats, 75-cc high-swirl/high-quench combustion chambers, and 5/8-inch deck thickness. They will fit standard 390 4.780-inch bore with 2.200/1.650-inch valves. Exhaust ports are in the stock OEM location. The BBM head will accept OEM-spec rocker arm shaft and pedestal rocker arm systems with generous additional pad material cast into the head for durability. ■

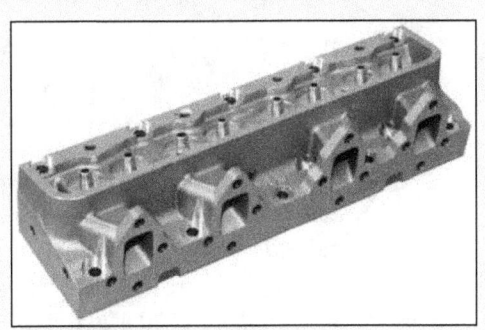

BBM reproduces the 427 Medium Riser cylinder head in high-tech cast aluminum along with its family of reproduction FE Side Oiler blocks. These heads are fitted with 2.150/1.650- or 2.200/1.650-inch intake/exhaust valves with lightweight 11/32-inch hollow stems. High-swirl combustion chambers are engineered for optimum quench.

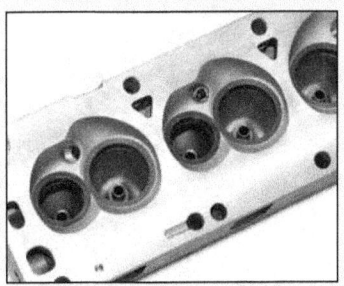

High-swirl/high-quench chambers allow for more aggressive ignition timing with today's more unforgiving pump gas. BBM heads flow 35 to 50 more CFM than current aftermarket FE heads with 3 to 5 degrees less ignition timing required. Optional CNC-ported FE aluminum heads with 2.250/1.710-inch intake/exhaust valves, which call for a larger 4.230-inch minimum bore size, are also available from BBM.

Development of the BBM FE cylinder heads from top to bottom involved test trials with a variety of chambers and port configurations. GEN 1 was a more typical FE shovel-shaped combustion chamber. GEN 2 (actually two GEN 2 heads) through GEN 3 evolved more toward a kidney bean–shaped chamber ultimately arriving at high-swirl and greater quench at GEN 4 through GEN 6.

CHAPTER 5

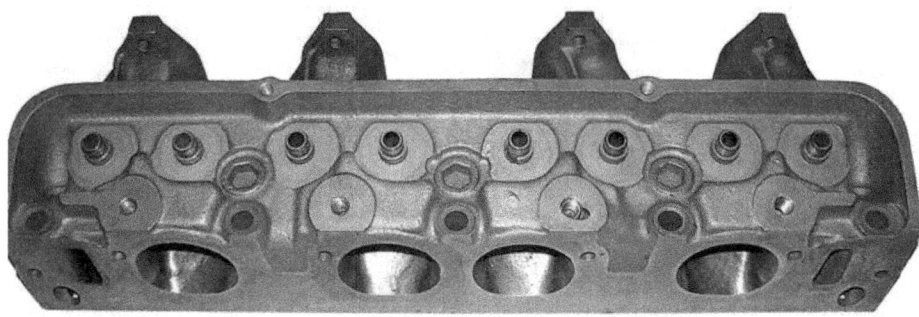

The 427 Tunnel Port C7OE-K head conceived for NASCAR was the ultimate FE wedge race head beyond the High Riser with a vast 2.170 x 2.340–inch intake and 1.780 x 1.300–inch exhaust ports. Exhaust port width is a pinch narrower for aggressive scavenging. The Tunnel Port concept was strictly for high-RPM use and never intended to be a street head. (Photo Courtesy Scott Walter)

The exhaust side of the C7OE-K Tunnel Port head shows generous port work in addition to size. These offer the correct sizing so that you have good flow but just enough restriction to step up velocity. (Photo Courtesy Scott Walter)

The Tunnel Port's 88- to 91-cc chambers are the typical FE shovel shape with plenty of quench. (Photo Courtesy Scott Walter)

Finned cast-aluminum FE valvecovers began appearing in 1966–1967 on the Shelby GT500 Mustangs atop the 428 and dealer-installed 427s. The Cobra and Cobra Le Mans covers are very popular and available as reproductions.

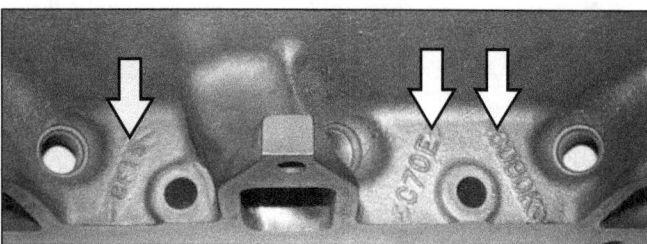

As with other FE head castings, the Tunnel Port head sports the Ford casting number of "C7OE-6090-K" (right arrows) along with the alphanumeric casting date code of "8F15" (left arrow), indicating June 15, 1968. These heads were never installed on a production vehicle and were made available to racers only. (Photo Courtesy Scott Walter)

Here's the stamped steel chromed "POWER BY Ford" FE valvecover. It arrived in 1967 and was in production through 1970.

This is the reproduction Cobra Le Mans finned aluminum valvecover in wrinkled black.

Repairing Damaged Threads

One thing you can expect to find with used castings is damaged bolt hole threads. There are many ways to fix damaged threads. Helicoil is one solution; it uses precision screw-in threaded inserts for damaged threads. Another is TIME-SERT, which is a thread-repair system for SAE and metric bolt holes. You would be amazed at how easy it is to install.

TIME-SERT is a solid bushing insert. This guarantees easy installation and allows for full load use of a tapped hole, ensuring protection against stress and vibration. It is thin-walled due to synchronized internal/external threading. A thin cross-sectional area allows for installation in areas of limited space and clearance material. Using TIME-SERT means positive placement. Having a flange on top ensures the insert will have positive placement and cannot wind down into the newly repaired hole. In addition, TIME-SERT is self-locking where bottom internal threads of the insert are cold-rolled to expand the mating external threads into the base material, which locks the insert in place. The locking mechanism is at the bottom of the insert. ■

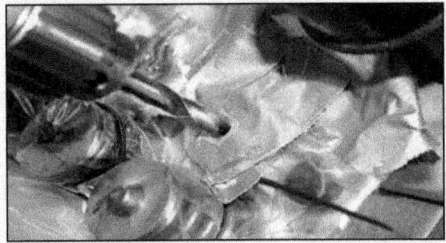

TIME-SERT installation begins by drilling out the existing bolt hole with the appropriate drill bit, which depends upon your application. If casting is installed on the engine, you will want to cover everything to prevent metal shavings from wandering down inside the engine. Use a vacuum to catch shavings. Even the smallest shaving can cause engine damage.

The drilled-out hole is beveled (countersunk) for easy TIME-SERT installation. Use compressed air and a vacuum to remove all debris from the bolt hole.

The hole is tapped for TIME-SERT installation. Again, use compressed air and a vacuum to rid the hole of debris.

The threaded bolt hole is now ready for the TIME-SERT. Be sure to inspect the hole for any debris.

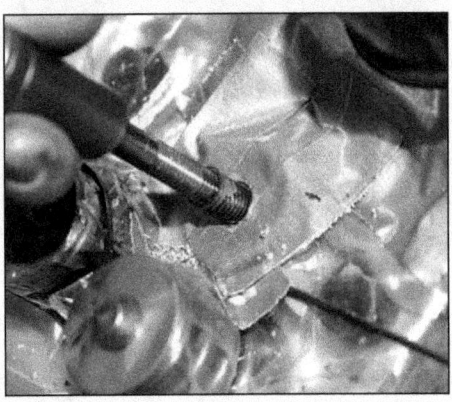

The TIME-SERT is threaded into the bolt hole and tightened until it locks.

The TIME-SERT is completely installed and ready for use. Check the bolt hole for any debris.

This is the finned aluminum Cobra Le Mans valvecover in natural metal finish.

When the 428 Cobra Jet arrived in 1968 it had chromed stamped steel "Power by Ford" valvecovers through the beginning of the 1970 model year. Early 1970 Cobra Jet models received the steel covers; these finned aluminum covers arrived shortly after the introduction of 1970 models. There are also finned aluminum covers void of any identification.

Chromed steel pent-roof FE valvecovers were common in the early to mid-1960s. Early versions were void of crankcase ventilation, which was located via the intake manifold.

6,500 to 7,800. The 427 Low Riser cylinder head isn't much different than a 1961–1962 390 High Performance casting, and is priced accordingly. It is a good performance head and advanced for its time.

The C7OE-K Tunnel Port head casting was a race-only cylinder head made available to racers. It was never installed on a production vehicle. Although there's a lot to be gained from a 427 Tunnel Port head in terms of performance, there are better heads out there today for competition FE engines.

The MEL

Because the MEL was developed as a large-displacement luxury car engine, cylinder heads didn't evolve much because they didn't need to. The MEL head isn't your typical Ford head. In fact, there's no other Ford cylinder head like it. It has a flat deck like a diesel cylinder head void of combustion chambers, which are at the top of each cylinder. Actually, combustion chambers, if you can call them that, were flat from 1958 to 1959. Where the MEL head varies is the pocketing of combustion chambers from roughly 1959-on in order to reduce compression and detonation (pinging) issues. Instead of a flat surface, these heads got small combustion chambers around the valves and spark plug.

This flat-deck head void of combustion chambers was designed that way, with the block deck cut at a 10-degree angle to the piston dome giving the top of the cylinder a wedge chamber instead of the cylinder head. Ford (and also Chevrolet with its 348/409-ci W Series big-block engines) did this as a means to compression control, although it didn't work very well.

When you're selecting pistons for your MEL project, it is crucial to keep cylinder head design in mind. Not all MEL heads have a flat deck surface at the valves and spark plug. Later heads have a small pocket chamber around the valves to reduce compression and change the dynamics of combustion. Piston dome size and shape determine compression in the MEL, as does cylinder head selection. This means you must be mindful of cylinder head type going in.

CYLINDER HEADS

MEL cylinder head selection directly affects piston selection. If you get this wrong, you can wind up with too much compression or not enough. If you opt for a flat-top piston, expect to lose compression, especially if you're using the later MEL head with the small chamber.

You will have to look to custom piston manufacturers, such as Wiseco and Egge, for your MEL project because pistons for these engines are not widely available. There's simply not enough demand for them. Before these companies can make a piston for you, they must know what you have for cylinder heads. The MEL piston was originally designed to not only compress the air/fuel mix and transfer power, but to manipulate how air and fuel were compressed. Ford learned this through trial and error with at least three known cylinder head revisions intended to eliminate rough running and detonation.

As MEL cylinder head design changed, so did pistons, which further punctuates why you must pay close attention to piston and cylinder head selection as a package. Because the MEL was a challenging engine, there were ongoing changes in cylinder heads, pistons, and induction.

The MEL cylinder head was produced in at least four casting types in its 10-year production life. Early in the 1958 model year, the MEL cylinder head sported large valves and enormous compression. Midyear, Ford reduced valve size to improve drivability and torque. In light of continuing detonation and rough operation, Ford engineers revisited the MEL cylinder head. They kept the same valve sizing but with reduced compression via pocket chambers.

The MEL's intake ports are huge, which helps horsepower, but doesn't do much for low- to mid-range torque. Horsepower isn't really necessary in a luxury car engine. However, it is important if you're going racing. Intake ports were later reduced in size to follow to improve low-to-mid-range torque. The torque advantage in the MEL comes from the tremendous arm of stroke.

The MEL's head deck surfaces are perfectly flat and void of combustion chambers. Because the block decks are 10 degrees off piston deck, the top of each cylinder bore is the combustion chamber, which leaves chamber size and shape up to the piston crown. The piston dome size and shape control the compression. Later on, MEL heads were changed with a small pocket chamber in the head surrounding the valves; it was employed to reduce the compression ratio.

The MEL's shaft-mounted rocker arms are lubricated the same way as the FE's via block and cylinder head galleys and pedestals.

This is a B9ME-6090-A MEL head casting. Note the oil galley that feeds the rocker arm assembly, visible through the bolt hole.

CHAPTER 5

Another issue for early MEL engines was excessive compression and low-octane fuels primarily with export vehicles. Ford issued a Low-Octane Fuel Adapter Kit (PN I-502592) consisting of cylinder head gaskets and spacers, intake manifold gaskets and spacers, head bolts and dowels, and longer pushrods. According to Ford documentation at the time, the Low-Octane Fuel Adapter Kit took compression from 10.5:1 to 7.14:1 on the Mercury 383 and from 10.5:1 to 7.25:1 on the 430. The Edsel 410 undoubtedly had the same kit for compression reduction. Ford/Lincoln/Mercury service departments had the option of retarding ignition timing prior to this kit. However, retarding ignition timing hurt power and fuel consumption.

385 Series

Cylinder head selection for the 385 Series 429/460 is straightforward compared to the FE. Throughout the lengthy production life of the 385 there were four basic cylinder head castings you should be concerned with. There is the standard 429/460 casting, Cobra Jet, Police Interceptor, and the Boss 429. The Boss 429

MEL Cylinder Head Identification

Some cylinder head castings may not be listed. ■

Displacement/Year	Casting/Part Number	Chamber Size	Valve Size (inches)	Other Information
383/410/430 ci 1958	5750064	N/A	2.140–2.150 Intake 1.770–1.780 Exhaust	Before 1/9/58
383/410/430 ci 1958	5750062	N/A	2.080–2.090 Intake 1.770–1.780 Exhaust	After 1/9/58
383/410/430 ci 1958	5750063	N/A	N/A	N/A
383/410/430 ci 1958	5750065	N/A	N/A	N/A
410 ci 1958–59	B9ME-6049-A	N/A	2.080–2.090 Intake 1.770–1.780 Exhaust	Edsel
410 ci 1959–60	B9ME-6049-B	N/A	2.080–2.090 Intake 1.770–1.780 Exhaust	Edsel
410 ci 1959–60	B9ME-6049-C	N/A	2.080–2.090 Intake 1.770–1.780 Exhaust	Edsel
383/410/430 ci 1959–60	B8S-6049-A	N/A	2.080–2.090 Intake 1.770–1.780 Exhaust	
383/430 ci 1960–61	C0ME-B	N/A	2.080–2.090 Intake 1.770–1.780 Exhaust	
430 ci 1961	C1VE-A	N/A	2.080–2.090 Intake 1.770–1.780 Exhaust	
430 ci 1961	C1VE-B	N/A	2.080–2.090 Intake 1.770–1.780 Exhaust	
430 ci 1963–64	C3VE-B	N/A	2.080–2.090 Intake 1.770–1.780 Exhaust	
430 ci 1963–64	C3VY-A	N/A	2.080–2.090 Intake 1.770–1.780 Exhaust	Prior to 6/1/64
430 ci 1963–64	C3VY-B	N/A	2.020–2.030 Intake 1.645–1.660 Exhaust	After 5/31/64
430 ci 1964–65	C3VY-C	N/A	2.020–2.030 Intake 1.645–1.660 Exhaust	
430 ci 1964–65	C4VE-A	N/A	2.020–2.030 Intake 1.645–1.660 Exhaust	
462 ci 1966–68	C6VY-A	N/A	2.020–2.030 Intake 1.645–1.660 Exhaust	With Thermactor Before 11/22/65
462 ci 1966–68	C6VY-C	N/A	2.020–2.030 Intake 1.645–1.660 Exhaust	Without Thermactor
462 ci 1966–68	C6VY-D	N/A	2.020–2.030 Intake 1.645–1.660 Exhaust	With Thermactor After 11/22/65

CYLINDER HEADS

The hydraulic-lifter 429/460 head is set up for bolt/fulcrum no-adjust rocker arms. Note the slotted rocker arm pedestals for the hydraulic lifter 385 Series 429/460-ci engines.

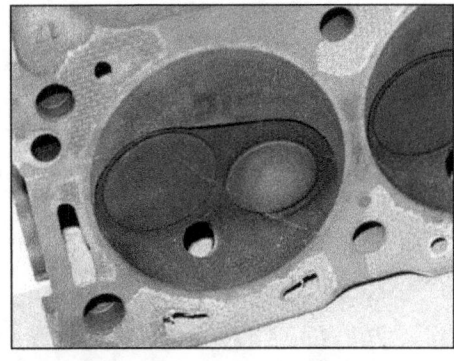

The 88-cc kidney bean chamber is common across the board for 429/460 engines. Valve sizing is 2.090-inch intake and 1.650-inch exhaust. The 429 Cobra Jet head goes larger at 2.190-inch intake and 1.730-inch exhaust valves.

This is a D0VE-C head casting even though it has been fitted with screw-in studs and pushrod guides. The D0VE-C casting is a standard production 429/460 head casting.

Here's an E6TE truck head casting with Thermactor provision (arrow), which is plugged for non-Thermactor emissions use. These Thermactor heads have minimal exhaust port restriction.

A D0VE-C 429/460 head void of Thermactor porting. This is a good cylinder head for port and bowl work along with larger valves.

cylinder head with its hemispherical chambers requires no introduction. It is a standalone head and engine.

Where the 429/460 wedge heads vary is in combustion chamber shape and size. In truth, the 429/460 cylinder head delivers excellent flow characteristics in all its forms. The most common 429/460 heads are the C8VE-A, C9VE-A, and D0VE-A, which are all basically the same cylinder head casting with 2.090/1.650-inch intake/exhaust valves and 2.180 x 1.870–inch intake ports and 1.990 x 1.300–inch exhaust ports. This is a head casting with 75- to 77-cc wedge chambers you can do port and bowl work on and wind up with significant flow improvement.

Another casting is the D2VE-A2A, which isn't much different than the aforementioned heads, except for a larger open 100-cc chamber, which delivers poor quench and reduced compression. The D2VE-A2A head is more prone to detonation due to its huge open chamber. The D3VE-A, D3VE-A2A and higher are emissions heads with open chambers with poor quench. Although they have smaller chambers they're a disappointment from a performance standpoint. Ford continued to cast the basic 460 head through the mid-1990s. When these engines were deleted from the option sheet in 1979, they continued in Ford F Series trucks and E Series vans. These head castings will show up as E7TE, E8TE, and so on, which are basically the D3VE-A casting with engineering revisions designed more for electronic fuel injection and reduced emissions.

The rarest 429/460 head is the 1970–1971 Cobra Jet casting, D0OE-R with 2.190/1.730-inch intake/exhaust valves, 2.510 x 2.110–inch intake, and 2.250 x 1.300–inch exhaust ports along with 71- to 75-cc chambers. Because the Cobra Jet head is rare and darned expensive you may opt for the 1972–1974 Police

CHAPTER 5

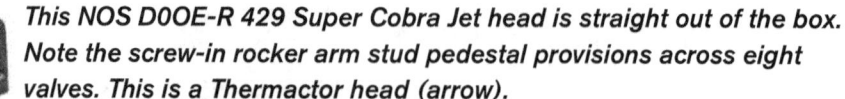

This NOS D0OE-R 429 Super Cobra Jet head is straight out of the box. Note the screw-in rocker arm stud pedestal provisions across eight valves. This is a Thermactor head (arrow).

The NOS 429 Super Cobra Jet head is shown from the chamber side. These are approximately 88-cc chambers with 2.190-inch intake and 1.730-inch exhaust valves.

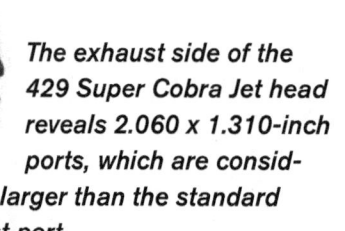

The exhaust side of the 429 Super Cobra Jet head reveals 2.060 x 1.310-inch ports, which are considerably larger than the standard 429/460 exhaust port.

Interceptor castings with the same valve sizing as the Cobra Jet head, yet with smaller ports and 88- to 91-cc chambers. Police Interceptor head port sizes are 2.200 x 1.930–inch intake and 2.060 x 1.310–inch exhaust ports, which means better low- to mid-range torque. Exhaust scavenging is debatable with these heads, with virtually little or no gain.

The Police Interceptor heads have hardened exhaust valveseats for use with the unleaded fuels introduced at the time. There are three Police Interceptor castings, D2OE-AA, D2OE-AB, and D3AE-FA, all with 88- to 91-cc chambers. The Police Interceptor head is an alternative to the more expensive Cobra Jet head because it offers better low-end torque for street use.

429/460 Cylinder Head Identification

Some cylinder head castings may not be listed. ■

Displacement/Year	Casting Number	Chamber Size	Valve Size (inches)	Port Size (inches)
429/460 ci 1968–72	C8VE-A		2.09 Intake 1.65 Exhaust	2.18 x 1.87 Intake 1.99 x 1.30 Exhaust
429/460 ci 1968–72	C9VE-A		2.09 Intake 1.65 Exhaust	2.18 x 1.87 Intake 1.99 x 1.30 Exhaust
429/460 ci 1968–72	D0VE-C		2.09 Intake 1.65 Exhaust	2.18 x 1.87 Intake 1.99 x 1.30 Exhaust
429/460 ci 1968–72	D3AE-A2A	88 cc	2.09 Intake 1.65 Exhaust	2.18 x 1.87 Intake 1.99 x 1.30 Exhaust
429 ci Cobra Jet 1970–71	**D0OE-R**		**2.19 Intake 1.73 Exhaust**	**2.51 x 2.11 Intake 2.25 x 1.30 Exhaust**
429/460 ci 1972–74 Police Interceptor	**D2OE-AA**	**88 cc**	**2.19 Intake 1.73 Exhaust**	**2.20 x 1.93 Intake 2.06 x 1.31 Exhaust**
429/460 ci 1972–74 Police Interceptor	**D2OE-AB**	**88 cc**	**2.19 Intake 1.73 Exhaust**	**2.20 x 1.93 Intake 2.06 x 1.31 Exhaust**
460 ci only 1973–74 Police Interceptor	**D3AE-FA**	**88 cc**	**2.19 Intake 1.73 Exhaust**	**2.20 x 1.93 Intake 2.06 x 1.31 Exhaust**

Bold indicates high-performance application or change in valve/port size.

CYLINDER HEADS

The 429 Super Cobra Jet's huge drive-through intake port measures 2.510 x 2.110 inches and leads into a 2.190-inch intake valve.

A closer look at the 429 Super Cobra Jet exhaust port. All it takes is a little bit of port and bowl work to get more power from these heads.

This 460 D3AE-FA Police Interceptor cylinder head has positive-stop rocker arm pedestals. This is typical of what you will find in truck head castings through the 1970s, 1980s, and 1990s.

The 429 Super Cobra Jet head has screw-in rocker arm studs and guide plates, which is what makes it different than standard 429/460 head castings. You can have the hydraulic lifter pedestals machined down and tapped for adjustable screw-in studs and guide plates.

A closer look at this Super Cobra Jet head reveals the casting date code of "9J25" indicating September 25, 1969.

Boss 429

Any way you look at the hemi-head Boss 429, it is not the same as a conventional 429/460. This engine was born for NASCAR competition. There are many variables when it comes to cylinder heads and what to do with them. The street Boss 429 is a detuned version of an all-out factory-born racing engine. There are two basic Boss 429 cylinder head castings: C9AE-A and D0AE-AA. There are also race and experimental cylinder head castings circulating out there. One Boss 429 expert states that he believes there are at least 50 different cylinder head castings out there. Some differences are subtle while others are more obvious.

Chances are slim that you're building a Boss 429. However, there are two basic Boss 429 street heads: C9AE-AA and D0OE-AA. This is a pair of D0OE-AA castings with 2.380/1.900-inch intake/exhaust valves. The Ford part number is D0AZ-6049-C. The C9AE-AA cylinder head has 2.280/1.900-inch intake/exhaust valves.

CHAPTER 5

Boss 429 Cylinder Head Identification

Some cylinder head castings may not be listed.

Displacement/Year	Casting Number	Chamber Size	Valve Size (inches)	Port Size (inches)
Boss 429 1969–70	C9AE-AA	100 cc	2.280 Intake 1.900 Exhaust	2.360 x 2.360 Intake 2.040 x 1.680 Exhaust
Boss 429 1969–70	D0AE-AA	100 cc	2.280 Intake 1.900 Exhaust	2.360 x 2.360 Intake 2.040 x 1.680 Exhaust

An overhead view of the D0AE-AA Boss 429 cylinder head shows its true crossflow design with the most unusual valvetrain the Ford big-block has ever had. The Boss 429 was Ford's answer to Chrysler's 426-ci Hemi.

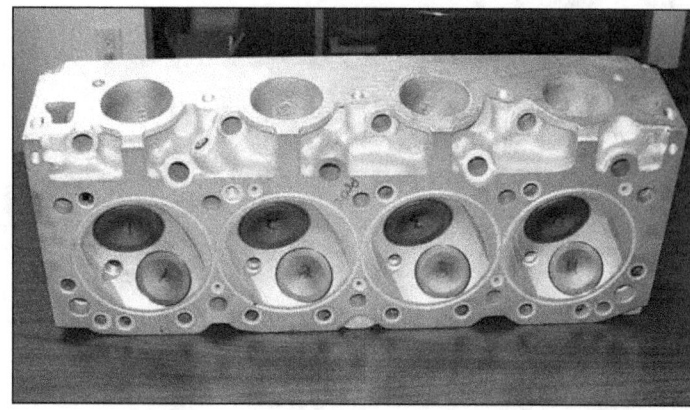

Although the Boss 429 was called a hemi, the street head didn't sport a full hemispherical chamber. Some call these "semi-hemis."

Boss 429 valvecovers are specific to the Boss Nine.

The Boss 429's right-hand valvecover looks like this when installed. These valvecovers are identical from side to side. They are available as a special order from Tony D. Branda.

FORD BIG-BLOCK PARTS INTERCHANGE

CHAPTER 6

CAMSHAFT AND VALVETRAIN

Big-block Ford valvetrain systems cover the gamut from shaft-mounted adjustable and non-adjustable rocker arms on the FE Series, MEL, and Boss 429 to adjustable stud and bolt-fulcrum non-adjustable on the 385 Series. Ford big-block valvetrain systems are plenty rugged from the factory unless you're running an aggressive camshaft. The stamped steel rocker arms on the 385 Series big-blocks can stand up to a tremendous amount of punishment before it becomes necessary to run aftermarket roller rockers. The same can be said for the FE and MEL. Both have rugged valvetrain systems engineered to take a lot of abuse. Each had its share of challenges, problems Ford engineers had to work out over time.

FE Series

The FE and FT Series engines were equipped with shaft-mounted rocker arms. The main difference lies in mechanical versus hydraulic, which affects rocker arm ratio, adjustability, and pushrod type. Four rocker arm shaft types were used during the production of FE and FT engines from 1958 to 1976. The original B8AZ-A rocker arm shaft was designed for mechanical lifter engines only. Look for the shaft with eight holes along the bottom. The B8AZ-D rocker arm shaft was conceived for hydraulic lifter engines and has 16 oil holes.

A revised rocker arm shaft, C3AZ-A, which is very similar to the B8AZ-A shaft, has adjustable rocker arms and two additional oil holes. The C5AZ-A shaft is also a mechanical lifter shaft designed for use on the 427 Medium Riser and Tunnel Port engines. Dove Performance offers heavy-duty rocker arm shafts for FE engines best used with some type of end support system for solid integrity.

Two rocker arms were used throughout FE and FT production. The adjustable B8A-B and B8AZ-B rocker with a 1.76:1 ratio is for use with mechanical lifters and ball/cup pushrods. The cup end of the pushrod mates with the adjuster in the rocker arm, with the other end seating in the mechanical lifter.

The B8AZ-C non-adjustable rocker arm at 1.73:1 is designed for use with hydraulic lifters. This calls for the use of a ball and ball, or tip and tip, pushrod where either end can be seated in the rocker arm or hydraulic lifter. You may also use the B8A-A or B8AZ-A adjustable rocker arm with a ball/cup pushrod and hydraulic lifters, which eliminates having to try different pushrod lengths. The B8A-A and B8AZ-A rocker arm also has the 1.76:1 ratio advantage because it affords you more valve lift.

The standard FE rocker arm and shaft system looks like this with 1.73:1 non-adjustable rocker arms and ball-end pushrods. The FE/FT and MEL engines share the same rocker arms. They do not share shafts and pedestals. The MEL rocker shafts are different.

FORD BIG-BLOCK PARTS INTERCHANGE

CHAPTER 6

Non-adjustable FE rocker arms use ball-end pushrods such as these. Use the one-piece machined pushrods with thicker .080-inch walls for durability.

There are two types of rocker arm assemblies for the FE/FT engines. At the top is the adjustable type with adjustable 1.76:1 rocker arms. At the bottom is the non-adjustable rocker with a 1.73:1 ratio.

A closer look at FE rocker arms shows adjustable 1.76:1 (left) and non-adjustable 1.73:1 (right). These rocker arms call for different shafts as well due to oil distribution.

This is an adjustable FE rocker arm assembly with iron pedestals on a 427. Check out the rare factory aluminum-head castings.

Adjustable FE rocker arms make it easier to maintain valve lash on both mechanical- and hydraulic-lifter engines. When you use adjustable rockers, you get the benefit of 1.76:1 ratio for additional lift.

Assembly of the FE rocker shaft includes shimming rockers for proper spacing.

When you use non-adjustable rocker arms with hydraulic lifters, you will need to use a pushrod checker to verify geometry and valve lash. You can take up excessive valve lash by opting for a longer pushrod. By using a pushrod checker, you run less chance of making a mistake. Five basic pushrod Ford part numbers were originally available for FE engines in the following dimensions.

C0AE-J	9.590 inches
C8AZ-A	9.590 inches
C4TZ-B	9.620 inches
C4TZ-D	9.560 inches
C3SZ-A	9.770 inches

CAMSHAFT AND VALVETRAIN

Of course, the aftermarket offers an infinite number of pushrod lengths for FE/FT engines and they can be ordered in custom lengths. Required pushrod length is going to depend upon how much the cylinder heads and block have been milled. This is why your best decision is to use a pushrod checker going in.

Another very important issue to consider is lifter type for your FE/FT. FE/FT engines were originally fitted with three potential types of lifters: mechanical, shell, and hydraulic. It is crucial to properly match the correct lifter with the corresponding pushrod. Check lifter height as well as pushrod length and type.

Always check static valve lash before firing the engine. There should be appropriate clearance when the engine is cold and lifters have bled down. Make allowances for this beforehand. Allow the engine to get to the proper operating temperature before checking valve lash again.

Valvespring selection is centered on cam profile and suggested spring pressure and height. A radical camshaft and corresponding maximum RPM expected are going to mandate the use of greater spring pressures. Likewise, a milder street cam is going to call for lighter spring pressures. Look to Crane, Comp Cams, Crower, and other cam grinders for appropriate spring pressures. Every cam grinder offers kits with compatible profiles and spring pressures.

While you're thinking about rocker arm shafts and rockers for your FE project, be mindful that Ford produced at least four rocker shaft pedestals for this engine during its production life. Most FE/FT engines used the C2AZ-6531-B pedestal, which is aluminum and can take a lot of abuse if you're running a mild street cam. However, if you're opting for a more aggressive cam profile, you're going to want one of four high-performance pedestals Ford produced for the FE or an aftermarket pedestal. The C3AZ-A cast-iron pedestal is an easy bolt-in swap for the C2AZ-B aluminum piece.

When Ford introduced the 427 High Riser race head and induction system late in 1963, it released the C3AE-A cast-iron pedestal for the FE. This pedestal is only for the High Riser and cannot be used with any other FE head. The reason this pedestal is High Riser specific is height, which is 1.720 inches compared to the standard FE pedestal height of 2.200 inches. It also measures 1.100 inches wide compared to the standard pedestal's width of 1.020 inches.

The C5AZ-A cast-iron pedestal is Medium Riser and Tunnel Port specific, which means it is not intended for any other FE cylinder head. This pedestal measures 2.200 inches in height, as does the C3AE-A piece for the High Riser. Pedestal bolts come in various lengths for each pedestal type. The taller the pedestal, the

Adjustable FE rocker arms get cup-style pushrods. Note the oil deflection shield, which carries oil promptly to the drain-back holes. Some aftermarket rocker arm assemblies will not clear these shields.

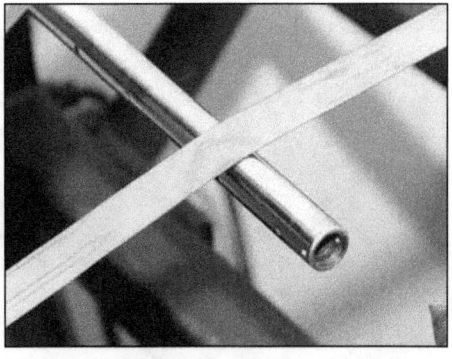

Unless a rocker shaft is scored badly it can be polished as shown and pressed back into service. Measure shaft diameter for evidence of wear and tear. While you're at it, make sure you have a straight shaft. As a rule, these shafts can be used again and again as long as wear isn't excessive.

FE/FT engines benefit greatly from a hot aftermarket roller cam, which reduces friction and allows a more aggressive cam profile. Note this new cam plate and Grade-8 hardware.

FORD BIG-BLOCK PARTS INTERCHANGE

CHAPTER 6

Crane offers almost everything you're ever going to need for an FE/FT valvetrain. This is a complete roller cam/roller rocker setup with billet pedestals and hardware.

longer the bolt. Don't make the mistake of installing bolts that are too long for the pedestal and bolt holes.

The aftermarket offers you billet rocker shaft pedestals available from a number of sources for the FE. The stock iron and steel pedestals will withstand up to .500-inch lift and 350 pounds of spring pressure. However, if you're planning greater than .500-inch lift and 350 pounds of spring pressure, go with billet pedestals. Budget permitting, you should outfit your FE with aftermarket roller rockers for reduced friction and greater durability along with billet pedestals.

FE Camshaft, Lifters, Timing Set

FE/FT camshafts were supported by five 2.124-inch bearings and oiled via the main journal galleys. Number 2 and number 4 bearings must have an oiling groove in their centers if you're running a 427 Side Oiler block. You won't need them on the rest of the FE engine family. Camshaft selection isn't so much about swapping, but about selection alone. In selecting a camshaft, you should consider how the engine will be used most of the time.

The FE/FT camshaft employs a single dowel pin at the front of the cam, which is a snug fit but not an interference fit. Originally, the dowel pin was pressed into the Ford timing gear. Today's aftermarket cam kits are just the opposite where the dowel slips into the cam and sprocket.

With one-piece fuel pump eccentrics, the dowel pin must be the correct length to make it through the timing sprocket and be flush with the eccentric. When you have the later two-piece fuel pump eccentric, the dowel pin should be recessed just enough in the sprocket to clear the eccentric tab. This is where you must have the proper combination of parts. The cam bolt is 7/16-4. Expect to see either coarse or fine thread. You must use a Grade 8-bolt in any case.

With the cam seated in the block, the forward-most point of the cam rides against the thrust plate bolted to the front of the block. Two 7/14-14 bolts secure the thrust plate to the

This is one of at least two or three timing pointers (two-bolt shown) for the FE. It is a 1968 390 High Performance engine. Earlier FE engines have a long pointer with two small screws.

block. From the factory, Ford used Phillips or button-head bolts to clear the timing sprocket. Not all aftermarket Grade-8 bolt heads will clear the sprocket, making this a trial-and-error situation. You must have at least .060 inch of clearance. Camshaft endplay should be around .005 inch. Blue Thunder is one source for camshaft thrust plates. You can even fit your FE with Torrington needle bearing thrust plates for reduced friction.

Most FE engines had flat-tappet hydraulic lifters from the factory. The earliest production 332/352 FE engines were fitted with mechanical flat-tappet lifters.

FE Power offers this adjustable timing set that allows you to change cam timing at the cam gear. If you need to change valve timing, all you have to do is pull the water pump, remove the plate on the special FE Power timing cover, and adjust the timing at the cam gear. The FE Power timing cover and adjustable timing set gives you the same functionality as a belt-drive timing system without the excessive cost of a timing belt. (Photo Courtesy FE Power)

CAMSHAFT AND VALVETRAIN

FE engines were originally fitted with flat-tappet mechanical and hydraulic lifters. At introduction, the 332 and 352 were fitted exclusively with mechanical-tappet cams. When Ford realized that competition from the rest of Detroit had hydraulic lifters standard, it quickly converted the FE engines to hydraulic lifters, even though high-performance versions, including the 352 in 1960, still received mechanical cams. (Photo Courtesy Crane Cams)

The FE Power cast-aluminum billet timing cover is unique because it has a removable front plate that allows access to the adjustable cam sprocket. This removable plate is sealed with an O-ring for easy service and timing adjustment. The FE Power timing cover also has additional bosses to allow bracket attachment for mounting additional engine accessories or perhaps a motor plate. The FE Power timing cover is a suitable replacement for the stock cover, especially if you're an avid racer. (Photo Courtesy FE Power)

Mechanical-tappet FE engines got ball-and-cup pushrods. These are three-piece pushrods. For durability, the best choice is the thick-wall one-piece pushrod. (Photo Courtesy Crane Cams)

Although FE engines were originally factory fitted with three-piece pushrods, it's a good life insurance policy to fit yours with one-piece .080-inch thick-wall pushrods. These are for hydraulic lifters with non-adjustable rocker arms. (Photo Courtesy Crane Cams)

FE engines fitted with hydraulic lifters can benefit from using a pushrod checker, which helps to confirm proper pushrod length during valve lash setup. A pushrod check enables you to set valvetrain geometry accurately before ordering pushrods. (Photo Courtesy Crane Cams)

When Ford discovered that buyers didn't care for periodic valve adjustment, the FE went hydraulic lifter throughout with the exception being high-performance applications. Lifter bore diameter through FE production is .874 inch. Because the FE oils its valvetrain through the block, head, pedestal, and shaft, lifters are not equipped with oil holes.

One option you have today for your FE project is mechanical or hydraulic roller lifters for reduced friction and allowance for a more aggressive cam profile without the

Valvespring pressure should correspond directly with cam profile. When you're shopping for a valvetrain system, opt for a matching cam profile and valvespring. Too much spring pressure can be as bad as not enough because you can wipe a cam with too much pressure. By the same token, too little spring pressure will cause valve float at high RPM.

CHAPTER 6

This is a Crane dual-roller high-performance timing set for high-revving FE applications. Even if you're building an FE stocker, a dual-roller chain reduces internal friction. (Photo Courtesy Crane Cams)

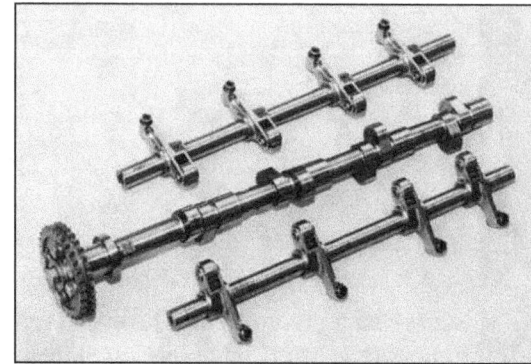

The 427 SOHC sports an incredibly complex valvetrain system. This is the Robert Pond cam and rocker arm assembly for one cylinder head. Pond components are race-ready pieces that have evolved from those that Ford produced a half-century ago.

This is the stub cam for the 427 SOHC, which is installed in the block where an OHV cam would ordinarily be fitted. Shown here is a stub cam with sprocket and one without. Robert Pond Motorsports produces and sells pretty much everything for the FE Series big-blocks. You can build an entire Robert Pond FE engine and never use a Ford part.

disadvantages of a hot cam. You can top the package with roller rockers for a drastic reduction in internal friction.

427 SOHC

Where the FE engine gets beyond the norm is the SOHC version of this engine displacing 427 ci. Although the SOHC isn't heavily addressed in this book, it is important to understand the idiosyncrasies of Ford's most extraordinary big-block V-8 in the valvetrain. On top are two cast-alloy camshafts with induction-hardened lobes. Journals are located close to the lobes. There are five cam journals on the driver's side and six on the passenger's side. Rocker arms are of nodular iron. These shaft-mounted nodular-iron rocker arms are bronze-bushed.

Early 427 Cammers were fitted with non-adjustable shaft-mounted rocker arms that were adjusted via lash caps. In time, Ford went to adjustable rocker arms; these could be adjusted in a more conventional manner. Rocker arm ratio on the SOHC is 1.3:1 due to the very nature of the beast. With the 1.3:1 ratio, a .500-inch lift cam winds up .650 inch at the valve.

Where the SOHC becomes complex is the involved timing package in front with a complex series of chains and sprockets. There are two complete sets of timing gears supporting each bank of cylinders. At the block, there's a stub shaft where an in-block camshaft would ordinarily sit in a wedge engine. The stub shaft is driven by a conventional timing chain. From the stub shaft and sprocket onward this beast becomes complex and tricky to time. The secondary chain is 6 feet long and winds around two tensioner gears and a pair of idler gears before it spins the camshafts. Two chain guides keep things on course.

Of course, the Cammer's timing system is notorious for its challenges. However, if timed and adjusted properly it is a proven, reliable system. The aftermarket has offered its share of gear drive systems to replace the

Here's the Robert Pond 427 SOHC stub cam, sprocket, and timing chain installed. The stub cam fits in place of the wedge-style cam in the SOHC. The crank drives this timing package, which drives the SOHC chains. The stub cam also runs the oil pump and distributor.

88   FORD BIG-BLOCK PARTS INTERCHANGE

CAMSHAFT AND VALVETRAIN

Cammer's involved timing chain system. The 427 SOHC is easily the most involved FE engine ever conceived, and I won't go into this engine in depth because it is so rare.

The 427 SOHC's original factory cams were iron sticks with user-friendly lobe ramps offering good stability and, as a result, longevity. The Cammer's lobe profile offered extended seat-to-seat time and lengthy duration. The replacement steel billet cams available today from Comp Cams offer a more aggressive profile with greater lift for the Cammer. Robert Pond offers a huge array of Cammer parts as well.

The MEL

The MEL rocker arm is completely interchangeable with the FE rocker arm. They are the same with a 1.73:1 rocker ratio for the non-adjustable rocker arm. If you want an adjustable MEL rocker arm with the 1.76:1 ratio, search for the B8A-6064-B rocker in the Ford box. They will fit all MEL model years from 1958 to 1968. The MEL's rocker arm shaft does not interchange with the FE because the MEL sports a completely different cylinder head and pedestals. You may opt for roller

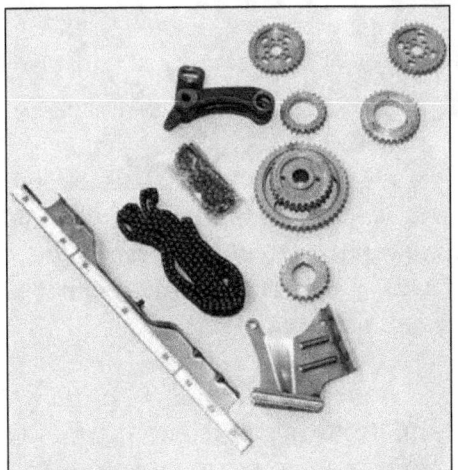
The 427 SOHC's complex timing chain system is shown in pieces from Robert Pond Motorsports. With an appropriate amount of cash in hand, you can build a 427 SOHC from scratch using Robert Pond parts. Pond's extensive experience in FE drag racing dates back decades. These are well thought-out pieces developed through the rigors of racing.

The MEL rocker arm assembly is strikingly similar to the FE shaft. The only differences are shafts and pedestals. The rocker arms are identical.

The MEL's timing cover has a mechanical fuel pump provision on top with pushrod actuation. This feature is what makes the MEL quickly identifiable.

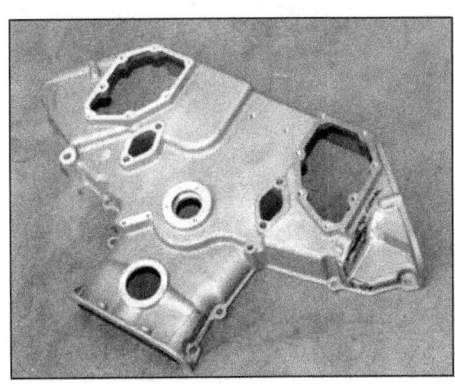
The Robert Pond cast-aluminum timing cover for the 427 SOHC has a number of design improvements. The stamped steel cover plate is also available.

MEL big-blocks were originally fitted with nylon-coated camshaft sprockets, which are not recommended in any form. This is an aftermarket MEL timing set, which will last for the life of any MEL engine. MEL timing components do not interchange with any other Ford big-block.

MEL timing covers are identified by the Ford casting number found inside. This is a 1958–1959 vintage MEL timing cover.

FORD BIG-BLOCK PARTS INTERCHANGE

To clarify a rumor often discussed in 429/460 circles, the 385 Series big-block was never factory fitted with hydraulic roller lifters, not even when small-blocks were roller-tappet equipped in the 1980s and 1990s. Ford saw an end coming for 385 production during the 1990s, which is why it never invested in the engineering and tooling necessary to cast a 460-roller block.

On top, the 460 head is almost the same as early 429/460 heads with bolt-fulcrum stamped steel rocker arms. The basic 429/460 head casting and valvetrain didn't change much during this engine's production life.

rockers for your MEL build because this engine shares a valvetrain with the FE, which gives you all kinds of options.

Harland-Sharp is a good source for FE/MEL rocker arms. Its bronze-bushed rocker system features Oilite bushings that fit on stock diameter shafts. If you go with adjustable 1.76:1 rocker arms on your MEL, don't forget to order ball/cup pushrods for use with the adjuster. You will have to check pushrod length with a pushrod checker to get pushrod length in the neighborhood. Non-adjustable rocker arms are 1.73:1.

385 Series 429/460

From the time the 385 Series engines displacing 429/460 ci were introduced in 1968 until production ended in the 1990s, the valvetrain didn't change much. The standard and Cobra Jet engines had non-adjustable bolt-fulcrum stamped steel rocker arms (C8SZ-6564-A) that were employed for the majority of this engine's production life. A revised bolt-fulcrum package (D0OZ-6A527-A) came later for the 429/460 engines. The 429 Super Cobra Jet sporting mechanical lifters had a fully adjustable valvetrain with screw-in rocker arm studs (C9ZZ-6A527-A) and stronger stamped steel rocker arms (C9ZZ-6564-A).

This is the 429 Super Cobra Jet with its aggressive mechanical cam calls for screw-in rocker arm studs and guides for durability. You can convert a standard 429/460 head to screw-in studs and guide plates by milling the bosses, then drilling and tapping the bolt holes.

Camshaft selection with the 385 mill isn't any different than shopping for any other high-performance engine. All 429/460 engines were fitted with a hydraulic flat-tappet camshaft; the exception was the 429 Super Cobra Jet equipped with a flat-tappet mechanical cam. The 429/460 was never factory fitted with a roller cam even when Ford was installing them in 5.0-liter High Output engines. The aftermarket offers a wealth of hydraulic and mechanical roller cams for the 429/460.

The 429 Cobra Jet engines were factory fitted with the C9AZ-6250-A hydraulic flat-tappet cam. The Super Cobra Jets got an aggressive mechanical cam, D0AZ-6250-A. Look for the "BJB" on a new old stock (NOS) Super Cobra Jet cam and an "8J" on a hydraulic.

Camshaft selection for your 429/460 build project boils down to what you want the engine to do. You want a matched camshaft kit with cam, lifters, and valvesprings. This gets all components on the same page. Cam profile and valvespring pressure

CAMSHAFT AND VALVETRAIN

The 429/460 timing package shown here has a dual-roller timing set for durability and reduced friction. Note the two-piece fuel pump eccentric for reduced friction. The endless debate over one-piece versus two-piece asks which eccentric is more durable. Both offer durability, but the two-piece eccentric yields less friction.

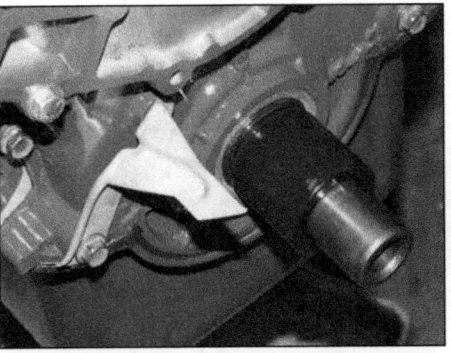

One of the 385 Series timing pointers and crank spacer bear similarity to that found on the FE engines. They are not interchangeable. This is a 1970–1971 429 Super Cobra Jet.

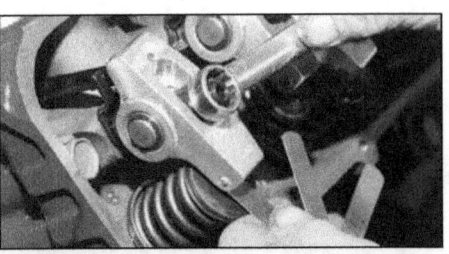

The 429 Super Cobra Jet's mechanical tappets call for screw-in studs and guide plates. This is true for any aggressive roller- or flat-tappet cam you have in mind for your 385 engine. Screw-in studs offer durability. Stock rocker arms are stamped steel. Here, I'm using a Crane roller rocker and performing valve lash adjustment.

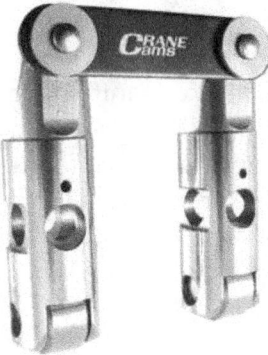

Although the 385 Series big-blocks were never factory equipped with roller tappets doesn't mean you have to live without them. All aftermarket cam grinders offer roller mechanical and hydraulic lifters, which reduce internal friction and free up power. (Photo Courtesy Crane Cams)

must match. Although roller cams are more expensive, you gain more efficiency and power when you use them.

Boss 429

The Boss 429 engine is a stand-alone big-block among 385 Series engines. These hemi-head engines were fitted with an exotic valvetrain, with intake valves actuated by short, shaft-mounted adjustable rocker arms (C9AZ-6564-C). Exhaust valves got the action via longer shaft-mounted adjustable rocker arms (C9AZ-6564-D). Pushrods for the Boss Nine are also distinctive due to the nature of the limited production cylinder heads. Intake pushrods are shorter (C9AZ-6565-A at 8.760 inches). Exhaust pushrods are longer (C9AZ-6565-B at 10.880 inches).

Down under are the dual-roller chain and sprocket. Regardless of the type of timing package you choose, always check clearance with the timing cover here at the crank.

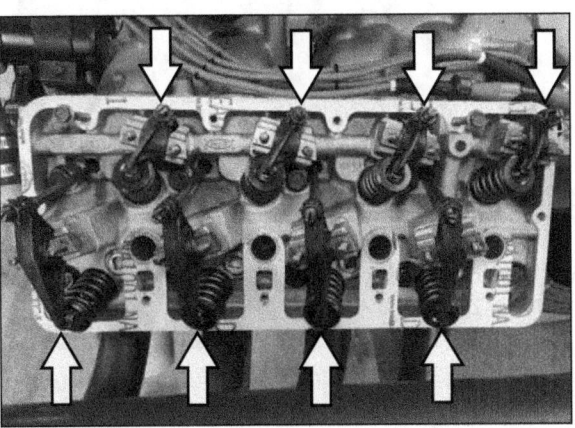

Boss 429 rocker arms are nearly impossible to install backward. Intakes (bottom arrows) offer a 1.53:1 ratio; exhausts (top arrows) have a 1.73:1 ratio and are much longer. Both are shaft mounted. The aftermarket has a good selection, including Jon Kaase Racing Engines. (Photograph Courtesy Dan Burrill)

CHAPTER 7

INDUCTION

A Ford big-block's induction system has always been a quick bolt-on source for performance. All three vintage Ford big-blocks (FE, MEL, and 385 Series) yield an array of performance options from both the factory and the aftermarket. Swap meets and online auctions remain good sources for big-block Ford induction systems. The FE big-block is undoubtedly Ford's most successful pedigree with a huge wealth of intake manifolds and carburetors to choose from out there. It is astonishing just how much there is, both new and used, for the FE.

If you're performing a restoration, you're naturally going to want casting number and date-coded correct pieces for your FE build. However, if you have the freedom of a resto mod–style build, options become many in both factory and aftermarket pieces. One option that excites enthusiasts is period speed equipment from the muscle car era of the 1960s. Classic Edelbrock, Offenhauser, Weiand, Holley, and Ford Performance induction systems thrust your restoration back to another era. Ford, especially, during the 1980s and 1990s, offered a wealth of performance pieces for the FE and 385 Series big-block Fords.

Even today, Blue Thunder, FE Power, and Survivor Motorsports, to name three, offer a wealth of big-block Ford intake manifolds for these engines if you are seeking an OEM look. Edelbrock has Performer Series manifolds for both the FE and 385 Series engines. Summit Racing Equipment offers a range of induction packages for both the FE and 385 Series engines.

Although the MEL big-block was originally conceived as a luxury car engine, it quickly developed a reputation as a brute high-performance engine long on torque and capable of a lot of horsepower, especially in powerboat and drag racing. The MEL's penalty was weight. It was undoubtedly the heaviest Ford big-block ever produced, except for the Super Duty truck engine.

The 385 Series 429/460 was conceived for the same reason as the MEL a decade earlier, to power big luxury cars beginning in 1968. Ford soon realized the great performance potential of the 429/460, introducing the 429 Cobra Jet and Super Cobra Jet in 1970.

FE Intake Manifold

The FE intake manifold and cylinder head relationship is certainly the most unusual in Ford history.

There's probably no greater selection of intake manifolds than those for the FE big-block. The best places to look for them are swap meets and online auctions. It is also good to put the word out on social media regarding what you're looking for, especially FE chat rooms. This is a small part of John Vermeersch's huge collection of FE and 385 Series parts at his Total Performance shop in Mount Clemons, Michigan.

INDUCTION

Here's a typical cast-iron 390 High Performance intake manifold for 1967–1969, which isn't much different than the standard 390 4V intake. If you gave a choice, sidestep this manifold and opt for the 428 Police Interceptor or a 427 Medium Riser.

If you're building a brute street 390 or 428, this is the manifold you want. The 428 Police Interceptor intake (C7AE-9425-F) offers lightweight cast aluminum and better heat transfer qualities. The high ports are an asset that deliver power at high RPM. Port length contributes to great low- to mid-range torque. This manifold will work with almost any FE cylinder head except the 427 High Riser. Before opting for this manifold, check the port match with your existing heads.

The cylinder head and intake manifold meet beneath the valvecover, which makes this engine one of the most unusual in Detroit history. Which intake manifold you choose has a direct effect on performance. Choice depends upon mission. How will your FE big-block be used most of the time? And, how much hood clearance do you have? Because the FE has an extensive performance history, an array of factory intake manifolds is available, some more elusive than others.

Factory experimental intake manifolds with the definitive X or XE in the casting number quicken the pulse because they're an integral part of Ford's factory racing history. Everyone has heard all the stories. Woodward Avenue and Telegraph Road in the Detroit suburbs were proving grounds for the Big Three to experiment with one-off experimental pieces that have found their way into swap meets. I have seen prototype induction packages that never made mass production, including super lightweight magnesium FE 427 intake manifolds conceived for Shelby and Le Mans.

Approximately 10 garden-variety intake manifold applications and port dimensions are available for the FE big-block. This means at least 10 potential port matches. When you're shopping for an intake manifold, both cylinder head and manifold port size should match. When they don't match you are courting turbulence issues that can cost you power. Measure cylinder head port size before laying down your money on an intake manifold. The cylinder head should always have slightly larger intake ports than what the manifold has if you're faced with different port sizing. Get this backward and you get into unwanted port turbulence where the two get together.

The more common FE intake manifolds from the factory and aftermarket are discussed in this book. It is impossible to cover every intake manifold ever produced for the FE from the factory and aftermarket because there were so many in the FE's peak production years. When you get into the aftermarket it becomes way more involved. There are obscure types found at swap meets and those rare factory experimental pieces that managed to slip out the back door at Ford a couple of generations ago. At times, their rarity makes them challenging to identify.

Jay Brown of FE Power can help identify the more obscure FE intake manifolds with *The Great FE Intake Comparo* manual, which is 288 pages of 150 dyno tests along with 600 images, charts, and graphs. *The Great FE Intake Comparo* is the result of four years of FE big-block dyno testing, during which nearly 40 intake manifold types were evaluated on 6 different engines ranging in power from 350 to 675 hp. The manifolds were often tested in port-matched or internally ported form, leading to more than 50 intake manifold configurations.

This is the 428 Police Interceptor intake (C7AE-9425-F) freshly tumbled and ready for installation. The PI intakes are becoming scarce with time because they're an excellent 428 Cobra Jet substitute. Blue Thunder offers a similar manifold.

FORD BIG-BLOCK PARTS INTERCHANGE

There are obvious FE intake manifold and cylinder head combinations designed to work only with each other. For example, the 427 SOHC intake manifold isn't going to fit your 390 GT engine. By the same token, 427 Tunnel Port heads were conceived only for the Tunnel Port intake. Not only do they not match, you couldn't even bolt this intake onto your standard FE wedge with a lot of imagination. More common intake manifolds, such as the 427 High Riser, won't bolt onto anything but a High Riser

Common FE Performance Intake Manifolds

Model Year	Part Number/Casting Number	Description
1958–59	5751087	Cast-Iron 4V
1961–62	C1AE-9425-B	Cast-Iron 4V
1963–64	No Part Number/Casting Number	Aluminum 6V Angle Deck
1963–64	No Part Number/Casting Number	Aluminum 6V Flat Deck
1963–64	C3AE-9424-E	Aluminum 4V Low/Medium Riser
1963–64	C3AE-9424-F	Aluminum 4V Low/Medium Riser Larger Ports
1963–64	C3AE-9425-A	Cast-Iron 4V
1963–64	C3AE-9425-H	Aluminum 8V Low Riser
1963–64	C3AE-9425-J	Aluminum 8V Low Riser
1963–64	C3AE-9425-K	Aluminum 8V Low Riser
1964	C4AE-9425-D	Aluminum 8V 427 High Riser (Fits High Riser Head Only)
1964	C4AE-9425-E	Aluminum 4V 427 High Riser (Fits High Riser Head Only)
1964	C4AE-9425-G	Aluminum 8V 427 High Riser (Fits High Riser Head Only)
1964		Cast-Iron 4V
1964	C4AE-9425-C	Cast-Iron 4V
1965	C5AE-9424-K	Aluminum 8V Low Riser
1965	C5AE-9425-C	Cast-Iron 4V
1965	C4AE-9425-K	Aluminum 8V Low Riser
1966	C6AE-9424-J	Aluminum 4V Sidewinder
1966	C6AE-9424-M	Aluminum 4V Sidewinder
1966	C6AE-9425-E	Cast-Iron 4V 428 Police Interceptor (Virtually the same as 427 Medium Riser)
1966	C6AE-9425-G	Cast-Iron 4V
1966	C6AE-9425-H	Aluminum 4V 428 Police Interceptor
1966	C6AE-9425-K	Aluminum 4V Medium Riser/Sidewinder
1967	C7AE-9425-A	Aluminum 8V Medium Riser
1967	C7AE-9425C	Aluminum 4V Medium Riser/Sidewinder
1967	C7AE-9425-E	Cast-Iron 4V
1967	C7OE-9425-A	Aluminum 8V Tunnel Port (Tunnel Port Heads Only)
1967	C7OE-9425-B	Aluminum 8V Tunnel Port (Tunnel Port Heads Only)
1967	C7ZX-9425-A	Aluminum 8V Medium Riser
1968	C8AE-9425-A	Cast-Iron 4V 390 GT
1968	C8AE-9425-F	Cast-Iron 4V
1968	C8AZ-9424-A	Aluminum 8V
1968	C8AX-9425-B	Aluminum 8V Tunnel Port (Tunnel Port Head Only)
1968	C8OE-9425-A	Cast-Iron 4V 428 Cobra Jet
1968	C8OE-9425-C	Cast-Iron 4V 428 Cobra Jet
1969	C9ZE-9425-B	Cast-Iron 390 GT
1970-On	CFMD-9425-C	Aluminum 8V

INDUCTION

This is the 427 Low Riser 8V dual-plane intake manifold (C3AE-9425-J). It bolts onto any FE big-block except the 427 High Riser, Tunnel Port, and SOHC. This manifold is designed for any of the square-flange 4V carburetors, including Holley and Carter AFB.

The same 8V manifold (C3AE-9425-J) is fitted with Holley carburetion. You can use any Holley 1850 or 4160 carburetor on this manifold. The Holley list includes 2652, 2652-1, 2804/2805, 2926/2927, 3300/3301, 3410/3411, and 4201/4201 as possible carburetor selections. Ford-spec Holleys have a Ford part number as well as the Holley list number.

The 390/406 Tri-Power intake manifold didn't have a Ford casting number. However, it is clearly recognizable. Intake ports are 2.140 x 1.160 inches. Holley carburetor list numbers are 2436/2437, 2497/2498/2499, and 3208.

This is the Ford FE Tri-Power manifold void of carburetion. Dozens of these manifolds have been seen through the years. I've never seen one with a Ford casting number, which indicates a Buddy Bar foundry (Los Angeles) casting.

This is a rare piece. The C8AX-9425-A factory experimental manifold for the FE is strictly a high-RPM manifold for off-road use because of its huge runners and dual-quads. This is not a street manifold.

head. The SOHC, Tunnel Port, and High Riser FE engines were never intended as street engines no matter how many of them you see on the street.

Port match on FE engines boils down to port floor positioning, according to Barry Rabotnick of Survival Motorsports, which specializes in Ford FE big-blocks. FE engines are all they do. Intake manifold selection begins with fitment and cosmetics. Bolt holes and ports must line up. Moreover, it is important to like what you see once the manifold is bolted on. Selection goes deeper than fitment and appearance. Choice depends upon how you intend to use your FE most of the time. Most factory intake manifolds are dual-plane with a common plenum for good low-to-mid-range torque. Torque is what you want most on the street. Horsepower is reserved for high RPM.

CHAPTER 7

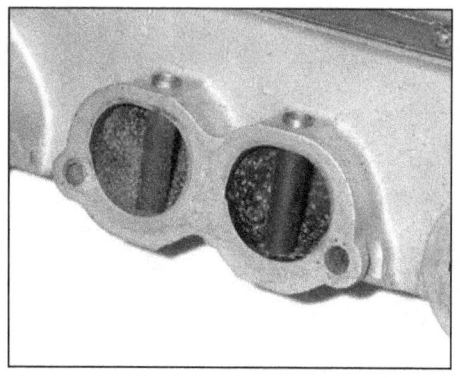

FE big-blocks were fueled by a wide variety of carburetors through their long production life. Basic 2-barrel FE engines were fitted with the Autolite/Motorcraft 2100 and 2150. However, you're not likely reading this book to learn about average big-block Fords with anemic

The C7OE-9425-A 427 Tunnel Port intake was conceived strictly for the Tunnel Port head. This is an all-out racing manifold and not recommended for street use. Pushrod tubes run through the intake ports.

Here's a close-up look at the Tunnel Port intake ports with pushrod tubes. Although the pushrod tubes appear restrictive, these manifolds and heads performed very well in high-RPM NASCAR competition.

Check out this factory experimental C7ZX-9425-A 8V High Rise. Parts such as this were released to racers. At times, they also slipped out the back door at Ford. They make for great conversation pieces, which are also beneficial to racers today.

This unusual manifold was found at John Vermeersch's Total Performance shop in Southeastern Michigan. It is an experimental NASCAR piece (PN SK-18455) with square bore flanges designed for the Holley 4150/4160.

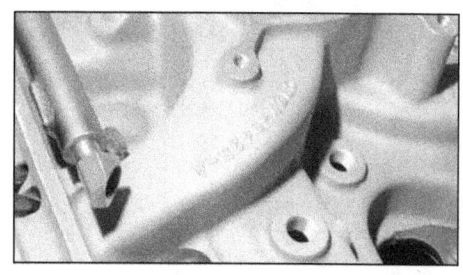

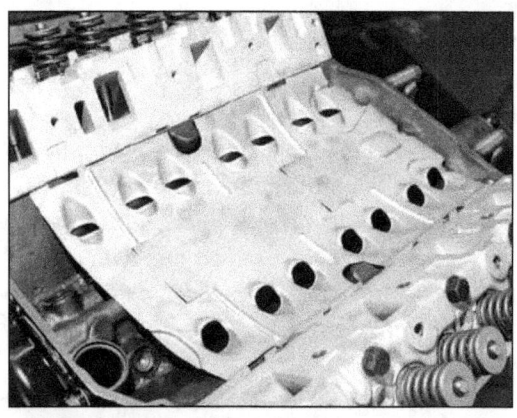

FE engines benefit from this factory intake manifold heat shield that keeps heat away from the intake. In fact, it keeps hot oil away from the manifold. Not everyone remembers to install these heat shields, but they do make a difference in induction temperatures. You're going to find that not every FE engine still has one.

The Ford experimental casting number eliminates any doubt as to the identity of this C7ZX-9425-A intake manifold. Swap meets and online auctions offer a wealth of limited production pieces such as this one.

Fel-Pro Print-O-Seal gaskets offer the best sealing of any intake manifold gasket if you're going racing. For street use, they suffer from leak issues where oil is ingested into the intake ports. Mr. Gasket composition gaskets and Edelbrock gaskets are much more durable for street/strip applications. Use light amounts of Permatex's The Right Stuff around cooling passages and along the bottom of each intake port. Use a thicker bead of The Right Stuff along the block rail ends instead of the cork/rubber gasket provided.

INDUCTION

This is a rare magnesium 427 Medium Riser intake manifold used in Ford's racing program in the 1960s. As you might imagine, there's no Ford casting number. The downside to these magnesium intake manifolds is corrosion. They pitted severely because racers ran straight water in most of them. When you mix in aluminum thermostat housings and steel bolts, corrosion becomes a reality.

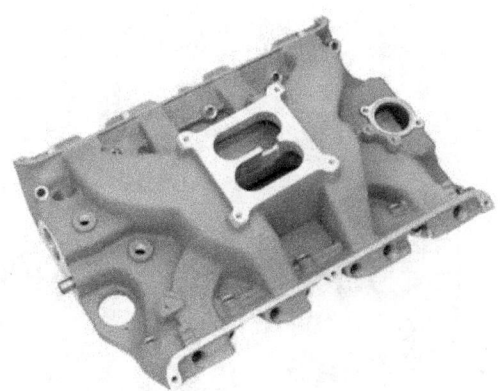

Blue Thunder reproduces the 427 Medium Riser intake manifold. However, they don't come cheap; they do enable you to score this manifold as new without an extensive search.

Swap meets yield odd-duck FE intake manifolds such as this 12-barrel designed for small base 2-barrel carburetors such as the Stromberg 97 and 2-barrel Holley carburetors. You have to admit, this isn't an induction package you see every day.

This Edelbrock Tri-Power F380 intake for FE big-blocks was spotted at Carlisle complete with carburetion. These manifolds were not designed for the Holley 2-barrel carbs commonly seen on a Tri-Power. These classic Edelbrock manifolds are from the 1950s and designed for Stromberg 97s and petite 2-barrel carburetors.

Although it's not a stock manifold, the Edelbrock Performer RPM dual-plane intake manifold is a suitable substitute for the 427 Medium Riser and 428 Police Interceptor. This manifold's square base plate will accommodate almost any Holley-style 4150/4160 carburetor. This is the Holley HP Series performance carburetor.

Shown here is the single 4-barrel C6AE-9424-J 427 SOHC Cammer dual-plane intake manifold. Although very few of you will be in the market for one of these, or have the bankroll necessary to buy one, they're entertaining when spotted at a swap meet. This one is in John Vermeersch's collection at Total Performance.

The Autolite 2100/2150 series 2-barrel carburetor, introduced in 1957, was employed on virtually every 2-barrel FE Series big-block. It remains the most reliable Ford carburetor ever produced. The 2100 was the first carburetor with annular fuel discharge–boost venturis produced in sizes ranging from 190 to 400 cfm. Bore sizes were .98, 1.01, 1.02, 1.08, 1.12, 1.14, 1.23, and 1.33 inches. The 2100 later became the 2150 as emissions standards increased in the 1970s and 1980s.

The Autolite 4100 is a 4-barrel version of the smaller 2100 2-barrel. Both carburetors evolved along much the same path with similar modifications and sizing. Known affectionately as the "shoebox" carburetor, the 4100 (as well as the 2100) are the most reliable Ford carburetors ever produced. The 4100 is equipped with annular discharge boosters and vacuum secondaries. Some are equipped with a hot idle compensator to increase idle speed when underhood temperatures get high. The 4100 was available in 1.08, 1.14, and 1.23 inches ranging from 480 to 600 cfm. This one is fitted with an anti-stall dashpot for automatic transmissions.

Popular FE Aftermarket Manifolds

Manufacturer	Part Number	Description
Blue Thunder	IM-428CVJ-4V	428CJ 4V High Riser Manifold
Blue Thunder	IM-428CJ-4VC	428CJ 4V High Riser Competition Manifold
Blue Thunder	IM-428CJ-D	428CJ Dominator High Riser Manifold
Blue Thunder	IM-428CJ-8V	428CJ 8V Manifold
Blue Thunder	IM-427MR-4V	427 Medium Riser 4V Manifold
Blue Thunder	IM-427MR-4VC	427 Medium Riser Competition 4V Manifold
Blue Thunder	IM-427MR-D	427 Medium Riser Dominator Manifold
Blue Thunder	IM-427MR-8V	427 Medium Riser 8V Manifold
Blue Thunder	48-IDA	Weber IDA 8V
Dove Manufacturing	N/A	High Rise 4V
Dove Manufacturing	N/A	Tunnel Ram
Edelbrock	2105	Performer RPM, Satin
Edelbrock	21053	Performer RPM, Black
Edelbrock	7105	Performer RPM, Satin
Edelbrock	71051	Performer RPM, Polished
Edelbrock	71053	Performer RPM, Black
Edelbrock	71054	Performer RPM, EnduraShine
Edelbrock	7505	Dual-Quad Air Gap, Satin
Edelbrock	75054	Dual-Quad Air Gap, EnduraShine
Edelbrock	2936	Victor 4V Single-Plane
Edelbrock	3205	Streetmaster Dual-Plane 4V
Edelbrock	F68	Aluminum 6V
Edelbrock	F262	Aluminum High Rise 8V
Edelbrock	F380	Tri-Power, Stromberg 97
Edelbrock	X-F66	Cross Ram 8V
Edelbrock	F427	High Rise 4V
Edelbrock	SP/2P	Aluminum Dual-Plane 4V
Mickey Thompson "M/T"	N/A	Power Ram
Offenhauser	5407	Dual-Quad
Offenhauser	6148	Port-O-Sonic
Offenhauser	5774	360 Dual-Port
Robert Pond Motorsports		SOHC 8V
Weiand	7282	Aluminum 4V

INDUCTION

The Autolite 4300 carburetor is easily one of the worst Ford has ever conceived in an effort to meet tougher federal emissions standards in 1967–1968. It promptly replaced the 4100. The 4300 was originally available in one size: 441 cfm on all Ford 4-barrel V-8 engines, including the 390 FE. It choked engines that needed great air and fuel flow. Engines that didn't get the 4300 in 1967 were the 289 High Performance V-8; 428 FE Police Interceptor, which received the 4100; and the Shelby GT350s and GT500s, which used Holley carburetors. The 4300 grew larger in 1968, becoming available in 600 cfm.

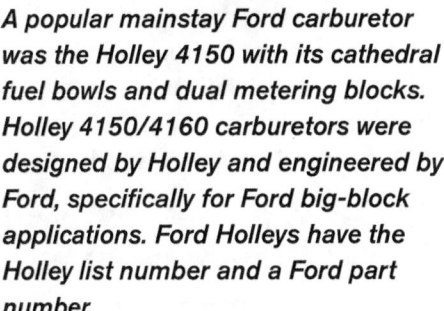

A popular mainstay Ford carburetor was the Holley 4150 with its cathedral fuel bowls and dual metering blocks. Holley 4150/4160 carburetors were designed by Holley and engineered by Ford, specifically for Ford big-block applications. Ford Holleys have the Holley list number and a Ford part number.

The Holley 4150 from a different angle shows just how Ford-specific this carburetor is. Linkage is set up for automatic transmission and factory fuel connections.

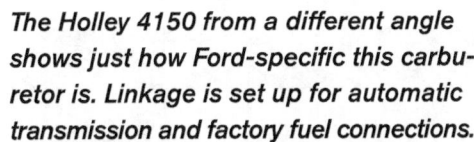

This is the Le Mans–bowl Holley 4150 for high-performance Ford small- and big-block applications. The Le Mans–bowl Holley was conceived for the Shelby 289 High Performance V-8 as well as the legendary 427 FE to keep floats stable during hard cornering. You can also take a 4150/4160/1850 Holley and install Le Mans bowls for racing or just for aesthetics.

This is 8V induction for the FE with a quartet of Weber IBA 2V carburetors, which can also be fitted with Inglese EFI throttle bodies from Fuel Air Spark Technology (FAST).

Here is a pair of modern Holley 4160s atop a Ford 8V FE induction package. When you can't find vintage Holleys, there are always new ones. These twin Holleys function via a progressive linkage. Cathedral-style fuel bowls will not fit in this configuration.

The FE Dual-quad package from the opposite side demonstrates vacuum secondaries and choke configuration.

CHAPTER 7

2-barrel induction. This book is more about how to get power from your FE and what works well together.

Most FE 4-barrel applications prior to 1967 were the Autolite 4100 carburetor. High-performance FE applications got the Holley 4150/4160 carburetors. Tri-Power FE engines got a trio of Holley 2-barrel carburetors. FE engines with dual quads got a pair of Holley 4160 carburetors. In both cases these special OEM Holley carburetors were given both Holley list numbers and Ford part numbers.

FE Aftermarket Induction

The FE aftermarket remains strong for enthusiasts still building these timeless Ford powerhouses. Edelbrock, Blue Thunder, Weiand, Offenhauser, Ford Racing, and a host of others have produced thousands of FE intakes since 1958. If you're scouting the swap meets, there are thousands of manifolds and carburetors out there for your FE project. If you're building a period hot rod or classic Ford muscle car, it is exciting to find old cast-aluminum Edelbrock or Offenhauser manifolds just waiting to be tumbled and made to look like new. If you're building a modern FE big-block, Edelbrock, Blue Thunder, and Summit Racing remain sources for FE intake manifolds.

Blue Thunder manifolds are generally difficult to come by. They are excellent manifolds of the highest quality. However, Blue Thunder does not keep them in stock and it is not unusual to wait more than a year for one of these fabulous intakes.

Popular FE Carburetors

Engine/Year	Make/Type	Ford ID Number	Other Information
332-4V 1958	Autolite 4100 4V	EDC-C and D	Manual Transmission
332-4V 1958	Holley 4160 4V	EDC-G and F	Manual Transmission
352-4V 1958	Autolite 4100 4V	EDT-B and C	Cruise-O-Matic
352-4V 1958	Carter AFB 4V	EDT-D	Cruise-O-Matic
332/352-4V 1959	Autolite 4100 4V	5752308 or 5752309	Manual and Cruise-O-Matic
332/352-4V 1959	Autolite 4100 4V	5752303	Cruise-O-Matic
352-4V 1960	Autolite 4100 4V	C0AE-J	Manual Transmission
352-4V 1960	Autolite 4100 4V	C0AE-K	Cruise-O-Matic
352-4V 1960	**Holley 4160 4V**	**C0AE-AA**	
390-4V 1961	Autolite 4100 4V	C1AE-AG	Manual Transmission
390-4V 1961–62	**Holley 4160 4V**	**C1AE-AM**	
406-4V 1962			
390-6V 1961–63	Holley 2300 2V (3)	C1AE-AV (Pri)	Full-Size Ford/Mercury
406-6V 1962–63		C1AE-AU (Sec)	Full Size Ford/Mercury
390-4V 1962	Autolite 4100 4V	C2AF-U, S, and Y	Manual Transmission
390-4V 1962	Autolite 4100 4V	C2AF-N, T, and Z	Cruise-O-Matic
390-4V 1963	Autolite 4100 4V	C3AF-S and N	Manual Transmission
390-4V 1963	Autolite 4100 4V	C3AF-T and R	Cruise-O-Matic
390-6V 1962–63	Holley 2300 2V (3)	C2SE-A C2SE-B C2SE-E	Ford Thunderbird Only
406-4V 1963	**Holley 4150 4V**	**C3AE-B**	
427-4V 1963–64			
406-8V 1963	**Holley 4150 4V (2)**	**C2AE-B**	
427-8V 1963			
352-4V 1964	Autolite 4100 4V	C4AF-N	Manual Transmission
352-4V 1964	Autolite 4100 4V	C4AF-R	Cruise-O-Matic
390-4V 1964	Autolite 4100 4V	C4AF-DH	Manual Transmission
390-4V 1964	Autolite 4100 4V	C4AF-DJ	Cruise-O-Matic

Bold indicates high-performance or significant change.

INDUCTION

Edelbrock is the better bet; the dual-plane Performer RPM intake is an excellent choice. The single-plane Victor intake is a great race manifold. You can order them and get them straight away.

The FE Power intake adapter (PN 13001) allows the use of 351C intake manifolds on the FE. With the FE Power intake adapter, an FE can run a tunnel ram, a Yates-style single-plane spider intake, or any number of other 351C manifolds. The FE Power intake manifold adapter makes it possible

FE Power makes it possible to install popular 351C intake manifolds onto your FE big-block. These FE Power intake adapters bolt onto FE engines and allow using a 351C intake manifold. They offer performance advantages because they turn every intake into an air-gap–style intake that lets the air/fuel mixture stay cool. They also allow use of some manifolds, such as tunnel rams, that are not available anywhere for the FE. What's more, they enable you to swap intakes without draining the cooling system.

Engine/Year	Make/Type	Ford ID Number	Other Information
427-8V 1964	**Holley 4150 4V (2)**	**C3AE-C**	
352/390-4V 1965	Autolite 4100 4V	C5AF-E and Z	Manual Transmission
352-4V 1965	Autolite 4100 4V	C5AF-F and AA	Cruise-O-Matic
390-4V 1965	Autolite 4100 4V	C5AF-H and AC	Cruise-O-Matic
427-4V 1965	**Holley 4150 4V**	**C5AF-BE**	
427-8V 1965	**Holley 4150 4V (2)**	C3AF-BK C3AF-BJ C4AF-CU C4AF-CV	All of these Ford part numbers have been found in this application.
352-4V 1966	Autolite 4100 4V	C6AF-L	Cruise-O-Matic
390-4V 1966	Autolite 4100 4V	C6AF-E	Manual Transmission
390-4V 1966	Autolite 4100 4V	C6AF-F	Cruise-O-Matic
390-4V 1966	Autolite 4100 4V	C6OF-D	Fairlane Manual Transmission
390-4V 1966	Autolite 4100 4V	C6OF-E	Fairlane Cruise-O-Matic
390-4V 1966	Autolite 4100 4V	C6OF-H	Fairlane/California Manual Transmission
390-4V 1966	Autolite 4100 4V	C6OF-J	Fairlane/California Cruise-O-Matic
390-4V 1966	**Holley 4150 4V**	**C6OF-M and N**	**Fairlane GT/GTA**
427-4V 1966–67	**Holley 4150 4V**	**C5AF-BV**	
427-8V 1966	**Holley 4150 4V (2)**	**C5AF-BD C5AF-BC**	
410-4V 1966	Autolite 4100 4V	C6AF-E	Manual Transmission
428-4V 1966			
410-4V 1966	Autolite 4100 4V	C6AF-F and BU	Cruise-O-Matic
428-4V 1966			
410-4V 1966	Autolite 4100 4V	C6AF-AB	**California**
428-4V 1966			Manual Transmission

Bold indicates high-performance or significant change.

FORD BIG-BLOCK PARTS INTERCHANGE

Popular FE Carburetors CONTINUED

Engine/Year	Make/Type	Ford ID Number	Other Information
410-4V 1966	Autolite 4100 4V	C6AF-AC	California
428-4V 1966			Cruise-O-Matic
390-4V 1967	Autolite 4300 4V	C7AF-C and AC C7OF-E	Manual Transmission
390-4V 1967	Autolite 4300 4V	C7AF-D and AD	Cruise-O-Matic
390-4V 1967	Autolite 4300 4V	C7OF-G	**California** Manual Transmission
390-4V 1967	Autolite 4300 4V	C7OF-H and AH	**California** Cruise-O-Matic
390-4V 1967	**Holley 4150 4V**	**C7OF-A**	Fairlane GT/Mustang GT Manual Transmission
390-4V 1967	**Holley 4150 4V**	**C7OF-B**	Fairlane GTA/Mustang GTA Cruise-O-Matic
390-4V 1967	**Holley 4150 4V**	**C7OF-C**	Fairlane GT/Mustang GT **California** Manual Transmission
390-4V 1967	**Holley 4150 4V**	**C7OF-D**	Fairlane GTA/Mustang GTA **California** Cruise-O-Matic
427-4V 1967	**Holley 4150 4V**	**C5AF-BV**	
410-4V 1967 428-4V 1967	Autolite 4300 4V	C7AF-AE	Manual Transmission
410-4V 1967 428-4V 1967	Autolite 4300 4V	C7AF-F, AD, AF, AV, BA and BJ	Cruise-O-Matic
410-4V 1967 428-4V 1967	Autolite 4300 4V	C7AF-J and AG	California Manual Transmission
410-4V 1967	Autolite 4300 4V	C7AF-K, AH, AY and BH	**California** Cruise-O-Matic
390-4V 1968	Autolite 4300 4V	C8AF-A and AR	Manual Transmission
390-4V 1968	Autolite 4300 4V	C8AF-B and AS	Cruise-O-Matic
390-4V 1968	**Holley 4150 4V**	**C8OF-C**	Manual Transmission
390-4V 1968	**Holley 4150 4V**	**C8OF-D**	Cruise-O-Matic
427-4V 1968	**Holley 4150 4V**	**C8AF-AD**	
428-4V 1968	Holley 4150 4V	C8ZX-A	Shelby GT500 Manual & Cruise-O-Matic
428-4V 1968 **Cobra Jet**	Holley 4150 4V	C8OF-AA	Mustang/Fairlane/Torino Cyclone/Cougar Shelby GT500KR Manual Transmission
428-4V 1968 **Cobra Jet**	Holley 4150 4V	C8OF-AB	Mustang/Fairlane/Torino Cyclone/Cougar Shelby GT500KR Cruise-O-Matic
390-4V 1969	Autolite 4300 4V	C9ZF-E	Manual Transmission
390-4V 1969	Autolite 4300 4V	C9ZF-F	Cruise-O-Matic
428-4V 1969–70 **Cobra Jet**	Holley 4150 4V	C9AF-M	Mustang/Fairlane/Torino Cyclone/Cougar Shelby GT500 Manual Transmission
428-4V 1969–70 **Cobra Jet**	Holley 4150 4V	C9AF-N	Mustang/Fairlane/Torino Cyclone/Cougar Shelby GT500 Cruise-O-Matic

Bold indicates high-performance or significant change.

INDUCTION

MEL Induction

Although the Ford MEL was conceived as a low-revving high-torque luxury car engine, it has also enjoyed an exceptional racing history. As a result, many induction options are available for MEL enthusiasts. There are even adapter options where you can bolt a 385 Series intake manifold onto the MEL, which increases your performance options.

Ford MEL parts shelf intake manifold and carburetion options are few. The MEL was fitted with both 2V and 4V intake manifolds from the factory. Especially rare is the Mercury Super Marauder 6V manifold and Holley carburetion package for 1958 only. It made 400 hp, which was outrageous for the era. The Super Marauder was a flash in the pan at the MEL's birth because it didn't last. On the rare occasion that these exotic 6V manifolds come up for sale, they are expensive regardless of condition.

The most common MEL intake manifold was the cast-iron 4-barrel dual-plane, which was cast in a number of Ford casting and part numbers and was basically the same manifold for this engine's decade-long

Here's the FE Power intake adapter with an Edelbrock Super Victor 351C single-plane manifold. The FE Power intake adapter gives you more options and improved induction without having to search for obscure FE manifolds.

This FE Power intake adapter shows a tunnel ram setup. The FE Power adapter opens up your FE options and makes light work of intake manifold swaps. This piece saves you all kinds of time because you won't have to remove valvecovers, valvetrain, or the distributor. It begs the question: Why didn't Ford think of this a half-century ago?

to bolt more common induction systems onto your FE. What's more, it makes for an easier swap.

FE engines have always had raw torque on their side thanks to good bore and stroke combinations. On the street, you're going to want a dual-plane intake manifold. Runners with high ceilings help an FE come on strong at high RPM. This is what makes Edelbrock's Performer manifolds a good choice. They deliver excellent low-end torque. In addition, when it's time to pin the butterflies, the Performer works exceedingly well at high RPM. Blue Thunder and Survival Motorsports, which are Ford focused, offer the FE performance buff what's easily the greatest selection of FE intake manifolds.

Popular MEL Intake Manifolds

Model Year	Part Number/Casting Number	Description
1958	B9ME-9424-A B9ME-9425-A	430-4V
1958	B8M-9424-A 5750620	430-6V Super Marauder
1958	B8S-9424-A EDG-9424-A	383-4V Mercury
1959	PR9M-9424-A 5752089 5752090	383-2V
1961–64	C1VE-9424-C	430-2V
1963–64	C3VY-9424-B	430-4V
1966–68	C6VY-9424-A	462-4V

The beasty MEL was fitted with one of three basic factory induction packages: 2V, 4V, and the super rare 6V Mercury Marauder. This is a first-year EDG-9425-A 430-ci MEL 4V intake manifold.

FORD BIG-BLOCK PARTS INTERCHANGE

CHAPTER 7

A closer look at the EDG-9425-A shows the casting number and related specifics. The "1" is likely a cavity number.

production run. There was also a 2-barrel intake manifold, which had a brief production life for the Mercury 383 and Lincoln 430.

The MEL was fitted with the Holley 4150, 4160, and Carter AFB. For the majority of the MEL's production life it was fueled by the Carter AFB, which performed very well atop this engine.

Easily the best carburetor the MEL ever had was the Carter AFB

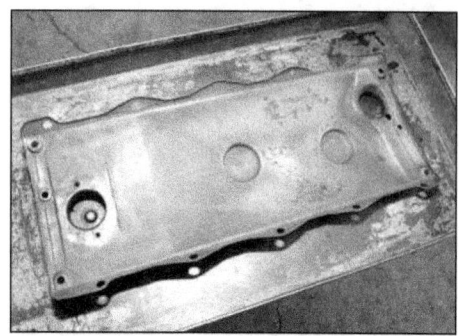

Like its FE cousin, the MEL intake manifold had this valley heat shield designed to keep the intake manifold and carburetor cooler and to keep oil where it belongs. Every MEL engine must have this shield.

While most Ford big-blocks of the period were fitted with Autolite or Holley carburetion, the MEL big-block was topped with a Carter AFB, although it does not appear to be original equipment. The Carter AFB is an exceptional, easy-to-maintain, and simple-to-tune 4-barrel carburetor for the MEL. A similar square-flange Holley or Autolite will fit the MEL manifold. The 2-barrel versions of the MEL were fitted with a Carter ABD. The 1958 Super Marauder was fitted with a trio of Holley 2-barrel carburetors atop a special manifold.

Popular MEL Carburetors

Model Year	Part Number/Casting Number	Description
1958	EDJ-A	Holley 4150 4V
1958	5750897	Holley 4160 4V
1958	EDG-C EDG-D	Holley 4150 4V
1958		Holley 2300C 2V Super Marauder
1958–59	5751682 5751683	Autolite 4100 4V
1959	5752004	Autolite 2100 2V
1959	5752040	Carter AFB 4V
1960	C0LE-A	Carter AFB 4V
1960	C0LE-D C0LE-G	Carter ABD 2V
1960	C0ME-G C0ME-K	Autolite 2100 2V
1961	C1VE-A C1VE-B	Carter ABD 2V
1962	C2VE-A C2VE-B C2VE-C	Carter ABD 2V
1963–64	C3VE-A C3VE-B C3VE-D C3VE-E	Carter AFB 4V
1965	C5VF-A C5VF-B	Carter AFB 4V
1966	C6VF-A C6VF-B	Carter AFB 4V
1967	C7VF-A C7VF-B C7VF-C C7VF-D	Carter AFB 4V
1968	C8VF-C C8VF-D	Carter AFB 4V

INDUCTION

The MEL's conventional fuel pump and glass-bowl filter sat in an unconventional location. It was fitted on top of the timing cover and actuated by a pushrod off the fuel pump eccentric below.

for its tunability and performance. The Carter's equal is the Holley 4150/4160. Ironically, the MEL was never fitted with the shoebox Autolite 4100, which was very common in other Ford car lines.

MEL Aftermarket Induction

Because the MEL has been out of the mainstream for so long, it is unknown just how many aftermarket performance manifolds and carburetors were produced for this engine in its peak years. Edelbrock catered to the MEL performance enthusiast with at least two manifolds: the L300

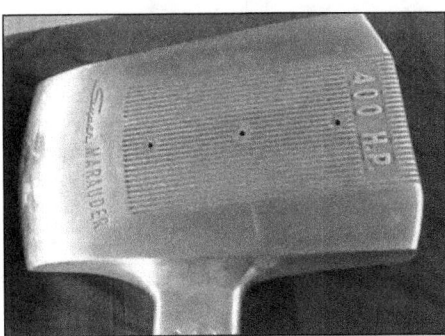

No Super Marauder package is complete without the polished cast-aluminum air cleaner. And yes, that's really 400 hp from 430 ci in 1958. (Photo Courtesy Royce Brechler)

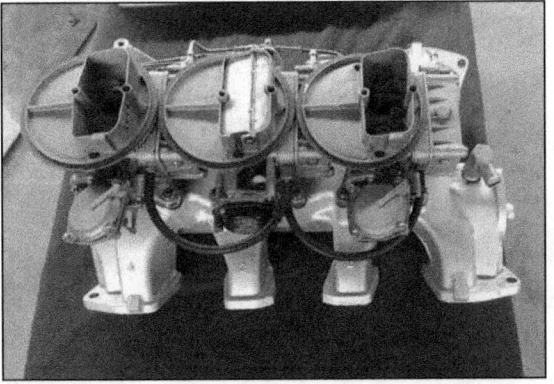

Mercury's Super Marauder 6V setup for 1958 sports three Holley 2300C 2-barrel carburetors on top of a special aluminum manifold. Don't expect to see many of these in your travels. They're a rare swap meet item commanding thousands when they do show up for sale. Moon cast this induction system for the Super Marauder option. (Photo Courtesy Royce Brechler)

The other side of the Marauder 6V Holley induction package shows progressive throttle linkage and fuel feeds. This is a nice and surely rare piece for MEL buffs. They cost thousands whenever they come up for sale because Mercury built so few of them. (Photo Courtesy Royce Brechler)

The 430 Super Marauder fuel pump and filter package looks exotic and is surely rare. However, it is little more than a pump and filter combo. If you happen to find a Super Marauder induction package, make sure it is all there. (Photo Courtesy Royce Brechler)

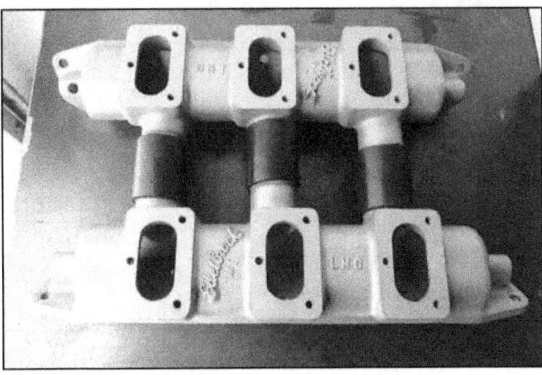

The Edelbrock LM6 is a 12V manifold designed for six Stromberg 97-style 2-barrel carburetors. There was also the cast-aluminum L300 6V manifold designed for Strombergs/Holleys.

CHAPTER 7

The 385 Series 429/460 4-barrel cast-iron intake manifold is easily one of the heaviest Ford has ever produced. This is the D0OE-9425-C, which is the most common 429/460 manifold out there in all its casting numbers. There's also a 2V intake that you don't see very often.

6V cast-aluminum intake and the P6 12V, designed for the Stromberg 97 and other similar Holley 2-barrel carburetors of the era.

429/460 Induction

Ford's original intent for the 385 Series 429/460 engine was as a drop-in replacement for the MEL 430/462 mid-year 1968. Like the MEL, the 429/460 was to be purely a low-revving luxury car engine engineered to haul the high-end Ford, Lincoln, and Mercury around in quiet high-torque comfort. It wasn't long before the 429/460 became high-performance big-blocks for Mustang, Torino, Cougar, Cyclone, and full-size beasties including the Galaxie XL.

The 429/460 story across the board is a simple one sporting the Autolite/Motorcraft 2100/2150 2-barrel carburetor with huge 1.230-inch throttle bores. Going in with 4-barrel carburetion, the 429 was equipped with the 605-cfm Autolite/Motorcraft 4300. In 1970–1971, the 429-4V was fitted with the GM Rochester Quadrajet. It was never fitted with the shoebox 4100.

When it comes to factory iron intake manifolds for the 385 Series engines, there were two basic 4-barrel manifolds: the Holley flange and the Quadrajet flange. The spread-bore Quadrajet flange was short-lived in 1970–1971 for Ford-spec 715-cfm Quadrajet carburetors only. Ford opted for the use of GM's Rochester Quadrajet carburetor due to tougher federal emissions standards until it could get the Autolite/Motorcraft 4300 dialed in from an emissions and drivability standpoint. The 4300 was used on some Ford and Mercury Division 429 engines beginning in 1969. Quadrajet filled the gap for 1970–1971 until Ford went back to the 4300 in 1972.

The 429 Cobra Jet available in 1970–1971 only was built with the 715-cfm Rochester Quadrajet. The uprated 780-cfm 429 Super Cobra Jet was fitted with the Holley 4150. The Boss 429 for 1969–1970 held a 780-cfm Holley 4150.

Where the 460 induction system changed dramatically was when Ford went to Sequential Electronic Fuel Injection (SEFI) in the late 1980s. None of them were passenger car applications because the 385 Series big-block became truck and van only at the end of the 1970s. The 460's SEFI induction package consists of a lower intake manifold setup for port injection coupled with an upper intake manifold and twin-bore throttle body. This induction system didn't change much during the course of production, which ended in the 1990s.

Popular 429/460 Intake Manifolds

Model Year	Casting Number	Description
1968–69	C8SE-9425-B	Cast-Iron 4V, Square Flange
1969	C9VE-9424-A	Cast-Iron 4V, Square Flange
1969-on	C9XE-9424-G	Aluminum Racing 4V, Dominator Flange
1970	D0OE-9425-B	Cast-Iron 4V, Square Flange, Also Super Cobra Jet
1970	D0OE-9425-C	Cast-Iron 4V, Square Flange, Also Super Cobra Jet
1970	D0OE-9425-D	Cast-Iron 4V, Spread Bore, Quadrajet Flange
1970	XE-152211	Cast-Iron 4V, Spread-Bore, Quadrajet (Experimental)
1970	D0VE-9425-B	Cast-Iron 4V, Square Flange
1971	D1AE-9425-BA	Cast-Iron 4V, Spread Bore, Quadrajet Flange
1976	D6VE-9425-A3A	Cast-Iron 4V, Spread Bore, Quadrajet Flange
1987–97	E7TE-9K501	Lower SEFI Intake Manifold
1987–97	F2TZ-9E926-H	Twin Bore Throttle Body

INDUCTION

Popular 429/460 Carburetors

Engine/Year	Make/Type	Ford ID Number	Other Information
429-4V 1968	Autolite 4300 4V	C8SF-A, E, and G	Cruise-O-Matic w/o A/C
429-4V 1968	Autolite 4300 4V	C8SF-B	Cruise-O-Matic w A/C
429-4V 1968	Autolite 4300 4V	C8SF-G and H	Cruise-O-Matic
429-4V 1969	Autolite 4300 4V	C9AF-R	Cruise-O-Matic
429-4V 1968–69	Autolite 4300 4V	C9LF-A	Manual and Cruise-O-Matic
429-4V 1969	Autolite 4300 4V	C9AF-G	Manual Transmission
429-4V 1969 Boss 429	**Holley 4150 4V**	**C9AF-S**	Also known as C9AZ-S
429-4V 1968–69	Autolite 4300 4V	D0PF-AF	Manual and Cruise-O-Matic
429-4V 1970	Autolite 4300 4V	D0AF-K, AG, AM, and AN	Cruise-O-Matic
429-4V 1970	Autolite 4300 4V	D0AF-L and AL	Manual Transmission
429-4V 1970–71 Cobra Jet	**Rochester Quadrajet 4V**	**D0OF-A**	Manual Transmission w/o A/C
429-4V 1970–71 Cobra Jet and Police Interceptor	**Rochester Quadrajet 4V**	**D0OF-B**	Cruise-O-Matic and Manual Transmission w/and w/o A/C
429-4V 1970 Cobra Jet	**Rochester Quadrajet 4V**	**D0OF-E**	Cruise-O-Matic w/A/C
429-4V 1970 Cobra Jet	**Rochester Quadrajet 4V**	**D0OF-F**	Manual Transmission w/A/C
429-4V 1970 Super Cobra Jet	**Holley 4150 4V**	**D0OF-N**	Manual Transmission
429-4V 1970 Super Cobra Jet	**Holley 4150 4V**	**D0OF-R**	Cruise-O-Matic
429-4V 1970	Autolite 4300 4V	D0SF-A, E, and F	Cruise-O-Matic
429-4V 1970 Boss 429	**Holley 4150 4V**	**D0OF-S**	Also known as D0OZ-S
429-4V 1970	**Holley 4150 4V**	**D0ZF-G, H, U, T, AA, AB, AC, AD**	Also known as D0ZZ-H
429-4V 1971	Autolite 4300 4V	D1AF-MA	Cruise-O-Matic
429-4V 1971	Autolite 4300 4V	D1OF-GA	Manual Transmission
429-4V 1971	Autolite 4300 4V	D1SF-AA	Cruise-O-Matic
429-4V 1971 Super Cobra Jet	**Holley 4150 4V**	**D1ZF-YA**	Manual Transmission
429-4V 1971 Super Cobra Jet	**Holley 4150 4V**	**D1ZZ-XA**	Cruise-O-Matic
429-4V 1972	Motorcraft 4300 4V	D2AF-AA	
429-4V 1972	Motorcraft 4300 4V	D2AF-BA	
429-4V 1972 Police Interceptor	**Motorcraft 4300D 4V**	**D2AF-KA**	California
429-4V 1972 Police Interceptor	**Motorcraft 4300D 4V**	**D2AF-LA**	49-State
429-4V 1972 Police Interceptor	**Motorcraft 4300D 4V**	**D2PF-TA**	
429-4V 1972	Motorcraft 4300 4V	D2SF-AA	
429-4V 1972	Motorcraft 4300 4V	D2SF-BA	California
429-4V 1972	Motorcraft 4300 4V	D2AF-AB	
429/460-4V 1972	Motorcraft 4300 4V	D2PF-SA	
429-4V 1972	Motorcraft 4300 4V	D2SF-AB, AC, and BB	
429-4V 1972–75	Motorcraft 4300 4V	D5PE-FB	
460-4V 1972	Motorcraft 4300 4V	D2VF-AA	
460-4V 1972	Motorcraft 4300 4V	D2VF-FB	
460-4V 1972–75	Motorcraft 4300 4V	D5PE-FB	
460-4V 1972–75	Motorcraft 4300 4V	D4PE-FB	
460-4V 1972–75	Motorcraft 4300 4V	D5PE-GB	

Bold indicates high-performance or significant change.

CHAPTER 7

This is a 385 Series cast-iron intake for the 429/460 equipped with the spread-bore Rochester Quadrajet carburetor Ford used in 1970–1972. This particular manifold is an XE-152211 experimental version. The production 4V spread-bore manifold (D0OE-9425-D) is identical.

A close-up of the XE-152211 manifold casting number gives you an idea of what you may find out there for your 429/460.

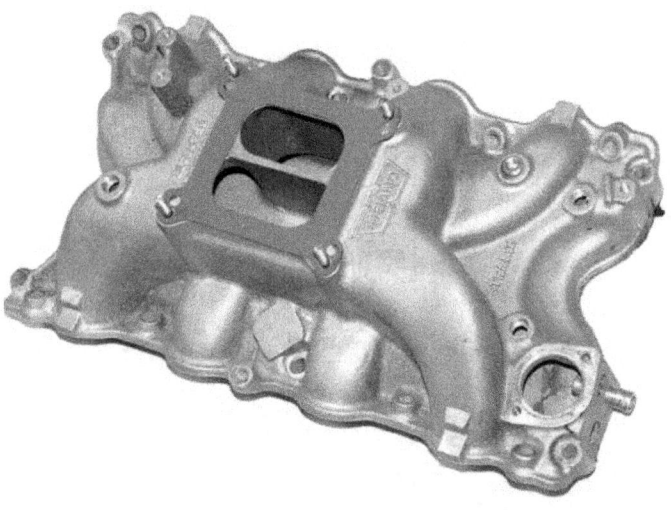

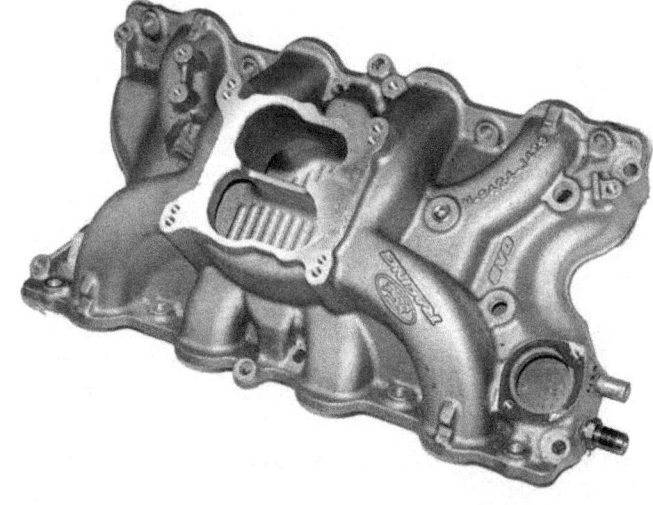

The Weiand Stealth high-rise cast-aluminum dual-plane intake manifold gets the weight off and offers great low- to mid-range torque. Because it has long, high ceiling runners, it also delivers horsepower at high RPM.

Ford Performance has long offered many options for the 385 Series enthusiast. This is the spread-bore–style M-9424-J429 dual-plane intake manifold for the 429/460. You can find these at swap meets from coast to coast and in online auctions.

Fel-Pro Print-O-Seal performance gaskets do the best job of engine sealing. Use a thin film of Permatex's The Right Stuff around cooling passages and along the bottom of each intake port for added measure. This is suggested because not all machine shops have their milling act together. Heads, block, and manifold can be off-angle with an excessive gap along the bottom of the intake manifold.

INDUCTION

Popular 429/460 Aftermarket Intake Manifolds

Manufacturer	Part Number	Description
Blue Thunder	IM-429CJ-4V	429/460 CJ High Rise 4V
Blue Thunder	IM-429CJ-4VC	429/460 CJ High Rise 4V Competition
Blue Thunder	IM-429CJ-D	429/460 CJ High Rise Dominator Flange
Blue Thunder	IM-429S-D	429/460 Standard Port High Rise Dominator Flange
Blue Thunder	IM-429-8V	429/460 8V High Rise
Blue Thunder	IM-429CJ-8V	429/460 8V CJ Port-matched
Blue Thunder	IM-429B-4V	Boss 429 4V Reproduction
Blue Thunder	IM-429B-8V	Boss 429 8V Reproduction
Blue Thunder	IM-429 CJ-I	429/460 Race Injection
Blue Thunder	IMW-429-S	429/460 IDA 8V Straight
Blue Thunder	IMW-429-A	429/460 IDA 8V Angle
Edelbrock	7166	Performer RPM 460, Satin
Edelbrock	71661	Performer RPM 46, Polished
Edelbrock	7566	Air Gap 46, Satin
Edelbrock	75661	Air Gap 46, Polished
Edelbrock	5066	Torker II 460, Satin, Single-Plane
Edelbrock	50661	Torker II 460, Polished, Single-Plane
Edelbrock	50665	Victor 460 EFI Needs 3645 Fuel Rail
Edelbrock	2966	Victor 460, Satin, Square Flange
Edelbrock	29661	Victor 460, Polished, Square Flange
Edelbrock	2965	Victor 460, Satin, Dominator Flange
Edelbrock	29651	Victor 460, Polished, Dominator Flange
Ford Performance	M-9424-C460	Single-Plane 4V Dominator Flange
Trick Flow	TFS-5340012	R-Series Single-Plane Dominator Flange
Trick Flow	TFS-55400111	R-Series PowerPort Single-Plane Dominator Flange
Trick Flow	TFS-53400111	Track Heat Single-Plane Square Bore
Weiand	8012	Stealth 4V Dual-Plane
Weiand	8021	Stealth 4V Dual-Plane

Ford looked to GM's own Rochester Quadrajet carburetor for 1970–1971 429 engines as a substitute for the 4300 and 4300D. According to reliable sources at Ford, the company couldn't get the 4300 through federal emissions on the 429. The Quadrajet was a quick fix. The Ford Quadrajet is different from the GM Quadrajet at the fuel line. It also has quite the complement of vacuum connections (arrows). The GM version is hardlined from the fuel pump to carburetor. The Ford Quadrajet has a hose and filter at the inlet.

CHAPTER 7

When you're shopping for a Ford Quadrajet, make sure you're getting a Ford-spec Quadrajet. They are different from the GM Quadrajet. This is a GM Quadrajet. Do you see the difference at the fuel line/filter connection?

This is the Boss 429 intake manifold, which is Boss 429–specific and designed for the Holley square flange. At a glance, it doesn't look like a Boss 429 manifold. Flip it over and the difference in port design makes it immediately identifiable.

The Thermactor emissions air pump system first appeared on Ford engines in the 1966 model year on California vehicles only. It began appearing in 49 states beginning in 1968 and mostly on manual-transmission cars. On the Boss 429, for example, the Thermactor pump has a larger pulley to keep RPM down. Thermactor parts and systems are very hard to come by. Mustangs Etc. has a wealth of Thermactor parts and the means to get them.

429/460 Aftermarket Induction

If ever there has been an equal to the FE Series big-block it is the 385 Series 429/460 engine family. The aftermarket offers you a wealth of options when it comes to intake manifolds and carburetors for the 429/460. The challenge is figuring out which intake manifold and carburetor combination will work best for your application. It is common knowledge dual-plane manifolds work best for street and strip. Single-plane manifolds are best for drag racing and some road racing.

Air Cleaners

Ford produced more air cleaners for the FE, MEL, and 385 than could ever be listed here. Each vehicle type had a unique air cleaner for the application. High-performance air cleaners date back to a simple open-element air cleaner found on the first 352, 390, 406, and 427 High Performance FE big-blocks. Beginning in 1966, the FE took on a more involved closed air cleaner with inlet grilles instead of an open element to reduce induction noise and improve emissions. That was followed by closed-crankcase ventilation.

Thermactor/IMCO

Thermactor is an air-injection system designed to feed air into the exhaust manifolds to help burn residual hydrocarbon emissions. In short, its purpose is to clean up the exhaust. IMCO (Improved Combustion) is, as the name implies, a system of spark control regulated by engine coolant temperature and acceleration versus deceleration. It was phased in during 1968. During acceleration, IMCO allows spark advance. During deceleration and high vacuum, it retards the spark to reduce exhaust emissions. There are other aspects to IMCO, including carburetor jetting and spark timing curve.

CHAPTER 8

IGNITION, CHARGING AND STARTING

Big-block Ford ignition, starting, and charging systems are your vehicle's support system. Charging systems keep the battery charged to give you lights, accessories, and starting power. Starting systems get your Ford moving to begin with to get that cycle of power going. Ignition systems keep the fire lit to keep you rolling down the road.

With all that said, the components you choose for each of these systems depend on how you will use your Ford, Lincoln, or Mercury most of the time. If you're performing a concours restoration you're going to want these electrical components to conform to restoration standards practiced by most of the classic national car clubs and those who are seasoned in the subject.

If you're going to drive your vehicle daily, you may want to reconsider component selection and opt for more current technology in your starting, charging, and ignition systems. Sometimes you can get away with a little of both.

Keep in mind as you cruise the accompanying tables that not all information on starters, generators, alternators, and distributors is going to be here. I have made the decision to cover the more common part numbers and types, which are shown here. Because Ford is notorious for a lot of running engineering changes and revisions, it is impossible to cover them all.

Starting

Ford big-block V-8s employed two basic styles for mounting starters: two-bolt and three-bolt. The FE Series big-block and MEL use a three-bolt starter. The 385 Series 429

This is the original-style Ford starter with an external inertia Bendix drive that made a distinguishable hiss at start up. These were used on Fords prior to 1964 with a few exceptions. You won't see them on small-blocks. However, you will see them on the FE, MEL, and Y-block V-8s. This is a three-bolt start for the MEL.

and 460 use a two-bolt. In fact, the FE and MEL share the same bellhousing bolt pattern, which makes an engine swap easier if you decide to sideline the MEL and opt for an FE.

Not only am I talking about starter fitment, but also starter type. Prior to 1964, Ford starters employed a different external inertia drive than they did from 1965-on. There's also a clear difference in the way these

In the early 1960s, Ford went to this more compact Autolite 4.5-inch starter with an internal Bendix drive. This is a three-bolt starter for the FE and MEL. It was also intended for the 144/170/200/250-ci 6s. The 385 Series 429/460 uses a two-bolt starter as does the small-block. Starter selection boils down to starter-to-bellhousing fitment and whether the starter drive reaches the flywheel/flexplate.

FORD BIG-BLOCK PARTS INTERCHANGE

CHAPTER 8

Shown are three generations of Ford starters. At the far left is the traditional Autolite/Motorcraft two- and three-bolt starter. In the middle is the downsized Motorcraft starter developed during the 1980s and early 1990s to reduce vehicle weight. It will fit in place of the early Autolite/Motorcraft starter on the left. However, you are advised to stick with the larger 4.5-inch on your Ford big-block. On the right is the super compact Motorcraft PMGR starter with integral solenoid/drive, which first appeared in 1992.

This is an original NOS Ford starter solenoid made of Bakelite. When you buy a solenoid, opt for the best quality. The cheaper ones have a bad habit of sticking, causing significant panic for those behind the wheel. Never overtighten battery and starter terminals because it can distort the housing and cause solenoid sticking.

two types of starters sound. Ford FE and MEL starters prior to 1964–1965 spin the engine and disengage the flywheel/flexplate with a hiss as these engines come to life, which is the starter drive. These are known as inertia drive or external drive starters.

You can purchase new starters that resemble the factory originals from any of the discount automotive warehouses. The downside, perhaps, is the made-offshore status. If authenticity is what you desire, find a good core and have it rebuilt by a qualified rebuilder. If pure function in a driver is what you desire, there are more choices, including offshore reproduction starters and lightweight/high-torque starters.

When it comes to factory Ford starters, there were four basic types. The external inertia drive starter was used from 1958 to 1964. Internal positive engagement drive was most common from 1964 through 1980. A more compact version of this positive-engagement Motorcraft starter was common in the 1980s. The compact Motorcraft mini PMGR high-torque starter first saw application in 1992 and remains very common today.

Let's first look at the 4.5-inch positive engagement starters most of us are familiar with. These starters are easy to identify via the Ford part numbers stamped in the case along with a corresponding date code. These starters were produced in two- and three-bolt versions with various noses and drives depending upon application. Most of the time it was manual versus automatic along with flywheel/flexplate size. None of these starters were fitted with a solenoid, which was instead mounted to the inner fender apron.

Keep in mind that the FE and MEL engines share the same three-bolt starter with the Falcon/Mustang inline 6s. Although the six-banger's three-bolt starter fits, it isn't always going to make the torque necessary to start an FE or MEL. Where it gets confusing is what looks like the same basic three-bolt starter for a broad spectrum of Ford applications that use the same starter. Begin your search by observing the Ford part number and date code and go from there. Then, look at the casting number on the nose/drive housing and reference from there.

At the beginning of the 1980s, Ford downsized its positive engagement direct-drive starter to get the weight out. This likely isn't the starter you're going to want for your big-block project.

Early in the 1990s, Ford ditched its traditional heavyweight large-diameter starter. It took a new approach to starting with a lightweight reduction gear starter known as the PMGR (Permanent Magnet Gear Reduction). What makes the Motorcraft PMGR starter different from traditional starters is the planetary gear package between the starter motor and the starter drive. The planetary gear package takes the starter motor's torque and multiplies it significantly. Less weight. More torque.

Another big difference in these starters is the built-in solenoid, which not only energizes the motor but also engages the starter drive into the flywheel/flexplate. These PMGR starters are also available aftermarket from sources such as Powermaster and Summit Racing Equipment. They take up less space and weigh less. In addition, they're easy to install and connect. The PMGR starter entered service on new Fords in 1992 and remains original equipment today.

IGNITION, CHARGING AND STARTING

Big-Block Starter Identification

Engine/Year	ID Number Service Replacement	Other Information
383/410/430 1958–59	P86M-A	
430/462 1960–68	C6VY-A	
352/390/427 1965–67	C5AF-A	C3OZ-C (SA-628)
352/390/410/427 1966–67	C7AF-A	C3OZ-C (SA-628)
352/390/427/428 1966	C6VY-A	C6VY-A or C3OZ-C
428 1966–68	C6AF-A	C6AZ-A (SA-648)
	C7AF-E	
390/427 1968–71	C7AF-C	C3OZ-C (SA-628)
	C7OF-A	
427/428 1968–70	C8AF-A	C8AZ-A (SA-659)
429/1968	C8VF-A	C8VY-A or C8VY-C (DA-652)
429/1968–74 Including Boss 429	C9AF-A	C8VY-C (SA-658)
429/1970–74 Including Boss 429	D0VF-A	D0VY-A or D4VY-A (SA-663)

Big-Block Generator Pulley Identification

ID Number (10130)	Part Number (10130)	Diameter (inches)	Number of Sheaves
C2OF-A (GP-384)	C2OF-A	2.67	1
C2OF-B	C2OZ-B	2.67	2
C3OF-B High Performance	C3OZ-B (GP-397)	4.32	1

Bold indicates high-performance application.

Generators were common prior to 1964. Some were similar to this with a rubber dust boot while others sported a metal shield. Which was fitted depended upon application and model year. Six generator part numbers were available along with three pulley sizes: 2.670-inch diameter with one rung or two (two-rung shown) and the larger 4.230-inch for high-revving applications to reduce generator speed. Note the Bakelite solenoid on the left. Lincolns used 40- and 50-amp generators. The 50-amp generator was a Bosch unit for air-conditioned cars only.

Generator and Alternator

From 1958 to 1964 most FE engines were fitted with 30-amp generators with external voltage regulators. The MEL engines were fitted with 30-, 40-, and 50-amp generators depending upon application. Only those equipped with air conditioning received the 50-amp Bosch generator. These generators, on average, were virtually the same across these model years with the exception of the amp rating. There are six Ford part numbers for what is essentially the same generator. The main difference among Ford generators is in pulley size. There are two pulley sizes: 2.670 and 4.320 inches. The 2.670-inch pulley is the standard size found on most FE and MEL applications with either one groove or two. The 4.320-inch pulley is a high-performance pulley for high-RPM applications such as the 390 and 427 High Performance. The MEL was never factory fitted with the 4.320-inch pulley.

Alternator Types

Ford began using alternators on Lincolns in 1963 with those first 1G alternators. These were decidedly

Here's a generator with a metal/rubber dust shield. All Ford/Mercury generators were 30-amp units.

FORD BIG-BLOCK PARTS INTERCHANGE   113

different from the 1G alternators to come in mid-1964. Early 1G alternators had a slotted and open main case, which lacked the kind of support seen with 1G cases to come later.

Autolite/Motorcraft alternator identification and application boils down to having the correct combination of amperage, case halves, fan,

A rare very early Autolite 1G alternator bolted to a 427 SOHC. These early Autolites were found most often on 1963–1964 Lincolns. They sport the rounded case halves with a lot of cooling slots in back.

Big-Block Generator Identification

ID Number (10002)	Amperage	Description
FORD		
B6A-10002-A	30	Same as B6A-10002-H
B6A-10002-H	30	Two versions of this generator: one with bushing in rear frame and a later version with bushing in housing
B9A-10002A	30	Same as B6A-10002-A and B6A-10002-H
C0AF-10002-B	35	A/C Equipped
C0AF-10002-F	35	A/C Equipped
C0AF-10002-G	35	
C0TF-10002-C	30	
C1TF-10002-A	30	
C0AF-10002-A	35	
C0AZ-10002-C	35	
C0AF-10002-C	40	
C1AF-10002-G	40	
C1TZ-10002-A	30	
MERCURY		
B9LF-10002-A	40	A/C Equipped
FGV-10002-A	40	A/C Equipped
B8S-10002-A	30	
B9FM-10002-A	35	Automatic Transmission
C0MF-10002-A	35	Automatic Transmission
C0TF-10002-B	40	
C1VF-10002-B	40	383, 430 MEL
C0TF-10002C	30	Manual Transmission
C0AF-10002-A	35	332, 352, 390 FE
C0AZ-10002-C	35	332, 352, 390 FE
C0AF-10002-C	40	Optional, A/C Equipped
C1TZ-10002-A	30	
LINCOLN		
B8QH-10002-A	40	
FGV-10002-A	40	
B9LF-10002-A	40	Bosch Unit, A/C Equipped
C1VF-10002-A	40	
B9LF-10002-B	50	Bosch Unit, A/C Equipped
C1VF-10002-C	40	

Big-Block Autolite/Motorcraft Alternator Identification

ID Number (10300)	Service Replacement (10344)	Amperage	Number of Grooves	Pulley (10A310)	Fan (10A344)	Spacer
C5AF-A	D2AZ-C (GL-89A)	42	1	C5AZ-K (GP-493)	D0AZ-B (GP-473A)	C5AZ-B (GY-808)
C5AF-B	D2AZ-C (GL-89A)	42	1	C5AZ-K (GL-493)	D0AZ-B (GP-473A)	C5AZ-B (GY-808)
C5AF-C	D2AZ-C (GL-89A)	42	2	C5AZ-L (GP-494)	D0AZ-B (GP-473A)	C5AZ-B (GY-808)
C5AF-D 390/427	**D2AZ-C (GL-89A)**	**42**	**1**	**C5AZ-H (GP-580)**	**D0AZ-B (GP-473A)**	**C5AZ-B (GY-808)**
C5AF-E	D2AZ-C (GL-89A)	42	2	C5AZ-L (GP-494)	D0AZ-B (GP-473A)	C5AZ-B (GP-808)
C5AF-F	D0AZ-F (GL-88)	55	2	C5AZ-L (GP-494)	D0AZ-B (GP-473A)	C5AZ-A (GY-700)
C5AF-G	D0AZ-F (GL-88)	55	1	C5AZ-K (GP-493)	D0AZ-B (GP-473A)	C5AZ-A (GY-700)
C5TF-A	D2AZ-C (GL-89A)	45	1	C5AZ-K (GP-493)	D0AZ-B (GP-473A)	C5AZ-A (GY-700)
C5TF-B	D2AZ-C (GL-89A)	45	2	C5AZ-L (GP-494)	D0AZ-B (GP-473A)	C5AZ-A (GY-700)
C5TF-E	D0AZ-F (GL-88)	55	2	C5AZ-L (GP-494)	D0AZ-B (GP-473A)	C5AZ-A (GY-700)
C5TF-F	D0AZ-F (GL-88)	55	1	C5AZ-K (GP-493)	D0AZ-B (GP-473A)	C5AZ-A (GY-700)
C5TF-AN	D2AZ-C (GL-89A)	38	1	C5AZ-K (GP-493)	D0AZ-B (GP-473A)	C5AZ-A (GY-700)
C5TF-AS	D2AZ-C (GL-89A)	38	2	C5AZ-L (GP-494)	D0AZ-B (GP-473A)	C5AZ-A (GY-700)
C6AF-A	D2AZ-C (GL-89A)	42	1	C5AZ-K (GP-493)	D0AZ-B (GP-473A)	C5AZ-B (GY-808)
C6AF-B	D2AZ-C (GL-89A)	42	1	C5AZ-K (GP-493)	D0AZ-B (GP-473A)	C5AZ-B (GY-808)
C6AF-C	D2AZ-C (GL-89A)	42	2	C5AZ-L (GP-494)	D0AZ-B (GP-473A)	C5AZ-B (GY-808)
C6AF-D 427	**D2AZ-C (GL-89A)**	**42**	**1**	**C5AZ-H (GP-580)**	**D0AZ-B (GP-473A)**	**C5AZ-B (GY-808)**
C6AF-E	D2AZ-C (GL-89A)	42	2	C5AZ-L (GP-494)	D0AZ-B (GP-473A)	C5AZ-B (GY-808)
C6AF-F	D2AZ-F (GL-88)	55	1	C5AZ-K (GP-493)	D0AZ-B (GP-473A)	C5AZ-B (GY-808)
C6AF-G	D0AZ-F (GL-88)	55	2	C5AZ-L (GP-494)	D0AZ-B (GP-473A)	C5AZ-B (GY-808)
C6DF-A	D2AZ-C (GL-89A)	38	1	C5AZ-K (GP-493)	D0AZ-B (GP-473A)	C5AZ-B (GY-808)
C6DF-B	D2AZ-C (GL-89A)	38	2	C5AZ-L (GP-494)	D0AZ-B (GP-473A)	C5AZ-B (GY-808)
C6GF-A	D2AZ-C (GL-89A)	45	1	C5AZ-K (GP-493)	D0AZ-B (GP-473A)	C5AZ-B (GY-808)

Bold indicates high-performance application.

Big-Block Autolite/Motorcraft Alternator Identification CONTINUED

ID Number (10300)	Service Replacement (10344)	Amperage	Number of Grooves	Pulley (10A310)	Fan (10A344)	Spacer
C6GF-B	D2AZ-C (GL-89A)	45	2	C5AZ-L (GP-494)	D0AZ-B (GP-473A)	C5AZ-B (GY-808)
C6TF-A	D2AZ-C (GL-89A)	38	1	C5AZ-K (GP-493)	D0AZ-B (GP-473A)	C5AZ-B (GY-808)
C6TF-B	D2AZ-C (GL-89A)	38	2	C5AZ-L (GP-494)	D0AZ-B (GP-473A)	C5AZ-B (GY-808)
C6TF-E	D0AZ-F (GL-88)	55	2	C5AZ-L (GP-494)	D0AZ-B (GP-473A)	C5AZ-B (GY-808)
C6TF-F	D0AZ-F (GL-88)	55	1	C5AZ-K (GP-493)	D0AZ-B (GP-473A)	C5AZ-B (GY-808)
C6TF-J	D2AZ-C (GL-89A)	45	1	C5AZ-K (GP-493)	D0AZ-B (GP-473A)	C5AZ-B (GY-808)
C6TF-K	D2AZ-C (GL-89A)	45	2	C5AZ-L (GP-494)	D0AZ-B (GP-473A)	C5AZ-B (GY-808)
C6TF-AH	D0TZ-B (GL-91A)	60	2	C5AZ-L (GP-494)	D0AZ-B (GP-473A)	C5AZ-B (GY-808)
C6TF-AJ	D0TZ-B (GL-91A)	60	2	C5AZ-L (GP-494)	D0AZ-B (GP-473A)	C5AZ-B (GY-808)
C7AF-A	D1AZ-A (GL-93A)	65	1	C7TZ-B (GP-485)	D0AZ-A (GP-496)	D0AZ-A (GY-974)
C7SF-B	D0TZ-B (GL91A)	60	1	C5AZ-K (GP-493)	D0AZ-B (GP-473A)	C5AZ-B (GY-808)
C7TF-A	D1AZ-A (GL-93A)	65	1	C7TZ-B (GP-485)	D0AZ-A (GP-496)	D0AZ-A (GY-974)
C7TF-C	D2AZ-C (GL-89A)	42	2	C5AZ-L (GP-494)	D0AZ-B (GP-473A)	C5AZ-B (GY-808)
C8LF-B	D0SZ-A (GL-90)	55	2	C5AZ-L (GP-494)	D0AZ-B (GP-473A)	C5AZ-B (GY-808)
C9AF-A	D2AZ-C (GL-89A)	42	1	C5AZ-K (GP-493)	D0AZ-B (GP-473A)	C5AZ-B (CY-808)
C9AF-B	D0AZ-F (GL-88)	55	2	C5AZ-L (GP-494)	D0AZ-B (GP-473A)	C5AZ-B (GY-808)
C9AF-C	D2AZ-C (GL-89A)	42	2	C5AZ-L (GP-494)	D0AZ-B (GP-473A)	C5AZ-B (GY-808)
C9AF-D	D1AZ-A (GL-93A)	65	1	C7TZ-B (GP-485)	D0AZ-A (GP-496)	D0AZ-A (GY-974)
C9SF-A	D0AZ-F (GL-88)	55	1	C5AZ-K (GP-493)	D0AZ-B (GP-473A)	C5AZ-B (GY-808)
C9SF-B	C8SZ-A (GL-79)	55	1	C5AZ-K (GP-493)	D0AZ-A (GP-473A)	C5AZ-B (GY-808)
C9SF-C	D1AZ-A (GL-93A)	65	1	C7TZ-B (GP-485)	D0AZ-A (GP-496)	D0AZ-A (GY-974)
C9ZF-A	D2AZ-C (GL-89A)	38	1	C5AZ-K (GP-493)	D0AZ-B (GP-473A)	C5AZ-B (GY-808)
C9ZF-C	D0ZZ-B (GL-92)	55	2	C5AZ-L (GP-494)	D0AZ-B (GP-473A)	C5AZ-B (GY-808)

Bold indicates high-performance application.

IGNITION, CHARGING AND STARTING

ID Number (10300)	Service Replacement (10344)	Amperage	Number of Grooves	Pulley (10A310)	Fan (10A344)	Spacer
C9ZF-C	D0ZZ-B (GL-92)	55	1	C5AZ-K (GP-493)	D0AZ-B (GP-473A)	C5AZ-B (GY-808)
D0AF-A	D1AZ-A (GL-93A)	65	1	C7TZ-B (GP-485)	D0AZ-A (GP-496)	D0AZ-A (GY-974)
D0AF-C	D2AZ-C (GL-89A)	42	1	C5AZ-K (GP-493)	D0AZ-B (GP-473A)	C5AZ-B (GY-808)
D0AF-E	D0AZ-F (GL-88)	55	2	C5AZ-L (GP-494)	D0AZ-B (GP-473A)	C5AZ-B (GY-808)
D0AF-F	D2AZ-C (GL-89A)	42	2	C5AZ-L (GP-494)	D0AZ-B (GP-473A)	C5AZ-B (GY-808)
D0AF-G	D2AZ-C (GL-89A)	42	1	C5AZ-K (GP-493)	D0AZ-B (GP-473A)	C5AZ-B (GY-808)
D0AF-H	D0AZ-F (GL-88)	55	2	C5AZ-L (GP-494)	D0AZ-B (GP-473A)	C5AZ-B (GY-808)
D0LF-A	D0SZ-A (GL-90)	55	1	C5AZ-K (GP-493)	D0AZ-B (GP-473A)	C5AZ-B (GY-808)
D0SF-A	D0AZ-F (GL-92)	55	1	C5AZ-K (GP-493)	D0AZ-B (GP-473A)	C5AZ-B (GY-808)
D0ZF-A	D0ZZ-B (GL-92)	55	1	D1ZZ-A (GP-465A)	D0AZ-B (GP-473A)	C5AZ-B (GY-808)
D0ZF-B	D2AZ-C (GL-89A)	38	1	C5AZ-K (GP-493)	D0AZ-B (GP-473A)	C5AZ-B (GY-808)
D0ZF-C	D0ZZ-B (GL-92)	55	2	C5AZ-L (GP-494)	D0AZ-B (GP-473A)	C5AZ-B (GY-808)
D1AF-AA	D0TZ-C (GL-95)	61	1	C5AZ-K (GP-493)	D0AZ-B (GP-473A)	C5AZ-B (GY-808)
D1AF-BA	D1AZ-A (GL-93A)	65	1	C7TZ-B (GP-485)	D0AZ-A (GP-496)	D0AZ-A (GY-974)
D1AF-CA	D1AZ-A (GL-93A)	70	1	D1AZ-A (GP-508)	D0AZ-A (GP-496)	D0AZ-A (GY-974)
D1ZF-AA	D0ZZ-B (GL-92)	55	1	D1ZZ-A (GP-465A)	D0AZ-B (GP-473A)	C5AZ-B (GY-808)
D2AF-AA	D2AZ-C (GL-89A)	42	1	C5AZ-K (GP-493)	D0AZ-B (GP-473A)	C5AZ-B (GY-808)
D2AF-AB	D2AZ-C (GL-89A)	42	1	C5AZ-K (GP-493)	D0AZ-B (GP-473A)	C5AZ-B (GY-808)
D2AF-BA	D0AZ-F (GL-88)	55	2	C5AZ-L (GP-494)	D0AZ-B (GP-473A)	C5AZ-B (GY-808)
D2AF-BB	D2AZ-D (GL-88A)	55	2	C5AZ-L (GP-494)	D0AZ-B (GP-473A)	C5AZ-B (GY-808)
D2AF-CA	D0TZ-C (GL95)	61	1	C5AZ-K (GP-493)	D0AZ-B (GP-473A)	C5AZ-B (GY-808)
D2AF-CB	D2TZ-B (GL-95A)	61	1	C5AZ-K (GP-493)	D0AZ-B (GP-473A)	C5AZ-B (GY-808)
D2AF-DA	D1AZ-A (GL-92A)	70	1	D1AZ-A (GP-508)	D0AZ-A (GP-496)	D0AZ-A (GY-974)

Bold indicates high-performance application.

Big-Block Autolite/Motorcraft Alternator Identification CONTINUED

ID Number (10300)	Service Replacement (10344)	Amperage	Number of Grooves	Pulley (10A310)	Fan (10A344)	Spacer
D2BF-AA	D2AZ-D (GL-88A)	55	1	D2AZ-D (GP-493)	D0AZ-B (GP-473A)	C5AZ-B (GY-808)
D2DF-AB	D2TZ-B (GL-95A)	61	2	C5AZ-L (GP-494)	D0AZ-B (GP-473A)	C5AZ-B (GY-808)
D2DF-AC	D2TZ-B (GL-95A)	61	2	C5AZ-L (GP-494)	D0AZ-B (GP-473A)	C5AZ-B (GY-808)
D2OF-AA	D2OZ-B (GL-101)	70	1	D2OZ-A (GP-511)	D2OZ-A (GP-510)	D2OZ-A
D2OF-BA	D2AZ-D (GL-88A)	55	2	D2AZ-D (GP-494)	C5AZ-L (GP-473A)	C5AZ-B (GY-808)
D2OF-BB	D2AZ-D (GL-88A)	55	2	C5AZ-L (GP-494)	D0AZ-B (GP-473A)	C5AZ-B (GY-808)
D2OF-CA	D2TZ-B (GL-95A)	61	1	C5AZ-K (GP-493)	D0AZ-B (GP-473)	C5AZ-B (GY-808)
D2OF-CB	D2TZ-B (GL-95A)	61	1	C5AZ-K (GP-493)	D0AZ-B (GP-473A)	C5AZ-B (GY-808)
D2OF-DA	D2AZ-C (GL-89A)	42	1	C5AZ-K (GP-493)	D0AZ-B (GP-473A)	C5AZ-B (GY-808)
D2OF-DB	D2AZ-C (GL-89A)	42	1	C5AZ-K (GP-493)	D0AZ-B (GP-473A)	C5AZ-B (GY-808)
D2OF-EA	D2AZ-D (GL-88A)	55	1	C5AZ-K (GP-493)	D0AZ-B (GP-473A)	C5AZ-B (GY-808)
D2OF-EB	D2AZ-D (GL-88A)	55	1	C5AZ-K (GP-493)	D0AZ-B (GP-473A)	C5AZ-B (GY-808)
D2OF-FA	D2ZZ-B (GL-92A)	55	1	D1ZZ-A (GP-465A)	D0AZ-B (GP-473A)	C5AZ-B (GY-808)
D2OF-FB	D2ZZ-B (GL-92A)	55	1	D1ZZ-A (GP465A)	D0AZ-B (GP-473A)	C5AZ-B (GY-808)
D2SF-AA	D0AZ-F (GL-88)	55	1	C5AZ-K (GP-493)	D0AZ-B (GP-473A)	C5AZ-B (GY-808)
D2SF-AB	D2AZ-D (GL-88A)	55			D0AZ-B (GP-473A)	C5AZ-B (GY-808)
D2UF-AB	D2TZ-B (GL-95A)	61	2	C5AZ-L (GP-494)	D0AZ-B (GP-473A)	C5AZ-B (GY-808)
D2ZF-AA	D2AZ-C (GL-89A)	42	1	C5AZ-K (GP-493)	D0AZ-B (GP-473A)	C5AZ-B (GY-808)
D2ZF-AB	D2AZ-C (GL-89A)	42	1	C5AZ-K (GP-493)	D0AZ-B (GP-473A)	C5AZ-B (GY-808)
D2ZF-AC	D2AZ-C (GL-89A)	42	1	C5AZ-K (GP-493)	D0AZ-B (GP-473A)	C5AZ-B (GY-808)
D2ZF-BA	D0ZZ-B (GL-92)	55	1	D1ZZ-A (GP-465A)	D0AZ-B (GP-473A)	C5AZ-B (GY-808)
D2ZF-BB	D2ZZ-B (GL-92A)	55	1	D1ZZ-A (GP-465A)	D0AZ-B (GP-473A)	C5AZ-B (GY-808)

Bold indicates high-performance application.

Autolite/Motorcraft Alternator Quick Facts

Amperage	Service Replacement Numbers
38	D2AZ-10346-C (GL-89A)
42	D2AZ-10346-C (GL-89A)
45	D2AZ-10346-C (GL-89A)
55	D0AZ-10346-F (GL-88)
61	D0TZ-10346-C (GL-95)
61	D2TZ-10346-B (GL-95A)
65, 70	D1AZ-10346-A (GL-93A)
70	D2OZ-10346-B (GL-101)

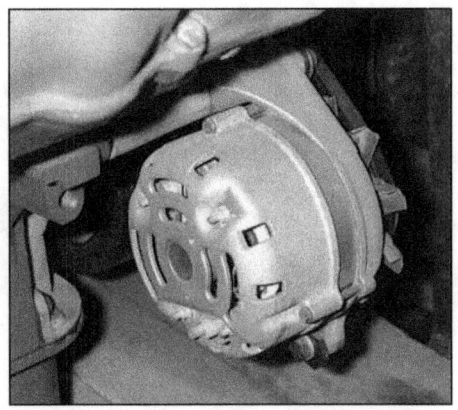

The back of the early Autolite 1G shows its ample cooling slots. Note the difference in connections compared to the more mainstream later-model 1G to. These were available in a variety of pulley sizes and configurations.

and pulley. It is important to understand original equipment alternator installation and what may have replaced it. There are seven basic 1G alternator types. Variations of the seven types can be found in the table above.

Several fans were used on the 1G alternator. The early 13-blade fan, C5AZ-10A310-B, was used on the 1G from late 1964 until late 1969. The D0AZ-10A310-A (GP-473A), which is the 10-blade stamping, was the most common 1G fan used on the 38-, 42-, 45-, 55-, 60-, and 61-amp alternators from November 1969–on. Two more fans were used on the larger 65- and 70-amp alternators: D0AZ-10A310-A (GP-496) from 1967 to 1970, and D2OZ-10A310-A (GP-510) from 1972-on.

There were also several pulley types and sizes used on the 38-, 42-, 45-, 55-, 60-, and 61-amp 1G alternators. Pulley diameter, width, and number of grooves are your most critical concerns. Several types were used on Ford big-block engines. The C5AZ-L (GP-494) is a dual-groove cast pulley with a 2.840-inch diameter and 1.400-inch width. The C5AZ-K (GP-493) is 2.840 inches in

The standard Autolite 1G employed throughout the 1960s had rounded case halves. These alternators were produced with a variety of pulley types and sizes. Amp ratings ranged from 38 to 55. Although some rebuilders claim they can get 65 amps from these alternators, I have never seen them make beyond 55. The stamp in the main case, which offers Ford part number and amp rating, identifies these alternators.

The large-pulley Autolite 1G alternator is for the high-revving 427 to keep alternator speed down. At the cusp of the 1970s, 1G alternators were stamped with a series of numbers and letters, including the Ford part number and amp rating. They were also color-coded to indicate amp rating.

The back of the rounded 1G case. In 1970–1971, the 1G had angular case halves, not rounded. In 1972, the name changed from Autolite to Motorcraft after Ford sold the Autolite name in the wake of a long and protracted federal lawsuit addressing anti-trust laws. Alternator harnesses varied, depending upon application and model year.

CHAPTER 8

It is best to use the Motorcraft solid-state voltage regulator for consistent charging. If you're performing a restoration you can use the cover from a mechanical regulator on the Motorcraft by drilling out the rivets and using screws.

diameter with a 1.015-inch width. The D1AZ-A (GP-465A) pulley is larger at 3.050 inches in diameter and just shy of 1.000 inch wide with a single groove.

High Performance Ford big-blocks such as the 390 and 427 engines had the large C5AZ-H (GP-580) pulley, which had a diameter of 3.900 inches in a single groove designed to keep alternator rotational speed down to prevent winding failure. The C7TZ-B (GP-485) is a 3.170-inch-diameter pulley 1.530 inches wide for the 65- and 70-amp alternators. Although it's easy to assume this larger pulley was developed to keep alternator speed down, it was intended to turn these behemoth dynamos more efficiently.

There were three more large pulleys produced for these 65- and 70-amp alternators. The D1AZ-A (GP-508) pulley is 3.120 inches in diameter with a .85-inch width in a single-groove design. The D2OZ-A (GP-511) is 3.150 inches in diameter with a wider .91-inch groove. There's also the D2AZ-A (GP-578) 3.150-inch pulley with a 1.490-inch width in two grooves. These high-amp alternators were engineered for luxury cars with huge current demands.

Autolite 1G alternator cases are identified by a series of numbers and letters stamped into the case. At the beginning of the 1970s, alternators were color-coded to indicate amp rating along with the Ford part number. Mass rebuilders tend to grind off these numbers; don't expect to see them on every core.

Most Autolite/Motorcraft alternators have been uprated to 55 amps over the course of mass production rebuilds. You can have yours tested to measure output by any reputable rebuilder or repair shop. And keep in mind that when these cores arrive at a mass rebuilder, cases and parts get mismatched because they're all thrown into huge bins where square cases get mixed up with round cases. When you find a suitable core, make sure both halves of the 1G case match: rounded/rounded and square/square.

In the late 1970s, Ford abandoned the time-proven 1G alternator for the internally regulated 2G alternator, which eliminated the external regulator entirely. The downside to the 2G is the terminals, which can get wet, short out, and catch fire. For those of you with 2G alternators, replace them with the 3G or 4G, which are more powerful and a lot safer. The 2G resembles the 1G and it's easy to get them mixed up. Don't make that mistake and wind up with the wrong alternator.

Ford replaced the 2G alternator with the 3G and ultimately the 4G, which were better high-output alternators. The beauty of these alternators is they are a drop-in replacement for the 1G and 2G with a minimum of fuss. All you have to do is install a V-belt pulley. You can get these alternators from Performance Distributors, Powermaster, and Summit Racing Equipment. Conversion kits are also available.

This is the Motorcraft 2G alternator, which entered service in the late 1970s and is internally regulated. The downside to the 2G is that its terminals run the risk of fire when they get wet and corroded.

The Motorcraft 3G high-amp alternator is a popular replacement for the 1G and internally regulated 2G alternators. The 3G is a direct bolt-in to replace the 1G and 2G. You will need a single-wire conversion kit from Painless Performance to complete the swap, but it's easy. You can use a V-belt pulley on the 3G.

Distributor

FE distributor identification is straightforward. The Ford part number is on the housing, but doesn't

IGNITION, CHARGING AND STARTING

The Autolite/Motorcraft single-point distributor for big-block Ford V-8s stayed basically the same throughout the FE and MEL production life until Duraspark arrived in the mid-1970s. These distributors underwent few production changes but did include the transition from one main bushing to two bushings, which made them better distributors. A weakness in these distributors has always been bushings and shaft wear from poor lubrication.

The Autolite dual-point distributor uses two sets of points for better coil saturation at high RPM. Early dual-point distributors are not equipped with a vacuum advance unit. At the cusp of the 1970s, Ford went to a dual-point distributor with a dual-advance unit in FE applications to reduce hydrocarbon emissions.

always fall in line with what you have in your hands. The Ford part number indicates what the distributor was when new. If it has been torn apart and rebuilt, it isn't always what it appears. All single-point FE distributors were of the dual-advance type meaning a vacuum advance and a centrifugal (mechanical) advance.

The FE never used the Load-O-Matic distributor. However, the MEL entered production with the Load-O-Matic distributor and eventually moved to the better dual-advance type. The Load-O-Matic single-point distributor was different than the dual-advance in that it had only a vacuum advance unit and no mechanical advance. Spark was advanced via load and power demand, which worked fine with low-revving engines such as the Falcon 6s and Lincoln MEL big-blocks.

Early Ford big-block distributors had an oil wick, which was used as a part of regular preventative maintenance using SAE 30-weight oil. Ford understood with time this oil wick served no real useful purpose

All Autolite and Motorcraft distributors are identified via a Ford part number (PN 12127), which is accompanied by a prefix and suffix to define application. They are also date-coded for quick identification. Reproduction distributors won't have this Ford part number and rebuilders have been known to remove it.

and went to Oil Lite bronze bushings and an improved system of spiraling engine oil up the shaft to the bushings. Ford also added a smaller bottom bushing to improve shaft support.

There's also a dual-point Autolite distributor for high-performance FE applications such as the 406 and 427 High Performance V-8s void of a vacuum advance. The use of two sets of ignition points enabled better ignition coil saturation for a hotter, more intense spark. Ford also produced a transistorized ignition system for these high-revving engines for better spark consistency. The transistorized ignition is extremely scarce these days; however, you do have options such as MSD, PerTronix, Accel, and others for spark enhancement.

In 1968, Ford went to a dual advance/retard distributor introduced as an important part of the Improved Combustion (IMCO) emissions control system. IMCO was a more precision form of spark timing control with two vacuum advance features and hoses that vectored vacuum where it was needed most. On acceleration with a warm engine, IMCO

Early Autolite distributors, both single- and dual-point, will have this oil wick (arrow) common from 1958 to 1964. The oil wick was phased out early in 1964.

Big-Block Distributor Identification

Engine/Year	ID Number	Service Replacement	Other Information
430 ci 1958–59	FEW-H	N/A	
383 ci 1958–59 410 ci 1958–59 430 ci 1958–59	B9S-B	N/A	
383 ci 1958–59 410 ci 1958–59 430 ci 1958–59	FEW-E	N/A	
383 ci 1958–59 430 ci 1958–59	B6MF-B	N/A	
430 ci 1960–63	C1VF-A	N/A	
430 ci 1963–64	C3VY-A	N/A	
430 ci 1964	C4VY-A	N/A	Transistorized Ignition
430 ci 1965	C5VF-B	N/A	Transistorized Ignition, Aluminum Casting, Stamped Advance Weights
430 ci 1965	C1VF-A C5VF-C	C5VY-B	Transistorized Ignition, Aluminum Casting, Stamped Advance Weights
462 ci 1966–68	C6VF-A	C6VY-A	
462 ci 1966–68	C6VF-B	C6VY-B	Transistorized Ignition
352 ci 1965	C5AF-A	C5AZ-A (DA-674)	All w/Manual Transmission
352 ci 1965	C5AF-B or C7TF-F	C5AZ-W (DA-913)	
352 ci 1966	C4AF-M or C5AF-BG	C4AZ-M or C4AZ-P	4V All
352 ci 1966	C6MF-A	C4AZ-P (DA-911)	4V All
352 ci 1966	C6AF-AG C6AF-L C6AF-U C6OF-G C6OF-H	C6AZ-L (DA-739)	With Transistorized Ignition
390 ci 1961–65	**C5AF-E**	**C5AZ-E or C0AZ-L**	4V/6V/8V Dual-Point
390 ci 1965	C5AF-C	C5AZ-C or C5AZ-W	4V Police
390 ci 1965	C7TF-F	C5AZ-W	With Transistorized Ignition
390 ci 1965	C5SF-B	C5SZ-B or C5AZ-W	With Transistorized Ignition
390 ci 1966	C6AF-A	C6AZ-A or C7AZ-A	2V w/Manual Transmission w/Transistorized Ignition
390 ci 1966	C6AF-K or C6OF-E	C6AZ-K or C8AZ-J (DA-738)	2V w/Manual Transmission w/Transistorized Ignition
390 ci 1966	C6AF-B	C7AZ-E (DA-784)	2V w/Cruise-O-Matic w/Transistorized Ignition
390 ci 1966	C6AF-T or C6OF-F	C6AZ-T (DA-740)	2V w/Cruise-O-Matic w/Transistorized Ignition
390 ci 1966	C6AF-L C6AF-U C6OF-G C6OF-H	C6AZ-L	4V w/Manual Transmission 4V w/Cruise-O-Matic w/Transistorized Ignition
390 ci 1966	C6AF-C	C6AZ-C or C7AZ-E	4V w/Manual Transmission
390 ci 1966	C6AF-D or C6MF-A	C4AZ-P (DA-911)	4V w/Cruise-O-Matic
390 ci 1966	C6OF-E	C6OZ-E or C0AZ-L	2V w/Manual Transmission w/Transistorized Ignition
390 ci 1966	C6OF-F	C6OZ-F or C6AZ-T	2V w/Cruise-O-Matic w/Transistorized Ignition

Bold indicates high-performance application.

IGNITION, CHARGING AND STARTING

Engine/Year	ID Number	Service Replacement	Other Information
390 ci 1966	**C6OF-J**	**C6OZ-J (DA-771)**	4V GT Engine
390 ci 1967	C7AF-A or C7AF-AD	C7AZ-A	2V w/Cruise-O-Matic
390 ci 1967	C7AF-C or C7AF-Z	C8AZ-J	2V w/Manual Transmission w/Transistorized Ignition
390 ci 1967	C7AF-B or C7AF-Y	C7AZ-B (DA-781)	2V w/Cruise-O-Matic
390 ci 1967	C7AF-AG	C7AZ-AG (DA-841)	2V w/Cruise-O-Matic
390 ci 1967	C7AF-E	C7AZ-E (DA-784)	4V w/Manual Transmission
390 ci 1967	C7AF-F	C7AZ-F or C6MY-B	4V w/Cruise-O-Matic
390 ci 1967	C7SF-A	C7SZ-D or C6MY-B	
390 ci 1967	C7MF-G	C7SZ-D or C6MY-B	4V w/Cruise-O-Matic
390 ci 1967	C7AF-H	C7AZ-H or C7SZ-B	4V w/Cruise-O-Matic w/Transistorized Ignition
390 ci 1967	C7SF-B	C7SZ-B	4V w/Cruise-O-Matic w/Transistorized Ignition
390 ci 1967	C7MF-H	C7SZ-H (DA-850)	4V w/Cruise-O-Matic w/Transistorized Ignition
390 ci 1967	**C7OF-H**	**C7OZ-H or C7AZ-U**	4V GT Engine w/Manual Transmission
390 ci 1967	**C7AF-U or C7AF-V**	**C7AZ-U (DA-796)**	4V GT Engine w/Cruise-O-Matic
390 ci 1967	C7MF-A	C6MY-A (DA-836)	4V w/Cruise-O-Matic
390 ci 1967–71	C7AF-D or C7AF-AA	C7AZ-D (DA-783)	2V w/Cruise-O-Matic/IMCO
390 ci 1967–69	C7AF-L or C7AF-AC	C7AZ-L (DA-790)	4V w/Cruise-O-Matic/IMCO w/Transistorized Ignition
390 ci 1967–69	**C7OF-F or C7OF-G**	**C7OZ-F (DA-807)**	4V GT Engine w/Cruise-O-Matic w/Transistorized Ignition
390 ci 1968	**C8OF-D**	**C8OZ-D (DA-881)**	4V GT Engine w/Manual Transmission w/Transistorized Ignition
390 ci 1968	C8AF-S	C8AZ-S (DA-876)	4V w/Manual Transmission
390 ci 1968	C8WF-B	C8WY-B (DA-906)	2V w/Cruise-O-Matic/IMCO
390 ci 1968	C8AF-R	C8AZ-R (DA-875)	2V w/Cruise-O-Matic/IMCO
390 ci 1968–70	C8AF-M	C8AZ-M (DA-873)	2V w/Manual Transmission/IMCO
390 ci 1968–70	C8AF-N	C8AZ-N or C7AZ-D	2V w/Cruise-O-Matic/IMCO
390 ci 1969	C9AF-J	C9AZ-B (DA-929)	w/Manual Transmission/IMCO
390 ci 1969	C9OF-J	C9OZ-J or C9AZ-D	4V w/Manual Transmission w/Transistorized Ignition
390 ci 1969	C9AF-K	C9AZ-D (DA-907)	4V w/Manual Transmission/IMCO
390 ci 1971	D1AF-LB	D1AZ-L (DA-1082)	2V w/Cruise-O-Matic
390 ci 1971	C7AF-AA	C7AZ-D (DA-783)	2V w/Cruise-O-Matic/ California
427 ci 1965–67	**C5AF-F**	**C5AZ-F or C0AZ-L**	4V/6V/8V w/Transistorized Ignition
427 ci 1965–67	**C5AF-E**	**C5AZ-E or C0AZ-L (DA-909)**	4V

Bold indicates high-performance application.

FORD BIG-BLOCK PARTS INTERCHANGE

Big-Block Distributor Identification CONTINUED

Engine/Year	ID Number	Service Replacement	Other Information
427 ci 1968	**C7OF-F** **C7OF-G** **C8AF-AD**	**C7OZ-F (DA-907)**	4V w/Manual Transmission
427 ci 1968	**C8OF-G**	**C8OZ-G (DA-927)**	4V w/Cruise-O-Matic w/Transistorized Ignition
428 ci 1966	C6AF-BA	C6AZ-BA or C7SZ-H	4V w/Manual Transmission w/Transistorized Ignition w/Thermactor
428 ci 1966	C6AF-E or C6AF-F	C6AZ-E or C4AZ-P	4V w/Cruise-O-Matic w/Manual Transmission w/Thermactor
428 ci 1966	C6AF-L or C6AF-U C6OF-G or C6OF-H	C6AZ-L (DA-739)	4V w/Cruise-O-Matic w/Transistorized Ignition w/Thermactor
428 ci 1966 **Police Interceptor**	**C6AF-M**	**C6AZ-M** C6AZ-Z C6AZ-L	4V w/Transistorized Ignition w/Thermactor
428 ci 1966 **Police Interceptor**	**C6AF-V**	**C6AZ-V** C6AZ-E C6AZ-L	4V w/Transistorized Ignition w/Thermactor
428 ci 1966 **Police Interceptor**	**C6AF-AH**	**C6AZ-AH (DA-756)**	4V
428 ci 1966	C7MF-H	C7SZ-H	4V w/Manual Transmission w/Transistorized Ignition w/Thermactor
428 ci 1966	C6MF-A	C4AZ-P (DA-911)	4V w/Cruise-O-Matic w/Thermactor
428 ci 1966	C6SF-B	C6SZ-B or C4AZ-P	4V
428 ci 1966	C6SF-D	C6SZ-D (DA-746)	4V w/Thermactor w/Transistorized Ignition
428 ci 1966–67	C7AF-J	C7AZ-J or C6MY-B	4V w/Manual Transmission w/Cruise-O-Matic
428 ci 1967	C7AF-AC	C7AZ-L (DA-790)	4V w/Cruise-O-Matic/IMCO
428 ci 1967	C7AF-M	C7AZ-M or C7SZ-B	4V w/Cruise-O-Matic w/Thermactor
428 ci 1967	C7MF-A	C6MY-B (DA-836)	4V w/Cruise-O-Matic
428 ci 1967 **Police Interceptor**	**C7AF-S**	**C7AZ-S or C8AZ-J**	4V w/Thermactor
428 ci 1967 **Police Interceptor**	**C7AF-N or C7AF-AF**	**C8AZ-J (DA-872)**	4V w/Cruise-O-Matic
428 ci 1967	C7SF-C	C7SZ-C or C7AZ-J	4V w/Thermactor
428 ci 1967	C7SF-E	C7SZ-E or C6MY-F	4V w/Thermactor
428 ci 1967	C7SF-F	C7SZ-F or C6MY-Y	4V w/Cruise-O-Matic/IMCO
428 ci 1967–69 **Cobra Jet/** **Police Interceptor**	**C7OZ-F**	**C7OZ-F (DA-807)**	4V w/Cruise-O-Matic/IMCO also w/Thermactor
428 ci 1968	C8AF-T	C8AZ-T (DA-877)	4V w/Manual Transmission w/Thermactor
428 ci 1968	C6AF-Y	C8AZ-Y (DA-905)	4V w/Cruise-O-Matic/IMCO
428 ci 1968–69	C8OF-D	C8OZ-D (DA-881)	4V w/Cruise-O-Matic w/Thermactor

Bold indicates high-performance application.

IGNITION, CHARGING AND STARTING

Engine/Year	ID Number	Service Replacement	Other Information
428 ci 1968–69 Police Interceptor	C8AF-J	C8AZ-J (DA-872)	4V w/Cruise-O-Matic w/Thermactor
428 ci 1969–70 Police Interceptor	D0AF-M	D0AZ-M (DA-998)	4V w/Cruise-O-Matic w/Thermactor
428 ci 1969	C8OF-J	C8OZ-J (DA-970)	4V w/Cruise-O-Matic w/Thermactor
428 ci 1969 Cobra Jet	C8OF-H	C8OZ-H (DA-969)	4V w/Manual Transmission
428 ci 1970 Cobra Jet	**D0ZF-C**	**D0ZZ-C (DA-1020)**	4V w/Manual Transmission w/Thermactor Dual Point
428 ci 1970 Cobra Jet	D0ZF-G	D0ZZ-D (DA-1021)	4V w/Cruise-O-Matic w/Thermactor
429 ci 1968–70	C8VF-A	C8VY-C (DA-885)	2V w/Cruise-O-Matic/IMCO 4V w/Cruise-O-Matic/IMCO
429 ci 1969 Police Interceptor	C8AF-AD	C7OZ-F (DA-807)	4V w/Cruise-O-Matic/IMCO
429 ci 1970	D0AF-Z	D0AZ-Z	4V w/Cruise-O-Matic
429 ci 1969 Boss 429	**C9ZF-D**	**C9AZ-U or C9ZZ-D**	4V w/Manual Transmission w/Thermactor Before 2/28/69
429 ci 1969–70 Boss 429	**C8VF-C**	**C9ZZ-D (DA-1094)**	4V w/Manual Transmission w/Thermactor After 2/28/69
429 ci 1969–70	C8VF-C	C9AZ-F (DA-933)	4V w/Manual Transmission/IMCO; w/Cruise-O-Matic 2V w/Cruise-O-Matic some w/Thermactor or IMCO
429 ci 1969–70	C9AF-Y	C9AZ-Y (DA-981)	4V w/Manual Transmission/IMCO
429 ci 1970–71 Cobra Jet	**D0OF-J or D0OF-AA**	**D0OZ-J (DA-1022)**	4V w/Manual Transmission w/Thermactor
429 ci 1970–71 Cobra Jet	**D0AF-Z**	**D0AZ-Z (DA-1034)**	4V w/Cruise-O-Matic
429 ci 1970–71 Cobra Jet	**D0OF-Y**	**D0OZ-K (DA-1014)**	4V w/Cruise-O-Matic w/Thermactor
429 ci 1971	C8VF-C	C9AZ-F (DA-933)	4V w/Cruise-O-Matic
429 ci 1971	D1MF-FA	D1MY-F (DA-1069)	4V w/Cruise-O-Matic/California
429 ci 1971 Cobra Jet Super Cobra Jet Police Interceptor	**D1AF-NA**	**D1AZ-N (DA-1080)**	4V w/Cruise-O-Matic
429 ci 1972	D2MF-FA	D2AZ-H (DA-1178)	4V w/Cruise-O-Matic/IMCO
429 ci 1972	D2MF-EA	D2AZ-J (DA-1179)	4V w/Cruise-O-Matic/IMCO
429 ci 1972	D2AF-MA	D2AZ-M (DA-1182)	4V w/Cruise-O-Matic/IMCO
429 ci 1972 Police Interceptor	D2AF-NA or D2AF-NC	D2AZ-N or D2AZ-R (DA-1224)	4V w/Cruise-O-Matic
429 ci 1972	D2AF-MB	D2AZ-R (DA-1224-A)	4V w/Cruise-O-Matic
429 ci 1972	D2SF-EA	D2SZ-E	4V w/Cruise-O-Matic
460 ci 1972	D2VF-AA	D2VY-A	4V w/Cruise-O-Matic
460 ci 1972	D2VF-BA	D2VY-B	4V w/Cruise-O-Matic

Bold indicates high-performance application.

CHAPTER 8

In 1968, Ford went to this advance/retard advance unit in an effort to reduce hydrocarbon emissions. This was known as the IMCO (Improved Combustion) emissions control system, which was controlled by a coolant vacuum valve at the thermostat. The advance/retard feature advances spark under acceleration (left arrow) and retards spark (right arrow) during deceleration (high manifold vacuum).

IMCO includes this distributor thermostatic vacuum control valve (also known as the Ported Vacuum Switch or PVS) that is activated by coolant temperature. It vectors vacuum to the advance/retard distributor to raise RPM if coolant the temperature becomes too high.

channeled vacuum to the advance side to advance spark for needed power. Upon deceleration, IMCO routed vacuum to the retard side to reduce hydrocarbon emissions.

In 1969, Ford introduced a dual-point distributor for the high-performance big-blocks with the IMCO dual advance/retard feature, which was employed to reduce hydrocarbon emissions.

In the mid-1970s, Ford introduced its first mass-produced electronic ignition system known as Duraspark. Duraspark greatly reduced incidents of misfire and high emissions from misfire. Duraspark distributors use a Hall effect module and reluctor wheel (magnetic pulse) to simulate the opening and closing of ignition points. Duraspark II, an improved form of Duraspark, was introduced a while later and was mainstream until 1985.

Three Autolite single-point breaker plates. From left is an original Autolite breaker plate and two aftermarket replacement breaker plates. If you can salvage the Autolite/Motorcraft version, it is the best breaker plate to use. It is by far the most stable example.

Autolite/Motorcraft distributor bushings, which are hard to come by, can be sourced through Mustangs Etc. From left are the B8QH-12120-A, C5AZ-12120-A, and C5AZ-12132-A. The main shaft bushings are shown left and center. Not all distributors have the bottom bushing (right), but you can add it for better support. Ideally, you will find a new shaft and bushings.

This is the main bushing, which is pressed into the housing. This single bushing is the weakness in these old distributors. It's just not enough support and it doesn't get enough lubrication, which snakes its way up the shaft from the engine. This is why adding the smaller bottom bushing is so important.

FORD BIG-BLOCK PARTS INTERCHANGE

IGNITION, CHARGING AND STARTING

In 1985, Ford went to the Thick Film Module (TFM) electronic Duraspark distributor, which did away with the vacuum advance. The thick film module advanced and retarded spark electronically. The downside to these TFM ignitions was engine heat and what it did to the modules. They became notorious for failure without notice, which left people suddenly stranded. In 1994, the TFM was moved away from the distributor.

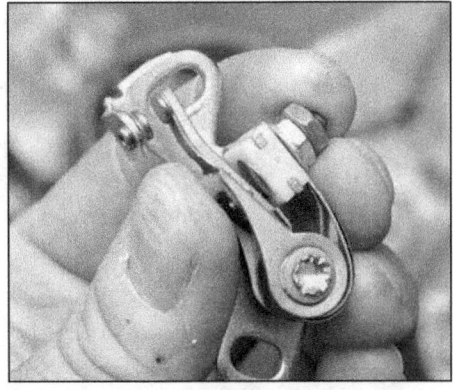

If you choose to stick with ignition points, opt for genuine Motorcraft parts with the phenolic pivot. Plastic pivots don't last, nor do non-ventilated contact points. The rub/cam block must be adequately lubricated.

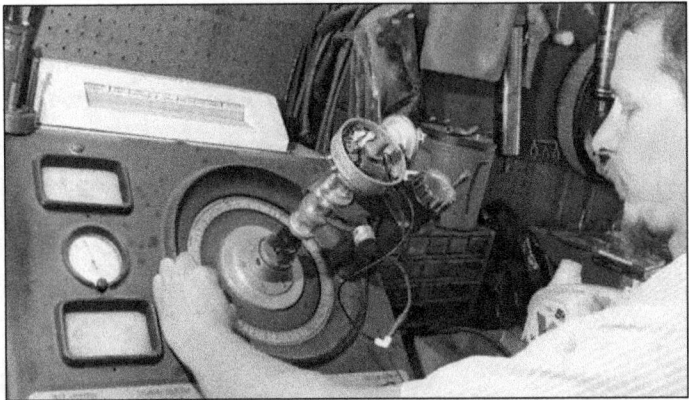

Two vacuum advance units for Ford distributors. The aftermarket advance unit (right), is adjusted with an Allen wrench via the vacuum port. On the left is original equipment, which is adjusted by adding or subtracting shims. Add to slow the rate of advance; subtract to speed up the rate of advance.

This is the Thick Film Module (TFM) distributor, which debuted in 1985. It is Ford's first real electronically controlled advance, which took the place of a vacuum advance unit. It was common throughout the mid-1990s. Problems with these distributors include heat and the TFM. They can fail on the fly. MSD has a replacement TFM designed to take the heat. In 1994-on, the TFM was moved away from the distributor.

The Ford part number on your FE, MEL, or 429/460 distributor isn't just about fit or authenticity. It is about how the distributor was factory curved. You want the mechanical and vacuum advances on the same page where the vacuum advance hands off to the mechanical advance as RPM increases. It takes a seasoned tuner to do this correctly. Curving begins on a distributor machine such as this. Tuning continues in the vehicle in gear under load.

This is the starter delay relay (C8AZ-11A126-A) common to 428 Cobra Jet–powered Fords and Mercurys after April 15, 1968, according to the 428 Cobra Jet Registry. This relay was designed to prevent any restart attempts within four seconds of a failed start attempt to prevent starter/flywheel damage.

FORD BIG-BLOCK PARTS INTERCHANGE

CHAPTER 8

Ford's Duraspark appeared for the first time in the mid-1970s. This is the Hall effect module; it is a magnetic trigger inside the distributor. This is an excellent upgrade for your FE or 429/460 program. Duraspark was never available for the MEL. Another option is the PerTronix Ignitor drop-in electronic ignition for those with the MEL. Painless Performance offers the Duraspark conversion kit, which includes the harness, resistor, and hardware.

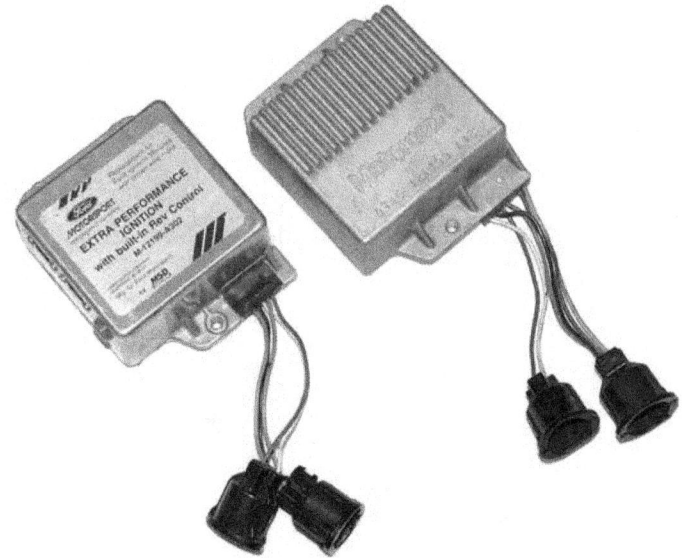

Shown here are Ford Duraspark and Duraspark II ignition modules, which first appeared in the mid-1970s. Duraspark is an excellent upgrade for any FE or 429/460 big-block. It was never available for the MEL. However, you can retrofit your MEL distributor with a PerTronix Ignitor module for the immediate benefit of electronic ignition.

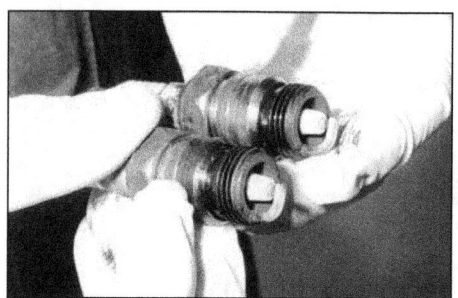

These fat-body 18-mm spark plugs were used from 1958 to 1976 in the FE and 1958–1968 in the MEL. They were never employed in the 429/460.

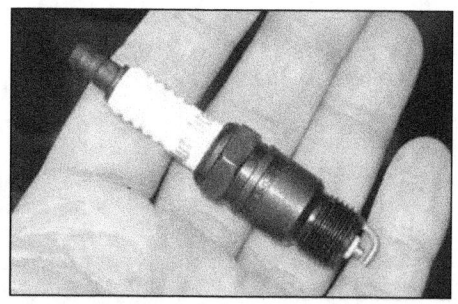

The 429/460 uses the more petite 14-mm taper-seat spark plug, which became the norm in all Ford V-8s in the 1970s.

Any Ford big-block build project should include senders. This is the water temperature sender for the temperature gauge. It operates on resistance to ground. The greater the resistance (colder coolant), the lower the reading. The lower the resistance (hotter coolant), the higher the reading. Some senders are a simple on/off affair where the switch closes (HOT light on) when coolant gets too hot.

This is an oil pressure sender for use with a gauge. It is a variable resistor to ground. With low resistance you get a high reading; high resistance to ground gives a low reading.

This is a simple oil pressure sending switch. When oil pressure drops to around 5 pounds, the switch closes to ground and you get an oil pressure light.

CHAPTER 9

EXHAUST

Exhaust systems have always been a quick and dirty means to improved performance, and Ford's family of big-blocks are no exception. If you're performing a concours restoration or perhaps you just want to keep your Ford close to stock, there is a plethora of factory Ford castings from which to choose as long as you keep fitment and clearance in mind. Most of us love the huge 406/427 cast-iron headers from the early 1960s. However, if you're planning to install them in a Ford or Mercury compact or intermediate, forget about it. Not only will they not fit the cylinder heads, they won't clear the frame rails and aprons.

When your goal includes enhancing performance, both stock and aftermarket options are available. FE big-blocks were packaged with a variety of exhaust manifolds for different applications. Thanks to their design, only the 406 and 427 High Performance exhaust manifolds flowed well; the cast-iron headers wound down each side like bananas to the exhaust system. The downside to these fabulous factory Ford headers is fitment. They don't fit anything except a full-size Ford or Mercury.

The 428 Cobra Jet engines weren't blessed with the 427's abundant factory exhaust headers because of their intended platforms. However, the Cobra Jet manifolds were still a big improvement over the run-of-the-mill FE log-style exhaust manifolds. However, you can bolt these guys onto any FE in a Ford compact or intermediate. When you are shopping factory exhaust manifolds for your FE, pay close attention to casting numbers and date codes.

Another important factor with FE exhaust manifolds is the manifold-to-cylinder head match. Most FE cylinder heads employ an eight-bolt exhaust manifold pattern with all bolts at 12 and 6 o'clock at each port. The diagonal 14-bolt pattern on compact and intermediate Ford/Mercury cylinder heads is common to Mustang, Cougar, Fairlane, Torino, and Cyclone with the 390, 427, or 428. Although 390 and 428 Cobra Jet

During the FE big-blocks' production life of almost two decades, dozens of exhaust manifolds were produced for this engine family. Your job is to find the correct manifolds for your restoration project. It is vital to know casting numbers and date codes along with knowing what fits and what doesn't.

FORD BIG-BLOCK PARTS INTERCHANGE

CHAPTER 9

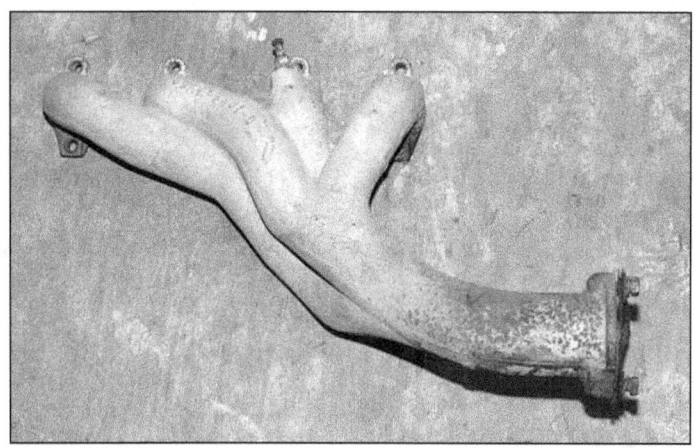

Ford went way out there to produce powerful factory high-performance big-blocks beginning in the late 1950s. These long-tube iron headers were conceived for the 406 and 427 High Performance FE big-blocks early in the 1960s. This pair was found at John Vermeersch's Total Performance shop outside Detroit, Michigan.

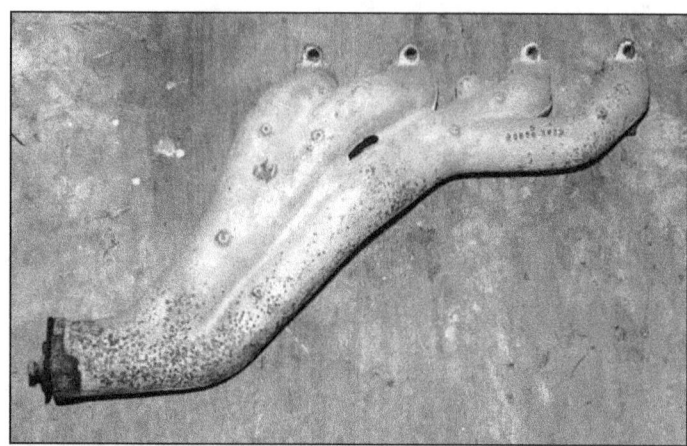

This is the passenger's side of the 406/427 High Performance header duo. These cast-iron bananas easily out-scavenge any Ford exhaust manifold. However, they were a brief flash in the pan as the Total Performance era unfolded in 1962–1964. They fit only full-size Fords and Mercurys.

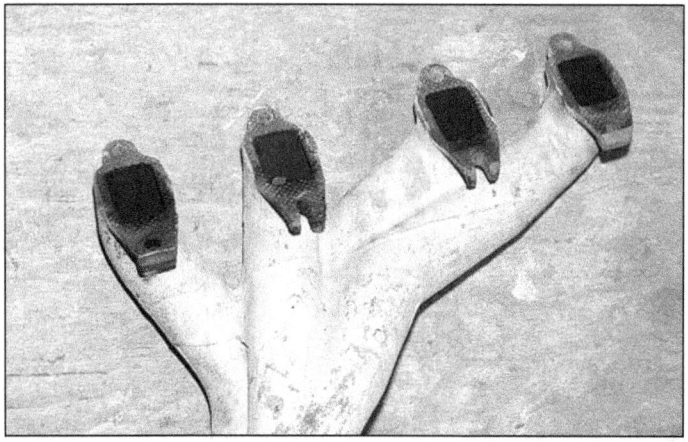

The 406/427 cast-iron exhaust header flanges are 12 and 6 o'clock bolt pattern (eight-bolt) and designed only for full-size Fords and Mercurys.

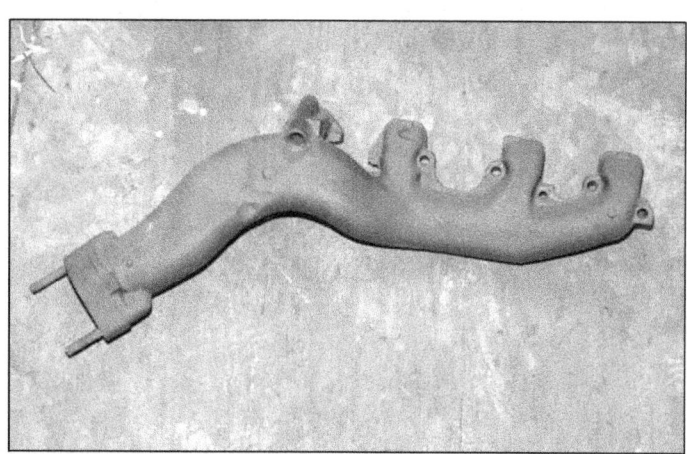

The 428 Cobra Jet exhaust manifolds are C8OE-9430-A (passenger-side) and C8OE-9431-A (driver-side). Exhaust manifolds are easily identified by their casting numbers and date codes.

Here is the Mustang/Fairlane/Cougar/Cyclone 390 High Performance exhaust manifold (passenger-side shown), which isn't much different than a bread-and-butter 390 manifold. Number-8 exhaust port has 12 and 6 o'clock bolt locations like its Cobra Jet counterpart. Pay very close attention to casting numbers and date codes.

EXHAUST

Check out these 406 shorty cast-iron headers for full-size Fords and Mercurys. These will not clear compact and intermediate applications because of shock tower interference.

exhaust manifolds may look similar they are not the same. Check casting numbers' appearances.

The MEL's exhaust manifolds depend primarily upon application, which was largely in Lincolns and to a lesser degree, Edsel, Mercury, and Ford Thunderbird. You will have to rely on Ford casting numbers and date codes for proper reference and vehicle application. There were no MEL high-performance exhaust manifolds from the factory. The only performance applications were the 1958 Mercury Super Marauder 430 and the 1959–1960 Ford Thunderbird 430.

Popular Big-Block Exhaust Manifold Castings

Model Year	Casting Number	Description
1960	C0AE-9430-B	352 High Performance (Passenger's Side)
1960	C0AE-9431-B	352 High Performance (Driver's Side)
1961	C1AE-9430-C	390 High Performance (Passenger's Side)
1961	C1AE-9431-C	390 High Performance (Driver's Side)
1962	C2AE-9430-B	406 High Performance (Passenger's Side)
1962	C2AE-9431-B	406 High Performance (Driver's Side)
1963–64	C3OE-9430-B	406/427 High Performance Long Tube (Passenger's Side)
1963–64	C3OE-9431-B	406/427 High Performance Long Tube (Driver's Side)
1965	C5AE-9430-H C5AE-9430-K	427 High Performance Long Tube (Passenger's Side)
1965	C5AE-9431-C	427 High Performance Long Tube (Driver's Side)
1966–68	C7OE-9430-C	390 High Performance (Passenger's Side)
1966–68	C7OE-9431-A	390 High Performance (Driver's Side)
1968–70	C8OE-9430-A	428 Cobra Jet (Passenger's Side)
1968–70	C8OE-9431-A	428 Cobra Jet (Driver's Side)
1958–59	B92M-9430-A	MEL (Passenger's Side)
1958–59	B8EL-9431-A	MEL (Driver's Side)
1970–71	D0OE-9430-A	429 Cobra Jet/SCJ (Passenger's Side)
1970–71	D0OE-9431-A	429 Cobra Jet/SCJ (Driver's Side)
1971	D1ZE-9431-CA1 D1ZE-9431-CA2	429 Cobra Jet/SCJ (Driver's Side)
1971–72	D2OE-9430-CA	429 Police Interceptor (Passenger's Side)
1971–72	D2OE-9431-AA1 D2OE-9431-AA2	429 Police Interceptor (Driver's Side)
1969–70	C9AE-9430-A	Boss 429 (Passenger's Side)
1969–70	C9AE-9431-A	Boss 429 (Driver's Side)

CHAPTER 9

At a glance, this passenger-side exhaust manifold resembles the Cobra Jet casting. It is a 390 High Performance manifold, which is similar, but does not flow anywhere even close to the Cobra Jet manifold.

This is the passenger's side of the 390 High Performance GT engine with its shorty header–style exhaust manifold, again similar in appearance to its Cobra Jet counterpart, yet inferior in performance.

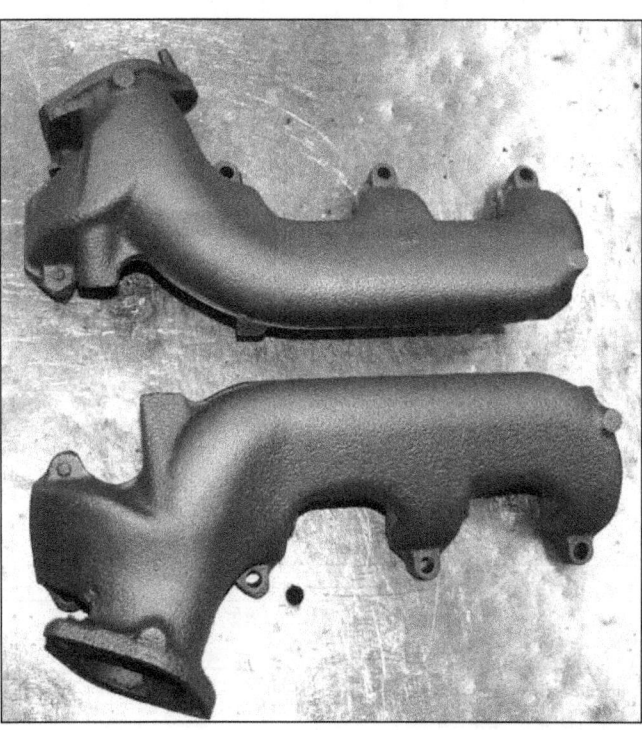

The 383/410/430/462 MEL exhaust manifolds don't sport a hint of performance, but I thought I'd show them to you anyway. The MEL was mainstream power for the Lincoln, Edsel, Mercury, and Ford Thunderbird. It isn't that the MEL was short on performance. Mercury understood its potential and got it to 400 hp. The MEL was a hands-down winner with the powerboat crowd.

The 429/460 385 Series engines never really had a broad range of exhaust manifolds. Of all the exhaust manifolds these engines were fitted with throughout their production life spanning 1968–1997, the best exhaust manifolds were the D0OE-9430-A and D0OE-9431-A for the 1970–1971 429 Cobra Jet and Super Cobra Jet.

Unless you are performing a concours restoration, the 429/460 will perform better using shorty or long-tube headers. The best headers are available from Ford Powertrain Applications (FPA) out of Everett, Washington, which have the best fit of any aftermarket header I have ever seen. They offer excellent fit for the FE and 385 Series big-blocks.

Because the 429 Cobra Jet and Super Cobra Jet were available only in Mustang, Cougar, Torino, Fairlane, and Cyclone, only a handful of castings were produced for these car lines. Most common are D0OE-9430-A for the passenger's side; D0OE-9431-A, D1ZE-9431-A, D1ZE-9431-CA1, and D1ZE-9431-CA2 for the driver's side. There are a greater number of driver-side manifolds due to broader applications.

Mufflers and Pipes

Although loud and obnoxious has always been in style among hot rodders, it can become very hard on your hearing over time, especially if you are in the silver-hair club. Regardless of whether you like loud or soft and tasteful, performance is always going to be in style. You want a muffler that flows well and an exhaust system that does a good job of scavenging. Aftermarket performance mufflers are generally loud regardless of manufacturer. Ideally, you will achieve a soft burble at the tailpipes and have a quiet cabin for the cruise.

EXHAUST

Flowmaster three-chamber mufflers, particularly the Series 50 Delta Flow mufflers, deliver great performance without being too loud. They don't resonate like traditional mufflers, which is the good news.

When it comes to pipes, size them with the level of performance expected. As a rule, big-blocks want 2½-inch pipes for adequate backpressure and good low- to mid-range torque, which is what you want from a big-block. Any time you venture beyond 2½ to 3 inches in pipe diameter you're bound to get into clearance issues and lose a certain amount of torque.

The debate continues over H-pipe versus X-pipe and even a mixture of the two. X-pipes provide better scavenging than H-pipes and this has been proven on chassis dynos around the world. The X-pipe provides a nice pulse rhythm between the two cylinder banks along with corresponding power and sound. Always run a balance tube between the sides regardless of what else you do.

Exhaust hanger technology has improved in recent years along with bolt-together exhaust pipe couplings from the aerospace industry, which makes muffler and pipe swaps easy. If you have an exhaust system fabricated, put it together with modern technology and save yourself from having to go back to the muffler shop.

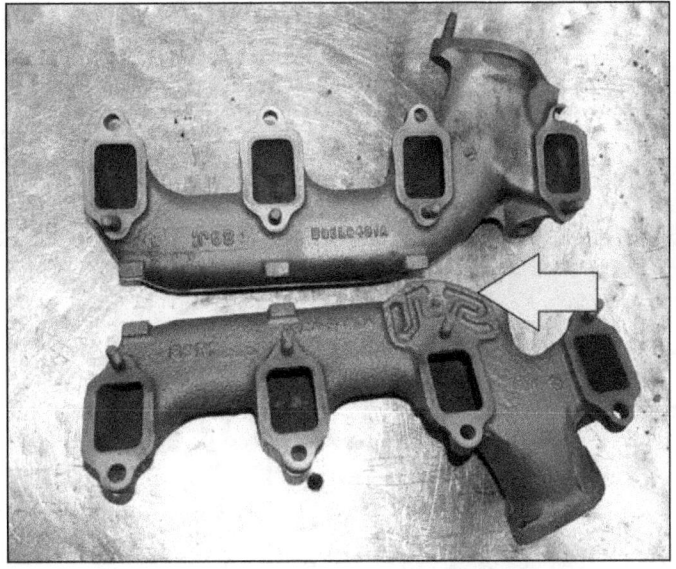

Flipped over, the MEL exhaust manifolds reveal more of what they're about. These castings are about scavenging and torque, not horsepower. The arrow indicates the choke stove for heating the automatic choke. Casting numbers tell you what you've found along with the date code.

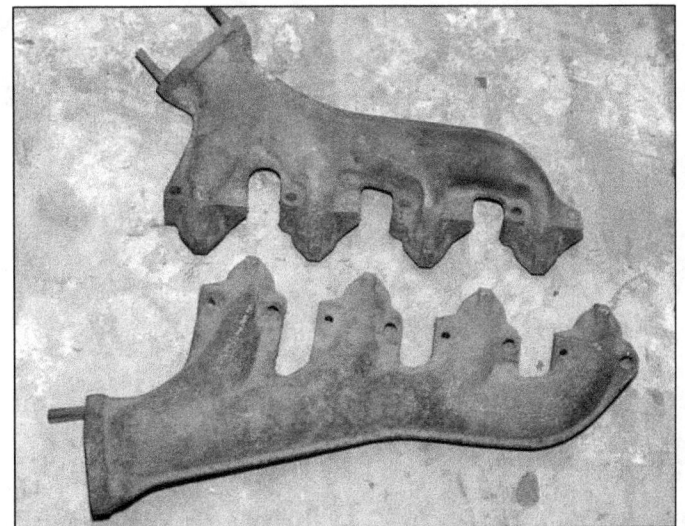

These are 429 Cobra Jet/Super Cobra Jet exhaust manifolds, which, to some degree, resemble shorty headers. They will fit nearly any 429/460 application. Look for D0OE-9430-A (bottom here, passenger's side) and D0OE-9431-A (top here, driver's side).

Although this interchange book is largely about factory components, it's productive to also show you what fits and works in big-block Ford applications. These are long-tube headers for the FE big-block from Ford Powertrain Applications (FPA). They offer the best fit of an aftermarket header along with ball and socket collectors for easy installation. FPA builds headers for the 385 Series 429/460.

CHAPTER 10

COOLING

Ford big-blocks haven't struggled as much with cooling issues as their small-block counterparts. These larger-displacement engines benefitted from improved cooling system engineering in larger vehicles along with better airflow. Ford engineers understood what it took to extract heat from these big iron behemoths, giving them larger radiators along with engine management devices, including hot-idle compensators and thermostatic vacuum control valves (1968-on) to increase idle speed to help cooling.

This is a typical FE cast-iron water pump. Because this one doesn't have casting numbers and a date code it is likely an aftermarket replacement. Most replacement water pumps are high-flow.

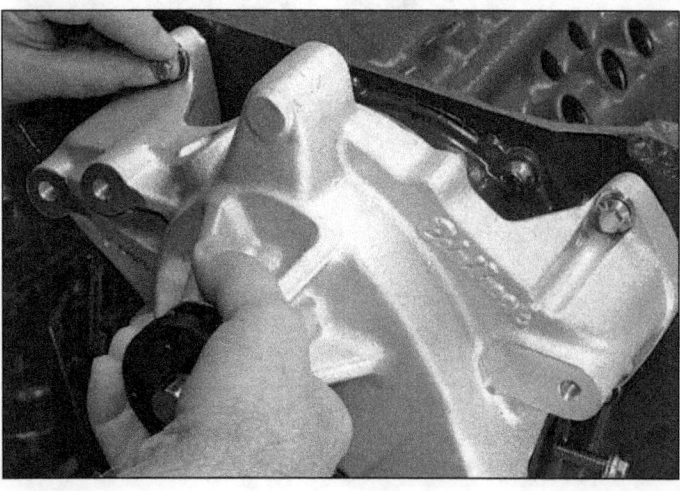

Edelbrock's high-flow water pump for the FE is constructed of cast aluminum, which gets weight out of the front of your FE big-block. This, coupled with a cast-aluminum intake manifold, sheds at least 100 pounds from the vehicle weight.

COOLING

The MEL water pump changed very little from this engine's 1958 introduction until production ended in 1968. The aftermarket doesn't offer a lightweight aluminum water pump for the MEL at this time. It is challenging to find an MEL water pump of any kind these days because these engines are no longer mainstream. Often, you need to find a rebuildable core and have it rebuilt.

Both the FE and MEL engines had coolant surge tanks, such as this one, in the early 1960s.

The aftermarket caters to the 429/460, as it does for the FE, with a wide variety of high-flow water pumps. Stock replacement cast-iron water pumps are also available for these engines. If you're performing a concours restoration you can have a stock casting rebuilt. This is the Edelbrock water pump (PN 88663) in black for the 429/460.

Radiator

Whether you're building an FE or facing the challenges of an MEL, shopping for a radiator has never been easier for the Ford big-block enthusiast. The aftermarket industry offers you a wealth of radiator choices including a stock replacement with more rows, a bold and effective aluminum heat exchanger, and more.

While you're shopping for a radiator, it's always good to go over-capacity, which is easier to control than under-capacity. It's always better to have too much radiator than not enough. If you have an automatic transmission, make sure there's a provision for cooler lines.

Another area that people generally don't give enough thought to is the fan and shroud. The fan and shroud relationship is a critical area that is overlooked too often. Fan depth into the shroud makes the difference between overheating and normal operating temperature.

Clutch fans, for example, must have a shroud and be properly spaced just inside the shroud. The same can be said for factory flex fans, which must also be fitted with a shroud. If the fan is too deep into the shroud,

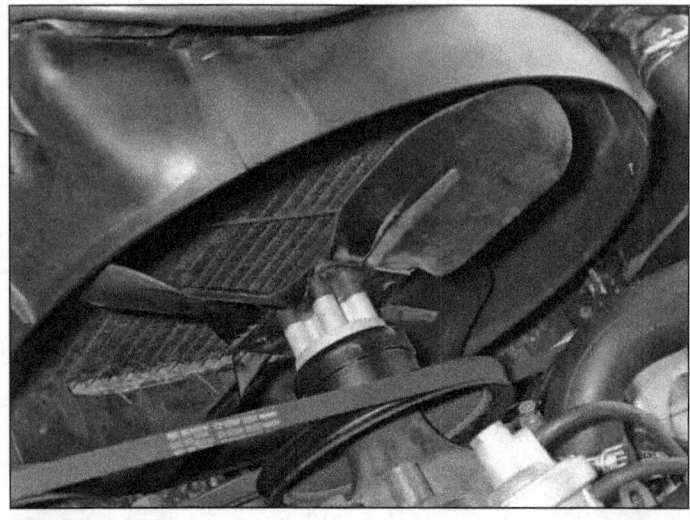

Effective cooling boils down to the fan, radiator, and shroud combo. The traditional stamped-steel, two-piece X fans don't require a shroud.

This is a shrouded six-blade aftermarket fan, which tends to be noisy and inefficient. Because these blades are in a fixed position, they move large quantities of air through the radiator all the time, which causes a power drain.

A cooling fan should be halfway (the width of the fan) into the shroud. If you opt for the original Ford fan spacer that the Master Parts Catalog calls for, the fan should be at the proper depth into the shroud. This Ford flex fan is most of the way into the shroud, with roughly 25 percent of the blades showing.

This is a 1967 Mustang with the 390 High Performance FE. In front is the proper fan clutch and seven-blade fan located halfway into the shroud. Clutch fans should always have a shroud. There are clutch fans and there are thermostatic clutch fans. Your Ford, if so equipped, should have a thermostatic clutch fan.

COOLING

The difference between a clutch fan and thermostatic clutch fan is the bimetallic coil in the middle of this fan clutch. If there isn't a bimetallic coil, it isn't a thermostatic fan clutch. Thermostatic fan clutches engage and spin because they are needed based on radiator temperature.

From the late 1960s into the 1970s Ford and other automakers conceived the flex fan, which flattens out at high RPM eating up less power in the process. The downside to these fans is noise and the risk of a stray fan blade flying off. Unless you're performing a concours restoration where a flex fan is required, it is best to stay away from them.

you're going to have air turbulence and stagnation issues. Outside the shroud you're not going to get the velocity needed through the radiator and shroud at low vehicle speeds. Fan blade tips must be in the position at which they are most effective.

The most efficient radiator-cooling fan is the thermostatic clutch fan. It cycles in and out as needed, depending upon coolant temperature. Remember, there are clutch fans and there are thermostatic clutch fans. You want the thermostatic clutch fan for greatest efficiency.

Radiator height is another issue. Mustang and Cougar, as examples, used radiators that were shorter by 1 inch compared to the full-size Ford and Mercury. A Galaxie or Fairlane radiator will not fit below a Mustang/Cougar hood line. With the exception of radiator height, fitment across Ford and Mercury car lines is good. The 1971–1973 Mustang and Cougar enjoy compatibility across all Ford/Mercury lines.

At the cusp of the 1970s, Ford began phasing in crossflow radiators, which are more efficient than vertical-flow radiators in the decades prior. Some of this was due to the quest for a lower hoodline. Apart from that, the crossflow design made more sense in terms of heat transfer and has been common ever since.

Water Pump

Big-block Fords offer greater simplicity when it comes to water pumps. The FE Series 332/352/360/361/390/406/410/427/428 use two basic water pump types, with endless variations in castings and good interchange. The two choices are standard and high-flow; that's it. The standard FE water pump is PN D0AZ-8501-D; it is one of dozens of Ford part numbers. The point is that the FE water pump fits virtually any FE.

If you're building a high-performance FE, you're going to want the C5AZ-8501-S high-flow water pump casting originally conceived for all FE big-blocks. You also have the option of Edelbrock and other aftermarket high-flow water pumps for a performance build. Almost all FE water pumps sold today are high-flow.

Don't panic if your replacement FE water pump doesn't have a casting number that applies to your Ford. One example is C9AE-8501-A, which is a random casting number for an FE water pump. There are dozens of others but they all interchange. If you find an FE water pump casting without numbers you've found an aftermarket replacement water pump. It will fit any FE big-block.

FE Power offers machined billet aluminum water pump adapters that allow the use of the CVR 55-gpm (gallons per minute) Pro-Flo Extreme electric water pump. This high-efficiency water pump made

FORD BIG-BLOCK PARTS INTERCHANGE

CHAPTER 10

Big-Block Radiator Identification (FE and 429/460 Only)

Big-Block Radiator Identification						
Engine/Year/Car Line	ID Number (8005)	Part Number (8005)	Core Width (inches)	Core Height (inches)	Core Thickness (inches)	Other Information
352/390 ci 427/428 ci 1965–67 Full-Size	C5AE-D C5AE-J C5AE-Z C6AE-T	C5AZ-H	23 3/16	17 3/8	2	w/A/C w/Cruise-O-Matic
428 ci 1966 Full-Size	**C6AE-AA**	C6AZ-S	N/A	N/A	N/A	Police Interceptor
390/428 ci 1967 Full-Size	**C7AE-T C7AE-U**	C7AZ-G	23 1/8	17 3/8	2 3/8	Police Interceptor
390/428 ci 1968 Full-Size	C8SE-A	C8AZ-C	21 3/4	18 1/2	1 1/2	w/o A/C w/Manual Transmission
390/427/428 ci 1968 Full-Size	**C7SE-D**	C8AZ-A	21 3/4	18 1/2	2 1/4	w/A/C w/Manual Transmission Police Interceptor
390/428 ci 1968 Full-Size	C8AE-R	C8AZ-B	21 3/4	18 1/2	2 1/4	w/A/C w/Cruise-O-Matic Police Interceptor
390/429 ci 1969 Full-Size	C9AE-J	C9AZ-D	21 3/4	17 3/8	1 1/2	w/Manual Transmission
390/429 ci 1969–70 Full-Size	D0AE-C	D0OZ-A	26	17 7/8	2 1/4	w/A/C w/Manual Transmission
390/428/429 ci 1969–70 Full-Size	**D0AE-G**	C9AZ-C	26	17 7/8	1 1/2	w/Cruise-O-Matic Police Interceptor
390/429 ci 1971 Full-Size	**D1VE-AA**	D1VY-A	26	17 3/8	2 1/4	w/A/C w/Cruise-O-Matic Police Interceptor
390/429 ci 1971 Full-Size	D1ZE-AB	D2ZZ-C	26	17 3/8	1 1/2	w/Cruise-O-Matic
429 ci 1971 Full-Size	**D1ZE-DA D1ZE-EA D1ZE-FA**	D1ZZ-B	26	17 3/8	2 1/4	w/A/C w/Cruise-O-Matic Police Interceptor
429 ci 1972 Full-Size	**D2AE-BB D2AE-GB D2AE-KA D2AE-VA**	D2AZ-B	26	17 3/8	2 1/4	w/A/C w/Cruise-O-Matic Police Interceptor
429 ci 1972 Full-Size	D2AE-JA	D3ZZ-A	26	17 27/32	1 1/2	w/Cruise-O-Matic
390/427 ci 1966 Intermediate	C6OE-F C6OE-H	C6OZ-F	23 1/4	17 3/8	2	w/A/C w/Cruise-O-Matic
390/427 ci 1967 Intermediate	C7OE-C C7OE-D	C7OZ-C	23 1/4	17 3/8	1 1/4	w/A/C w/Cruise-O-Matic
390 ci 1968 Intermediate	C8OE-A C8OE-B C8OE-D C8OE-F C8OE-H	C8OZ-C	24 1/4	17 3/8	1 1/2	w/o A/C w/Cruise-O-Matic
390/427/428CJ 1968–69 Intermediate	**C8OE-F**	C8OZ-B	24 1/4	17 3/8	2 1/4	w/A/C w/Cruise-O-Matic

Bold indicates high-performance application.

COOLING

Big-Block Radiator Identification

Engine/Year/Car Line	ID Number (8005)	Part Number (8005)	Core Width (inches)	Core Height (inches)	Core Thickness (inches)	Other Information
429 ci 1970 Intermediate Cobra Jet	D0OE-A D0OE-B D0OE-F D0OE-G D0OE-H	D0OZ-A	26	17³⁄₈	2¼	w/A/C w/Cruise-O-Matic CJ before 7/28/69
429 ci 1970 Intermediate Cobra Jet	D0OE-K	D0OZ-E	26	17³⁄₈	2¼	w/A/C w/Cruise-O-Matic CJ after 7/28/69
429 ci 1971 Intermediate Cobra Jet	**D2ZE-MB** **D2ZE-NA** **D2ZE-NB**	D1VY-A	26	17³⁄₈	2¼	w/A/C w/Cruise-O-Matic
429 ci 1971 Intermediate Cobra Jet	**D1ZE-DA** **D1ZE-EA**	D1ZZ-B	26	17³⁄₈	2¼	w/A/C w/Cruise-O-Matic Police Interceptor
429 ci 1972 Intermediate	D2OE-AB D2OE-DB D2OE-EB D2OE-EC D2OE-NA D2OE-UA D2SE-BB D2SE-EB	D2OZ-A	28	17³⁄₈	1½	w/o A/C w/Cruise-O-Matic
429 ci 1972 Intermediate	D2OE-CA D2OE-CB D2OE-CC D2OE-RA D2OE-RC D2OE-VA D2SE-AB D2SE-CB D2SE-DB D2SE-FB D2SE-GA D2VE-DA	D2VY-A	28	17³⁄₈	2¼	w/A/C w/Cruise-O-Matic Police Interceptor
390 ci 1967 Compact	C7ZE-G C7ZE-V C7ZE-Y C7ZE-Z	C7ZZ-C	23¼	16	2	w/A/C w/Cruise-O-Matic
390/427/428CJ Boss 429 1968–69 Compact	C8ZE-A C8ZE-B C8ZE-C C8ZE-K C8ZE-L C8ZE-M C8ZE-S	C8ZZ-C	24³⁄₁₆	16	2¼	w/A/C w/Cruise-O-Matic
429 ci 1971 Compact Cobra Jet	D1VE-AA D1VE-AB D1VE-AC D2ZE-ED **D2ZE-LB** **D2ZE-MB** **D2ZE-NA** **D2ZE-NB**	D1VY-A	26	17³⁄₈	2¼	w/o A/C w/Cruise-O-Matic
429 ci 1971 Compact Cobra Jet	**D1ZE-DA** **D1ZE-EA**	D1ZZ-B	26	17³⁄₈	2¼	w/A/C w/Cruise-O-Matic

Bold indicates high-performance application.

CHAPTER 10

There seems to be some confusion over which radiator cap to use. Most vintage Fords used a 7- to 10-pound cap. One thing to keep in mind is that the higher the pressure, the higher the coolant boiling point. You may go as high as 14 to 16 pounds if you have a solid cooling system as well as healthy gaskets and hoses. Use a 180-degree thermostat. Never run a Ford big block without a thermostat.

Another area of confusion is the lower radiator hose anti-collapse spring. Although some hose manufacturers state that you don't have to have an anti-collapse spring, you really must have one, period. Lower radiator hoses will collapse at higher RPM without this spring. This results in overheating on the open road.

possible for FE enthusiasts by the FE Power adapters, is the only 55-gpm electric water pump setup that bolts onto the FE big-block engine. In addition to mounting the water pump, the FE Power adapters use O-rings to seal to the engine block, with no gaskets required. These also offer mounting points for the factory alternator and power steering pump brackets.

A similar story can be told for MEL and 385 Series big-blocks. One basic water pump casting fits all years with a few exceptions. This means nearly any water pump specified for the 429/460 will fit your 385 Series big-block. Edelbrock, for example, offers one type of water

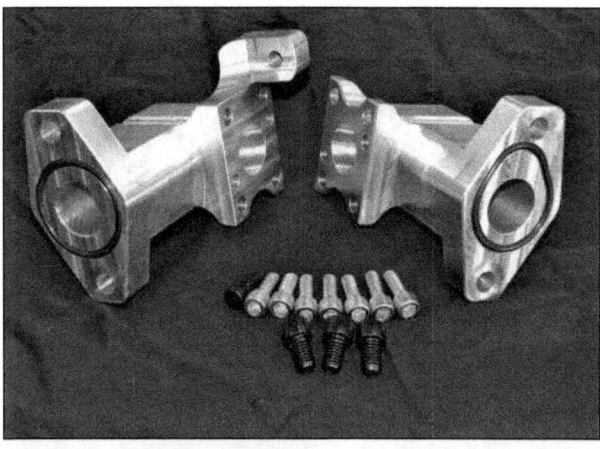

FE Power offers these machined billet aluminum water pump adapters that enable you to use the CVR 55-gpm Pro-Flo Extreme electric water pump on your FE big-block. Because these adapters are O-ringed, they're easy to service.

Here's the FE Power water pump adapter package complete with the CVR 55-gpm Pro-Flo Extreme water pump. This is a nice piece if you're seeking greater cooling system efficiency and good looks in an FE.

Although this isn't about parts interchange, it is worthy of note. Evans coolant is a non-aqueous coolant, which means that you run it at 100 percent with no added water. Evans will outlast your restoration because there's no electrolysis and no corrosion because there is no water (which causes corrosion). Your cooling system must be completely dry when you install it. Gaskets and seals must be in good condition. If you're going to run conventional coolant, run a 50/50 mix or even 60/40 antifreeze/water mix, which will minimize the risk of corrosion. Change conventional coolant every two years with a flush and fill.

COOLING

Fan Identification (FE and 429/460 Only)

Model/Year/Engine	Part Number (8600)	ID Number	No. of Blades/Fan Type	Diameter (inches)	Center Hole (inches)
352 ci 1965 Full-Size	D2OZ-A		4	18½	5/8
390 ci 1965 Full-Size	C6OZ-A		4	17½	5/8
390/428 ci 1965–66 Full-Size	D2OZ-A	C5AE-A	4	18½ Before 2/21/66	5/8
352/390 ci 1965 Full-Size	**C5AZ-F**	C5AE-G	5	18	5/8
352/390/428 ci 1965–66 Full-Size	**C5AZ-B**	C5AE-C	7 Clutch Type	19¼	2⅜
427 ci 1965 Full-Size High Performance	**C6OZ-A**		4 Before 1/25/65	17½	5/8
427 ci 1965–66 Full-Size High Performance	**C4SZ-A**	C4SE-A	7 Clutch Type From 1/25/65	18	2⅜
352/390 ci 1966 Full-Size	C1AZ-A	C6ME-C	5	18½	5/8
428 ci 1966 Full-Size	C1AZ-A	C6ME-C	5 From 2/21/66	18½	5/8
428 ci 1966 Full-Size	**C4SZ-A**	C4SE-A	7 Clutch Type Before 2/14/66	18	2⅜
428 ci 1966 Full-Size	**C5AZ-B**	C5AE-C	7 Clutch Type From 2/14/66	19¼	2⅜
428 ci 1966–68 Full-Size	**C6MY-A**		7 Clutch Type	19½	2⅜
390/428 ci 1967 Full-Size	**C5AZ-B**	C5AE-C	7 Clutch Type	19¼	2⅜
390/428 ci 1967 Full-Size	C7AZ-C	C7AE-C	4	19	5/8
390/428 ci 1967–68 Full-Size	C7AZ-A	C7AE-B	4	19	5/8
390/429 ci 1967 Full-Size	C1AZ-A	C6ME-C	5	18½	5/8
390/428 ci 1967 Full-Size	C6MY-B		6	18½	5/8
390/428 ci 1967 Full-Size	**C5AZ-B**	C5AE-C	7 Clutch Type	19¼	2⅜
390/428/429 ci 1967–69 Full-Size	C8AZ-D	C8AE-D	5	19	5/8

Bold indicates high-performance or heavy-duty application.

Fan Identification (FE and 429/460 Only) CONTINUED

Model/Year/Engine	Part Number (8600)	ID Number	No. of Blades/Fan Type	Diameter (inches)	Center Hole (inches)
390/428 ci 1968–69 Full-Size	C8AZ-B (YA-16)	C8AE-B D3OE-BA	7 Clutch Type	19½	5/8
427 ci 1968 Full-Size	C8AZ-A		5	19½	5/8
427 ci 1968 Full-Size	C5AZ-B	C5AE-B	7 Clutch Type	19¼	2⅜
390/429 ci 1969–71 Full-Size	C6MY-A		7 Clutch Type	19½	2⅜
390/429 ci 1969–71 Full-Size	D0AZ-B	D0AE-B	4	19	5/8
390/428/429 ci 1969–70 Full-Size	C8AZ-B	C8AE-B D3OE-BA	7	19½	5/8
390/429 ci 1969–70 Full-Size	C8AZ-D		7	19½	5/8
429 ci 1972 Full-Size	C8AZ-B (YA-16)	C8AE-B D3OE-BA	7	19½	5/8
429 ci 1972 Full-Size	C6MY-A		7 Clutch Type	19½	2⅜
390 ci 1966 Intermediate	D2OZ-A	C5AE-A	4	18½	5/8
390 ci 1966–69 Intermediate	**C6MY-B**		6 From 1/28/66	18½	5/8
390 ci 1966 Intermediate	**C6OZ-F**	**C6ME-B**	6	18½	5/8
390/427 ci 1966–67 Intermediate	**C6OZ-F**	**C6OE-F**	7 Clutch Type	18¼	2⅜
390 ci 1967 Intermediate	C7AZ-A	C7AE-B	4	19	5/8
390 ci 1967 Intermediate	C1AZ-A	C6ME-C	5	18½	5/8
390 ci 1968–69 Intermediate	C7AZ-C		4	19	5/8
390/427/428 ci 1968–69 Intermediate	**C8OZ-A**	**C8OE-B**	7 Clutch Type	18¼	2⅜
428CJ 1969–70 Intermediate	**C9ZZ-C**	**C9ZE-E**	7 Clutch Type	18¼	2⅝
428CJ 1969 Intermediate	**C9OZ-D**	**C9OE-H**	6	18	5/8
429 ci 1970 Intermediate	**D0SZ-A**	**D0SE-A**	7 Clutch Type	19	2⅜
429CJ 1970–71 Intermediate	**D0OZ-A** (YA-25)	**D0OE-A**	7	19	5/8

Bold indicates high-performance or heavy-duty application.

COOLING

Model/Year/Engine	Part Number (8600)	ID Number	No. of Blades/Fan Type	Diameter (inches)	Center Hole (inches)
429CJ 1970 Intermediate	C5AZ-K (YA-15)		5	18	5/8
429 ci 1972 Intermediate	**D0SZ-A**	D0SE-A	7 Clutch Type	19	2 3/8
429 ci 1972 Intermediate	**D0OZ-A** (YA-25)	D0OE-A	7	19	5/8
390 ci 1967 Compact	**C6OZ-F**	C6OE-F	7 Clutch Type	18 1/4	2 3/8
390/427/428CJ 1968–69 Compact	**C8OZ-A**	C8OE-B	7 Clutch Type	18 1/4	2 3/8
390/427/428CJ 1969–70 Compact	**C9ZZ-C**	C9ZE-E	7 Clutch Type	18 1/4	2-5/8
428CJ 1969–70 Compact	C9OZ-D	C9OE-H	6	18	5/8
428CJ 1970 Compact	**D0TZ-B**		7	18	5/8
429 ci 1969 Compact	**C9ZZ-D**	C9ZE-F	7	18	3/4
Boss 429 429 ci 1970 Compact	**D0ZZ-A**	D0ZE-A	5	18	1
Boss 429 429CJ 1971 Compact	**D0OZ-A**	D0OE-A	7	19	5/8

Bold indicates high-performance or heavy-duty application.

pump for the 429/460. The same can be said for everyone else in the aftermarket.

The C9VZ-8501-A water pump is specified for the 1968–1969 429/460; D1VY-8501-B is specified through 1972. The Ford part number changed again to D2VY-8501-A in 1972, and then to D4VY-8501-A in 1974. Although there have been countless part numbers since 1974, these pumps still interchange through 1997 when 385 Series big-block production ended at Lima, Ohio.

Of course, the aftermarket offers you plenty water pump-wise for the 429/460. Edelbrock, Weiand, and Ford Performance all have a generous lineup of water pumps for these engines. The best you can hope for with the MEL are rebuilt water pumps and perhaps NOS.

Cooling Fan

Cooling fan selection is straightforward with these big Ford V-8s. However, you must know exactly what you're doing when you're shopping for a fan because proper match is everything to cooling. Fans, shrouds, spacers, and radiators must all work together. As always, use the highest capacity available. Get the pulley size and width specified in the Ford Master Parts Catalog.

A 427, for example, must have a large-diameter water pump pulley (6.000- to 7.000-inch diameter) to keep pump speed safe. Too small and you can expect blown hoses, seals, or radiator.

FORD BIG-BLOCK PARTS INTERCHANGE

SOURCE GUIDE

American Muscle
877-890-4785
americanmuscle.com

ARP Bolts
800-826-3045
arp-bolts.com

BBK Performance
951-296-1771
bbkperformance.com

Blue Oval Performance
360-993-1745
blueovalperformance.net

Blue Thunder Auto
760-328-9259
bluethunderauto.com

Comp Cams
901-795-2400
compcams.com

Crane Cams
866-388-5120
cranecams.com

CJ Pony Parts
717-657-9252
cjponyparts.com

Cobra Automotive
203-284-3863
cobraautomotive.com

Dove Manufacturing
440-236-5139
dovemanufacturing.com

Federal Mogul/Speed Pro
federalmogal.com

FE Power
952-428-9035
jayb@fepower.net
fepower.net

Ford Performance Parts
800-FORD788
fordperformance.com

Ford Powertrain
  Applications
253-848-9503
fordpowertrain.com

Full Throttle Kustomz
Ray McClelland
805-200-5500
fullthrottlekustomz.com

Holcomb Motorsports
800-475-7223
holcombmotorsports.com

JBA Performance Exhaust
909-599-5955
jbaheaders.com

JGM Performance
  Engineering
661-257-0101

Jon Kaase Racing Engines
770-307-0241
jonkaaseracingengines.
  com

Livernois Motorsports &
  Performance
313-561-5500
livernoismotorsports.com

L&R Engines
562-802-0443

MSD Ignition
888-258-3835
msdignition.com

Mustangs Etc.
818-787-7634
mustangsetc.com

National Parts Depot –
  Michigan
800-521-6104
npdlink.com

National Parts Depot –
  North Carolina
800-368-6451
npdlink.com

National Parts Depot –
  Florida
800-874-7595
npdlink.com

National Parts Depot –
  California
800-235-3445
npdlink.com

Robert Pond Motorsports
909-376-2530
robertpondmotor
  sports.com

Roush Performance
800-597-6874
roushperformance.com

Stage 3 Motorsports
877-578-2433
stage3motorsports.com

Summit Racing Equipment
800-230-3030
summitracing.com

Survival Motorsports
248-931-0358
survivalmotorsports.com

Tony D. Branda Shelby &
  Mustang
800-458-3477
cobranda.com

Total Performance Parts
  Company, Inc.
586-468-3673
totalperformanceinc.com